FREE CAPITAL

HOW 12 PRIVATE INVESTORS MADE MILLIONS IN THE STOCK MARKET

GUY THOMAS

HARRIMAN HOUSE LTD

3A Penns Road
Petersfield
Hampshire
GU32 2EW
GREAT BRITAIN

Tel: +44 (0)1730 233870
Fax: +44 (0)1730 233880
Email: enquiries@harriman-house.com
Website: www.harriman-house.com

First published in Great Britain in 2011

ISBN: 978–1906–659–74–5

British Library Cataloguing in Publication Data
A CIP catalogue record for this book can be obtained from the British Library.

Set in Minion, Bebas Neue and FrutigerMW Cond.

Printed and bound in the UK by CPI Antony Rowe, Chippenham and Eastbourne.

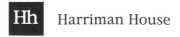

Harriman House

CONTENTS

A Note on Names and Details   vii
Preface   ix

Introduction   **1**

I – Geographers   **9**

    1. Luke: The Big Picture   13
    2. Nigel: Catching the Swings   29

II – Surveyors   **47**

    3. Bill: Just the Facts   51
    4. John Lee: Defensive Value and Dividends   69
    5. Sushil: The Apostate Economist   87
    6. Taylor: The Autodidact   107
    7. Vernon: Buying the Glitch   121

III – Activists   **145**

    8. Eric: The Networker   149
    9. Owen: Efficiency and Opportunism   165
    10. Peter Gyllenhammar: The Corporate Engineer   183

IV – Eclectics   **207**

    11. Khalid: The Day Trader   211
    12. Vince: The Tax Exile   231

Conclusion   **247**

    Characteristics of the Free Capitalists   249
    Life Choices and Chances   250

Attitudes   253
Working Methods   255
Summary Table of Investor Characteristics   260

A Note on Research Methods   263
Acknowledgements   265
Endnotes   267

Index   **273**

List of figures

Soco International plc: a 42-bagger from March 1999 to December 2009   19
AMEX Gold Bugs Index from January 2001 to December 2010   41
Value spider for Telford Homes as at February 2010   64
Value spider for KBC Advanced Technologies as at February 2010   65
Median compound growth as a function of leverage   98
Small engineering company: price chart from January 2001 to December 2010 102
Erinaceous price chart from January 2004 to April 2008   115
QXL Ricardo price chart from January 2004 to takeover in March 2008   131
Haynes Publishing price chart from January 2008 to December 2010   133
Hansard International price chart from January 2008 to December 2010   136
Ben Bailey plc: price chart from January 2001 to takeover in August 2007   156
Vodafone plc: price chart and 20-day RSI, January 2010 – June 2010   224
Payoff chart for covered straddle   241

A NOTE ON NAMES AND DETAILS

Throughout this book, biographical information which influenced the interviewees' psychological development as investors is generally accurate. In most chapters, real names and sometimes other non-investment details such as home towns and former employers have been modified or purposely left vague. This has provided a degree of anonymity to the subjects, allowing them to speak more frankly. Care has been taken to maintain the veracity of all investment details.

PREFACE

What this book covers

This book profiles 12 private investors. All of them have accumulated £1m or more – in most cases considerably more – mainly from stock market investment. Six of them have accumulated £1m or more in a tax-free Individual Savings Account (ISA), which is arithmetically impossible without exceptional investment returns.

The profiles cover the investors' backgrounds and how they first became interested in the stock market; how the interest progressed to the point where they gave up their day job; and how they spend their days now. They describe each subject's current investment approach, and reflect on lessons learnt from life as a full-time private investor.

Although a careful reading will yield many investment hints, this is not a how-to guide. The book aims to provoke reflection and provide ideas and inspiration, rather than the snake oil of simple prescriptions.

Who this book is for

Readers who may enjoy this book include:

- sophisticated private investors who want to compare their own approaches and experiences with others

- less experienced private investors who want to read about role models

- any reader of magazines like *Investors Chronicle* or *Shares*

- anyone who is curious about how stock market fortunes are made

- anyone who dreams of freedom and wealth!

Whilst the insights and reflections are at a level which should appeal to experienced investors, this is not a technical book. If a particular concept mentioned by any of the investors is obscure it can generally be skipped without impairing your enjoyment of the rest of the book.

How to use this book

The book consists of an introduction and conclusion surrounding 12 personal stories, which do not need to be read sequentially; the book can be dipped into at will.

As well as noting the investment hints and insights, readers may like to relate each profile to their own personality and experience. How well does the subject's approach match with your own temperament? Do you already possess skills or traits which would help in applying the approach?

For example, someone who needs activity and quick feedback to sustain their interest is likely to be a poor fit with the long-term strategic approach of Luke, which involves only a handful of trades every year. Someone who dislikes frenetic activity is likely to be a poor fit with the day-trading style of Khalid. Introverts who prefer to spend most of their time just reading and thinking may feel drawn to the styles of Bill or Sushil. Outgoing personalities who prefer to absorb information through one-to-one conversations may identify more with John Lee or Eric.

Free capital?

Free capital – a pot of money surplus to immediate living expenses – is the raw material with which the investors work. Free capital can also be thought of as their psychological habitat, free from the restrictions of conventional working life as an employee. Free capital also describes the footloose nature of their funds, which can be quickly redirected towards any type of investment anywhere in the world, without the mandate constraints institutional investors often face.

INTRODUCTION

Personal investing can radically change your life. It is probably not reasonable to plan on the basis that it *will*, but it *can*; and for each of the 12 investors profiled in this book, it *has*.

The freedom which investors enjoy from the drudgery of conventional careers is attractive to many people, but possible paths to achieving this through personal investment are obscure to most. Each of the profiles in this book illustrates one such path.

This is not a 'how-to' book or a manifesto, it is a collection of personal stories. But I hope that private investors who read it will, as well as enjoying the stories for their own interest, find some thoughts which can be used to improve their own investment performance.

The people in this book are not high earners who have accumulated wealth primarily through their salaries, nor entrepreneurs who have built and sold businesses for cash, nor trustafarians living idly off unearned inheritances.

> "Personal investing requires no deference, self-promotion, management skills or tact; it requires only a few good decisions."

Instead the people in this book are principally *investors*: they have accumulated free capital through their own decisions in the stock market, in most cases starting with modest savings from a salary. The skills and temperament required to do this are different from those required to advance in most careers and organisations, and also different from those of an entrepreneur. Personal investing requires no deference, self-promotion, management skills or tact; it requires only a few good decisions.

It is a field where outsiders can excel: an individualistic game loosely defined by rules which are sufficiently static to make experience valuable, but also sufficiently fluid to keep the game interesting.

The conditions under which the game is played now are not the same as 15 years ago, when it would have been more difficult to write this book. Then, access to real-time prices and company news cost thousands of pounds a year; brokerage and stamp duty 'round-trip' costs on a purchase and sale could easily amount to 3% or more; short selling was almost impossible for most private investors; and market-making spreads were unavoidable on all shares. This book highlights substantial technology-driven improvements in all these areas in recent years, which have facilitated self-directed investing, changing the world of private investors for the better.

I decided from an early stage that interviewees would generally appear in the book under disguised names. This was not the result of any great deliberation: it just seemed to me obvious (and still seems obvious) that many investors of the quality I wanted to interview would not be willing to talk freely about their personal finances without a degree of anonymity. Several interviewees made unprompted remarks confirming this early in our discussion. There were two exceptions to this principle of anonymity: Peter Gyllenhammar and John Lee, who agreed with my view that they were already public figures to such an extent that anonymity was not a realistic aspiration.

It would have been easy to write a book using real names about a different class of investor (or purported investor): those who are seeking publicity for investment seminars or coaching or share tips which they want to sell. But the claims of such self-promoting 'investors' usually do not withstand close scrutiny, and they are ultimately less interesting than the publicity-shy but genuinely successful investors in this book.

For the people in this book, I am convinced of the truth of Oscar Wilde's maxim: "*Man is least himself when he talks in his own person. Give him a mask, and he will tell you the truth.*"

Geographers, surveyors, activists and eclectics

Whilst each profile can be read on its own, further insight can be gained by classifying the investors into groups. The most salient classification to emerge from the interviews was a distinction based on how investors structure their thinking. This is the distinction between top-down analysis, focusing first on broad trends and macroeconomic conditions; and bottom-up analysis, focusing first on the idiosyncrasies of particular companies.

BACKGROUND: TOP-DOWN AND BOTTOM-UP EXAMPLES

As an example of top-down analysis, an investor might develop the view that interest rates are likely to fall next year; this leads to the idea that the housing market and therefore house-builders' shares will benefit; the investor then looks for the most attractive individual shares in the house-building sector.

As an example of bottom-up analysis, an investor might develop the view that a particular house-building company has exceptionally efficient building processes; this leads the investor to consider buying the company's shares; any view on the future course of interest rates is then noted as one factor amongst many which may affect the company. The bottom-up investor typically spends only a little time thinking about macro trends in the economy: his attention is directed mainly elsewhere, towards the attributes of individual companies.

The top-down versus bottom-up contrast can be thought of as a distinction between *geographers* and *surveyors*. Geographers have a top-down focus starting from the overall investment landscape; surveyors have a bottom-up focus starting from the individual elements of the landscape. Geographers start from the big picture and work down; surveyors start from the details of lots of small pictures and work up.

The *geographers* versus *surveyors* metaphor is inspired partly by the serendipitous fact that the interviewee in this book who places the greatest emphasis on top-down thinking is a former professional geographer. The metaphor can be illustrated by classifying some well-known investors. Examples of investment geographers include macro traders such as George Soros, and global investors such as the late John Templeton. Examples of investment surveyors include Warren Buffett, and the retired Fidelity fund manager Peter Lynch. The economist J. M. Keynes was initially a geographer, following his "credit cycle theory of investment" in the 1920s, until he made a radical shift to a surveyor's bottom-up philosophy after the 1929 crash.

Some investors are not easily characterised as either geographers or surveyors, so some further classifications are needed.

For a third group, the *activists*, their distinctive characteristic is active interaction with the management of companies in which they invest. Activists seek to influence company managers' decisions in line with their own views – by dialogue and persuasion, by using the votes on their shares, and if necessary by publicity (e.g. naming and shaming of inept and overpaid managers).

Activists share many of the habits of thought of surveyors, and vice versa: whenever a surveyor takes action to address a management problem which arises at a company in which he is invested, rather than just selling the shares, he draws on the activist's toolkit.

However, most surveyors try to avoid buying shares in companies which require management changes – that is, they do not go looking for trouble. The distinguishing characteristic of activists is that they are sometimes prepared to buy shares *knowing* that management changes are required. An activist is an investor who goes looking for trouble.

"An activist is an investor who goes looking for trouble."

The fourth and final group of investors, the *eclectics*, is a residual category. These investors are difficult to classify as either top-down geographers or bottom-up surveyors, and they are also not obvious activists. One eclectic is a fundamental investor who draws on both top-down and bottom-up analysis, with no clear predilection for either. The other is a day trader who trades partly on short-term news flow, and partly on technical analysis – that is, charts of recent share price histories. This approach falls outside both the *geographers* and *surveyors* classifications.

Performance records and ISA millionaires

It is not possible to identify from these interviews any one investment approach which is clearly better than all the others. Objective performance comparisons are difficult for people who all pay their very different living expenses from income or gains on their investments, and have varying exposure to tax depending on the past accumulation of their investments inside or outside tax-free vehicles such as ISAs.

Even with objective performance figures, the single historical realisation for each strategy over different periods for different investors means it would not be possible to eliminate the influence of luck.

Despite the lack of audited performance figures, there are some hard facts which verify the exceptional success of the investors profiled in this book.

Four investors (John Lee, Owen, Sushil and Vince) had already accumulated seven-figure sums in PEPs and ISAs by around 2003 or earlier. Vernon had done the same by 2005, and Luke by 2006. Owen and Sushil did not dissent from the inference that they had since multiplied this tax-sheltered sum several times over, albeit they were reticent about the exact figures.

Given the inability to borrow, and low contribution limits in PEPs and ISAs – £10,680 per annum in 2011-12, and for many years £7,000 per annum or less – these results are arithmetically impossible without exceptional investment returns.

Specifically, even if the *maximum* permissible contribution had been made *every year* since the inception of PEPs and ISAs in 1987, the total contributions up to and including the tax year 2003-04 would have been £126,200. Accumulation of these contributions to over £1m by the end of 2003 implies a compound growth rate of at least 23% per annum. With the exception of John Lee, most of the ISA millionaires had actually contributed for much shorter periods, implying much higher rates of return.

Although the 'ISA millionaire' tag provides a vivid and unambiguous confirmation of high investment returns for six of the investors, it would be a mistake to infer that these must be better models than the other six. There are good reasons why ISAs have been less significant to some. Peter Gyllenhammar – probably the book's wealthiest investor – is resident in Sweden, and therefore not eligible for ISAs. Khalid trades only in contracts for difference, which cannot be held in ISAs. Others were too poor to make significant contributions to PEPs in the 1990s, or have made larger withdrawals over the years to support their families or other spending needs.

For some of the investors, the regulatory requirement to declare publicly any shareholdings above 3% of a quoted company provided further evidence of their substantial free capital. Peter Gyllenhammar is named in many such announcements every year. Owen, Sushil and Vince have also been named in announcements on various occasions, although their anonymity in this book means that this is not verifiable by the reader.

No drama

A conundrum in writing a book such as this is that investment is a strictly results-oriented activity: success does not require that one be able to articulate one's methods, and the best investors are not necessarily the best raconteurs. This is a field where success can flow from passively observing the world and doing nothing more than making an occasional telephone call. This lack of drama is well illustrated by a story concerning the exceptional UK fund manager Anthony Bolton, the long-term manager of Fidelity Special Situations unit trust. A colleague who was asked to provide an anecdote about

Bolton for a book replied: "I have none. He is not an anecdote kind of person."[1] In this book, some of the investors are more "anecdote kind of person[s]" than others. My aim is realistic appraisal, rather than larger-than-life caricatures; wherever there is a choice, I have favoured authenticity over entertaining embellishment. I hope this choice will increase the value of the book to serious investors.

More casual readers may be disappointed by the lack of exciting struggles or psychological pathology. There is a simple riposte to this: quiet freedom is itself exotic. Most people in this book have been able to give up full-time employment for good in their 30s or 40s, to spend the rest of their lives doing something which they enjoy. They live comfortably, eschewing the hedonic treadmill of competitive materialism on which those possessed of high salaries or bonuses often seem to run.

Anyone who can do this without business success, inherited wealth or a lottery win is a person who has made some unusual and effective choices in life, and is interesting for that reason. It would be possible to pathologise these choices, to suggest that there is a price to be paid for the investors' success, and there were faint hints at what this might be in some interviews: for example, Vernon noted that "investing is not a team sport", and both he and Sushil used the word "misanthrope" about themselves. But in the end, it seems absurd to suggest that a youngish person with assets of several million pounds accumulated through his own decisions, who spends most of his time doing what he likes, is afflicted or dysfunctional compared with the general population. The straightforward view is that these are successful people living in relative happiness, and compared to the venality of many City high earners, perhaps even a degree of grace.

The role of luck

A more challenging critique than the absence of psychopathology is the pervasiveness of luck. This is a book about lucky people. Contrary to general human experience, they have reached middle age with lives which have turned out rather better than they expected, at least in a financial dimension. Some (not all) of the investors had thought carefully about this, and were anxious to highlight the role of luck in their own investment records.

A reasonable observation put to me by one of the interviewees (Vernon) is that there are two types of luck. The first type, 'lottery luck', is wholly random

– like winning a lottery – and exposure to its possibility requires negligible effort, like buying a ticket. But there is another type of luck characterised by a quotation attributed to the French microbiologist Louis Pasteur: "in the fields of observation, chance favours the prepared mind".

"In the fields of observation, chance favours the prepared mind."

More precisely, the point is not quite that chance 'favours' the prepared mind – chance is intrinsically impartial – but rather that exposure to some chances can only arise through deliberate and possibly unpopular and eccentric choices. For example, only a few investors around the millennium (in this book, Sushil and Vernon) both made *and kept* fortunes from investing in technology shares. These investors were lucky, but their exposure to the possibility of this luck arose from their obsessive interest and diligence in investing over much of the 1990s. Although all of the people in this book have probably been helped by some good luck, it has arguably been mainly Pasteur luck, rather than lottery luck.

Hearing that I was writing about successful investors, a sceptical friend pressed the point about luck by asking whether the book would include an equivalent sample of unsuccessful investors. The short answer is that it does not, although it does include unvarnished accounts of setbacks: Peter Gyllenhammar went bust twice earlier in his investment career. But this book is a work of observation; it makes no claim that what the investors have done is easy, or that there are simple recipes whereby anyone can do this. There must also be people who have lost fortunes as private investors; there may be an interesting book which can be written about them, if they can be persuaded to tell their stories; but it is a different book to this one.

Finally, a word about the separate panels in a different font at various points in the text. These give background information, usually on a technical topic, which may be helpful to some readers but can be skipped by those who either already know the topic or prefer to avoid it. Each chapter ends with a section summarising the main investment ideas. Careful readers may detect that I have not enforced strict consistency across the chapters in the summaries: different interviewees occasionally make contradictory recommendations. In these instances I hope that readers are stimulated by both sides of the argument, and remember Aldous Huxley's dictum: *"the only completely consistent people are the dead"*.[2]

1 GEOGRAPHERS

Geographers start from the big picture of the investment landscape. They take a top-down approach, thinking first about macroeconomic trends which make some investment sectors or countries or other themes more attractive than others at a particular time, and only then look for individual companies or other investments aligned with those themes.

1

LUKE
THE BIG PICTURE

LUKE: FACTS AND FIGURES

Age at interview	55
Age at leaving last full-time job	47
Background	Geography, transport planning; business school; investment banking (debt origination).
Style	Top-down selection of sectors and then a very few companies, held for several years.
Markets and sectors	Oil exploration and production.
Instruments	Shares
Typical holding period	Years
Performance indicators	Compound return above 30% per annum from 1995 to 2008; ISA millionaire by 2006 (despite contributing only from 1993 to 2003).
Quote	"Concentrate on quality of decisions, not quantity of decisions."
Phrases	The big picture; picking the right train; strategic lethargy.

T he scarcest resource for successful investors is not money but *attention*: how to manage the trade-off between time and rationality to best effect. There is not time in life to find out everything about every potential investment. Investment skill consists not in knowing everything, but in judicious neglect: making wise choices about what to overlook.

Top-down investors (geographers) start from the big picture and work down: they think first about macroeconomic themes such as interest rates and commodity prices, and only then look for individual companies aligned with those themes. Bottom-up investors (surveyors) start from lots of small pictures and work up: they think first about the attributes of individual companies, and

"Investment skill consists not in knowing everything, but in judicious neglect: making wise choices about what to overlook."

only then note any macroeconomic themes which affect those companies. Luke is an archetypal investment geographer, and as it happens a former real geographer, the inspiration for my use of the term in this book.

Apart from time and rationality, another trade-off is between dealing frequency and dealing costs: the more an investor deals, the higher the costs – both commission and bid-offer spreads, and the indirect costs of more avoidable errors through dealing on weaker information. Luke spends several hours every day observing and thinking about markets, and yet he deals only a very few times a year. He focuses on quality of decisions, not quantity of decisions, believing that "one of the big mistakes in investing is to think that you've always got to be doing something".

Geography

Luke is in his mid-50s and lives in a Suffolk coastal town, in a yellow detached house on a very wide and open street a few minutes from the sea. His childhood in South London was secure but not affluent: "there wasn't much money, but nor was there any particular hardship". He went to the local grammar school and then on to Exeter University in 1972 to study geography. After an MSc in transport planning, he spent the first six years of his career in this field in the South West, directly using both his academic degrees. He enjoyed his job, but in the early 1980s he gradually became aware of two structural problems which limited his long-term career prospects: his lack of a chartered engineering qualification, and the impact of Thatcherite cuts on local government.

In 1982, when he was 28, he resigned to spend two years doing an MSc in management, the forerunner of the MBA degree at the London Business School (LBS). "I gave up a reasonably secure job for two years of full-time education, with no guarantee of something better at the end of it. Many of my colleagues thought I was mad."

He enjoyed the MSc course, despite the fact that it was "quite tough from a personal life perspective, and I was very uncertain what I would do at the end of it." There was strong camaraderie amongst the students, with around a quarter who shared his motivation of escaping from poor pay and prospects in the engineering sector. He graduated in 1984, at the beginning of the boom leading up to the Big Bang reforms of the City in 1986, a period of strong demand for LBS graduates. After interviewing for fund management and analyst jobs he joined the small London office of an American bank, at a starting salary double what he had earned as a transport planner.

Into banking: a lucky break

Luke started his investment banking career in debt origination – identifying corporate clients who needed to raise money by issuing bonds to investors, and designing and marketing those bonds. After about 18 months, the American bank's bond syndicate manager resigned, taking his number two with him, so Luke stepped up into the job – a lucky break which turbo-charged his early career.

Three years later he moved on to a large British bank. The new job shifted his market focus from debt origination in the eurobond market to the same function in the embryonic medium-term note market. A medium-term note is a flexible debt security with a term usually between five and ten years, and often with features such as put options or warrants which give embedded optionality. Initially this was a small market in London, but it grew rapidly in the 1990s, creating strong career opportunities. Medium-term notes will be unfamiliar to many readers, but the details are not important. The significant point is that operating in this market required a particularly broad worldview, which has also shaped Luke's approach to personal investing.

> "In careers or in investment, it helps enormously to pick the right train – choose a field with long-term secular growth."

"The medium-term note market is a global market, so you need a model of the whole world in your head. Over the years I did deals in 15 to 20 currencies – different financial environments, different legal and tax regimes, different cultures. And because the embedded optionality in the notes often related to the commodity or equity markets, I needed to keep abreast of those markets as well."

This broad worldview helped with spotting opportunities for new issues which would appeal to both investors and issuers: "if say the Indonesian rupiah or Korean won were devalued, that might create an opportunity to do something based on Indonesian or Korean interest rates." Luke's long-standing habit of top-down thinking contrasts with the bottom-up surveyor investors in this book, who spent their formative investing years learning to analyse the accounts of individual companies, often giving little thought to the broader financial world.

The medium-term note market grew rapidly in the 1990s, creating strong career opportunities. Reflecting on this a decade after leaving banking, Luke noted the value of "picking the right train" in career decisions, a concept which has also informed his top-down investing. "By switching from local government into bond syndication, and from there into medium-term notes, I changed from a train going nowhere to a very fast train. In careers or in investment, it helps enormously to pick the right train – choose a field with long-term secular growth."

The job was often intense: he routinely left home before dawn for most of the year to be at his desk between 7 and 8 in the morning, and stayed until 7 or 8 in the evening. In these years he did little personal investing, apart from unit trusts and other collective vehicles. "The compliance requirements as an investment bank employee made dealing in individual shares difficult, and anyway I never had the time."

But he did make one big financial bet: in 1989, he sold his house west of London and moved to Suffolk, halving the size of his mortgage just before the property slump of the early 1990s. With 20 years' hindsight, this may seem an obvious market call, but few people found it obvious enough to act decisively at the time. For Luke the decision was based partly on his macroeconomic perspective, and partly on his geographer's sensibility: he foresaw trouble in the property market, and that the financial centre of London would probably drift eastwards towards Docklands. He repeated this type of call in 2006, downsizing to his present house as soon as his youngest child left home, partly because of his bearish macro view of the property market.

Leaving banking

By 1999, after nearly 15 years in investment banking, Luke had become weary of an intense job with a long daily commute from Suffolk and frequent international travel. Like many people in banking, he was wistful for a more relaxed lifestyle, but trapped by inertia and high financial rewards. The gilded cage was opened by dealing room ageism: "the bank had one of those periodic culls which indiscriminately target almost anyone over 45."

Soon afterwards he joined a small treasury consultancy, which offered advice to non-financial companies on dealing with banks. He aimed to develop a new service, advising companies on raising money in the securities markets rather than bank loans: "I was a poacher turning gamekeeper, or vice versa, depending on how you look at it." He persevered with this for about three years, but developing the business proved difficult. "The egos of the people to whom I was pitching often made it difficult for them to admit they needed help. And even if they knew it, their bosses didn't expect to pay for help."

In March 2000, Luke spent the whole month advising Marconi on its debt restructuring. After the month-end he realised that the movement in his personal share portfolio in March had been many times larger than his salary for that month, and indeed larger than the fee his firm had billed. "It made me reflect that perhaps I should be spending more time on investing, rather than earning." His employer's business suffered in the downturn after the September 2001 terrorist attacks, leading him to leave employment in early 2002. He was 47 years old. Apart from some sporadic ad hoc consultancy, he has been a full-time private investor since then.

The big picture: the neglected oil sector

When he began to spend more time on investment in the late 1990s, the habits of thought Luke had developed in his career made it natural to take a top-down perspective, scanning the whole investment landscape for value. In March 1999 this led him to focus on oil exploration and production companies. He had no particular expertise in the oil industry, and had never invested in the sector before, but thought that it offered clearly the best value in 1999. Although this may have seemed clear to Luke, it was a minority view at the time. On 4 March 1999 *The Economist* newspaper published its notorious "Drowning in oil" headline predicting a price of $5 per barrel of oil, almost to the day when Luke resolved to focus on the sector.

Luke made initial investments in a handful of what he thought were the best-value UK-listed oil explorers and producers. Over the next few years he increased these shareholdings, partly by investing consultancy earnings and partly by selling unit trusts and other collective vehicles in the technology sector in which he had invested during the 1990s. One of these oil stocks, Soco International, came to dominate his portfolio over the next decade.

Soco International plc: a 42-bagger from March 1999 to December 2009

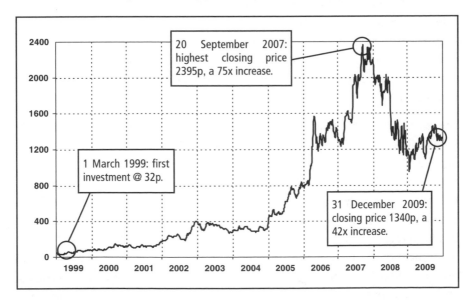

Source: data from ADVFN

From his earliest purchases in March 1999 at 32p the price rose *75 times* at its peak in September 2007, and was still up 42 times at the end of 2009. Although he made only a small part of his total investment in Soco at 32p, this spectacular rise illustrates the potential of focusing on "quality of decisions, not quantity of decisions." In almost every era of stock market history, there are a few shares like this, and if you can find them, buy them and sit tight, your life can be transformed. You only need to find one or two really good investment ideas to change your life.

Whilst Luke's investment process always starts with top-down analysis, this is a beginning, not an end: he also learns a great deal about each of the handful of companies he holds. Oil exploration has a substantial learning curve: terms such as *proven reserves, proven and probable (2P) reserves, possible reserves* and so on all have precise technical meanings, and their nuances can be of critical importance in interpreting news announcements from oil companies.

He has always invested in a very few stocks, usually no more than six. "My view is that most of the benefit from diversification comes from the first few stocks." Once he holds a stock, his ongoing research is focused on confirming that it retains "low downside and substantial upside." Provided that it does, he is indifferent to short-term price movements: "I try to watch the business, not the share price." Nor does he lose sleep over the possibility that some other stock might offer even higher returns over the next few weeks or months. "I think you are better off with a few good long-term choices, rather than flitting from one speculation to another, always chasing the latest hot stock in the market. Better to have a few good long-term friends, rather than change your friends every week for short-term advantage."

I remarked that the volatility of oil exploration companies meant that their investment clientele overlaps with the technology sector – both attract uninformed small investors with excessive enthusiasm for particular companies. Did Luke agree? "Yes, dumb money is common in both sectors. But because of new discoveries of oil, exploration is one of the few sectors where it is possible – and not even all that rare – to have a large change in the fundamentals of a company overnight. In that respect I think it is different from most of the tech sector." His bullish long-term view of the oil sector is predicated partly on the view that "oil and natural gas resources are limited, and ultimately we will see a buyer's scramble by resource-short nations like China. I do not know when, but I am convinced it will happen." His companies are picked partly for their plausibility as long-term targets of these strategic bidders.

Although his big picture approach has led to a portfolio weighted heavily in oils over much of the past decade, Luke also thinks deeply about other sectors; his many detailed bulletin board posts about the banking sector attest to this. But because he does no short selling, the banking part of his big picture did not lead to any useful investment ideas in the mid-2000s. "I didn't know precisely what the problems were at the banks, but I knew the nature of the games that were being played. My main conclusion for a number of years until early 2009 was that I didn't want to invest in them."

Leverage, shorts and squeezes

Most of Luke's half a dozen or so main investments are in fully listed stocks, partly because a substantial part of his portfolio has been accumulated in ISAs, which cannot hold most AIM stocks.[1] He began making contributions to a Personal Equity Plan (the forerunner of ISAs) in 1993; he ceased contributions in 2003 and has made some withdrawals since then. Despite this limited contribution period, his ISA passed the £1m mark in 2006. This result implies a compound growth rate of at least 27% per annum.

> "Leverage provides more juice, but in bad times that juice can quickly turn to hemlock."

He does not use spread betting or CFDs: he sees no need for leverage in a sector like oil exploration, which is operationally leveraged and volatile anyway. "Leverage provides more juice, but in bad times that juice can quickly turn to hemlock."

He has never been tempted to short a stock, having first-hand experience of executing a short squeeze in his bond market days. "We were launching a new bond issue in 1987, and before we could complete the syndication Paul Volcker announced he was not going to continue at the Fed. Six of the top ten eurobond houses shorted our bond at around 97, thinking that the Volker news was bad; but they didn't realise that they were all selling to us. We ended up owning 120% of the entire issue, which basically meant we had all six of them by the balls. We then just marked the bond up 2% a day for the next several days. Some quickly accepted their mistake and got out around 102 to 104; those who were more stubborn ended up paying around 115 to close the trade. At least one of the traders caught short lost his job. I have never wanted to short a stock since then."

A typical day

After many years as a crack-of-dawn commuter, Luke finds it easy to be in front of a screen at 7am to read the market news. On most mornings this is mainly for interest, and he will not actually trade anything. "But there is always a chance I might, if I have a compelling idea. I just don't feel compelled very often." He spends two or three hours looking at the markets, thinking things over, reading and drafting bulletin board posts, then usually takes a break to walk the dog. For the rest of the trading day, he doesn't feel tied to a screen in market hours, and doesn't necessarily have the Regulatory News Service (RNS) ticker running; but most days he spends a few hours on investment research.

Speaking or meeting with management plays little role in his initial selection of shares to buy, but after investing he may keep in email contact with management. He attends annual general meetings (AGMs) for his larger holdings, but generally not those of other potential investments. What about shareholder activism? "I have no interest in getting involved in any situation where I need to beat up the directors about something."

He tries to get hold of analyst research on his main holdings "not for new ideas, but to see the extent to which the market is already discounting my own views." Analysts' views often lag his own assessments of oil exploration and production stocks he knows well, which he thinks is partly for structural reasons related to analysts' typical valuation approach. "The most common way of valuing an exploration and production company is an appraisal of net asset value, based on a sum-of-the-parts approach. But most appraisals tend to ignore exploration assets which are not going to be drilled within some arbitrary time period, say the next 6-12 months. For some companies, much of the value is in assets which are not going to be drilled in the next year."

BACKGROUND: BULLETIN BOARDS

Prior to the late 1990s, the typical private investor had few sources of information or inspiration besides the business pages of newspapers, magazines such as *Investors Chronicle*, and company annual reports. Working with these generalist and non-interactive sources, collating investment ideas was laborious, time-consuming and sometimes not much fun. If the investor was lucky, he might have one or two friends who were interested in investment; but generally, private investors were not just autonomous, they were isolated.

Bulletin boards have relieved the private investor of much of this enforced solitude. The visible discussion on any board is often a misleading indication of readership and engagement: conversations with site operators suggest that for every visible participant, dozens or even hundreds of 'lurkers' read but seldom or never post. If one asks directors of quoted companies, City professionals or journalists about bulletin boards, many affect that such trivial matters are beneath them; but listening carefully over a longer period, it becomes obvious that many are avid lurkers on boards about companies with which they are professionally involved. Some CEOs post on bulletin boards, either openly or incognito, and companies have attempted defamation actions against bulletin board posters on both sides of the Atlantic.[2] Financial PR advisors and other corporate advisors also monitor many boards, and may attempt to steer discussions in directions favourable to their clients, either overtly or covertly.

The analogy is often made between bulletin boards and people chatting in a bar. As with bars, bulletin boards vary in character, popularity and longevity. At the time of writing, some popular boards can be characterised as follows.

- ADVFN (**www.advfn.com**) is more than ten years old and has established itself as the clear market leader in the UK as judged by independent measures of internet traffic.[3] With over *10,000* posts made every day, ADVFN is the Tower of Babel; but it is also an investor's reference library, with detailed company-specific threads on even the smallest UK quoted companies, populated by investors, customers, suppliers, business rivals and employees.

- Motley Fool (**www.fool.co.uk**) offers more restrained boards than the ADVFN free-for-all, with fewer company-specific boards and more general discussion; some sub-boards such as 'Paulypilot's Pub' and the 'Oil & Gas Board' have a high concentration of experienced investors.

- Interactive Investor (**www.iii.co.uk**) has a board on almost every UK quoted company, as well as videos, share tips and other articles from the site's editorial staff and columnists.

- Green Energy Investors (**www.gei.com**) is a relatively cerebral site, with a focus on green energy and macroeconomic discussion rather than individual shares.

- Stockopedia (**www.stockopedia.co.uk**) is a relatively new site with some novel web 2.0 interactive features.

30,000 posts

Luke is an enormously prolific poster on bulletin boards, not only in relation to his specialist interests of the oil and banking sectors, but also across many other topics. His persona as a bulletin board poster is often disputatious: more than one mutual acquaintance noted the curious contrast between his robust posting style and country-mouse manner in person. Given the depth of his own knowledge, which appears more sophisticated than many bulletin board posters, it is surprising that he posts so much – particularly when one notes that Owen, the other former investment banker in this book, spends no time at all on bulletin boards.

Why does Luke post so much? At Motley Fool, for example, his posting record runs to more than *30,000* posts over ten years, an astonishing number for a person who trades only a handful of times a year. Many of these are short replies of a sentence or two, but others are several paragraphs; if we allow even ten minutes per post including reading time, this implies 500 hours per year.

One answer is that bulletin boards are his filing system: he relies on his posts as a record of his thinking, and so keeps little in the way of paper files.

A second answer is that posting is a substitute for the morning meetings of a trading room. "Throughout my banking career I had the routine of a daily morning meeting to discuss the markets. Today I have that type of conversation via the boards."

A third answer is that posting on specialist oil and gas boards generates feedback from geologists and other experts in the oil and gas sector, which fills the gaps in his own knowledge.

Finally, I suspect that he also gets some personal validation from the many recommendations ('recs') his posts attract. Like many keen bloggers, he spends a lot of time looking over his shoulder for fear that he is not being followed.

Derision comes easily to professional investors at this point: bulletin board commentary can be (and often is) dismissed as a waste of time, the babble of uninformed amateurs. Such derision also emanates from professionals in other fields of expertise: medics who write diatribes like 'When the patient is a Googler', lawyers who deride determined litigants-in-person, and academic economists who disparage economics bloggers.[4] But the derision is not disinterested, because the professionals' real objection is the challenge to their authority and the erosion of their status and mystique.

Derision is easy because the quality of bulletin board discussion varies enormously, and the median is of low quality; but for an experienced skimmer who knows where to look, the median is beside the point. Finding one or two useful ideas often takes a few hours' reading, but it can sometimes make or save the investor tens of thousands of pounds. As Luke puts it: "I am not saying that most bulletin boards are useful, just that a few are. The boards which are most useful change over time. For example, the oil and gas board at Motley Fool a couple of years ago, or Stockopedia more recently. And the process of structuring my ideas into a post always clarifies my thinking."

Luke posts on many subjects and companies, but intriguingly even when he states clear views, he may not back them with his own cash. He prefers to bet only on his strongest views. As an example of not acting despite clear views, he pointed out several detailed bulletin board posts he had made in the spring of 2009, highlighting that banks and in particular Barclays were now cheap, after he had previously warned against investing in banks for several years. But he never quite pulled the trigger, which he later regretted.

For the future he has resolved that "if I can see a move of 20% or more, I will trade it. But for moves of 5% or 10%, I am not interested." With hindsight he thinks his main fault over the past few years has been *not trading enough*, an uncommon but relatively benign defect. "I am perhaps too prone to the status quo effect: as a long-term investor, when I feel I have superior knowledge about a share's long-term prospects, I find it difficult to sell even when I also expect a short-term fall. I hold the long-term view with greater confidence than the short-term one."

Conclusion

Of all the investors in this book, Luke is the most focused on the big picture of long-term, multi-year trends in global markets. This approach draws on his 15 years of following global markets for opportunities to originate bond deals, and also owes something to the eclectic and all-encompassing nature of his early career discipline of geography. His portfolio is very concentrated, holding a few stocks about which he knows a great deal. He is the least frequent trader in this book, but also the most prolific bulletin board poster.

He acts only on his strongest views, and this strategic lethargy is a critical ingredient of his success. "Most investors would have better performance if they thought more and did less. One of the great tricks in investment is learning to be happy doing nothing."

LUKE: INSIGHTS AND ADVICE

The big picture A broad view of the investment landscape can be a source of advantage.

Pick the right train Try to choose investment (and career) fields with long-term secular growth.

Just a few decisions Concentrate on quality of decisions, rather than quantity of decisions. You only need to find one or two really good investment ideas to change your life.

Stick with your best ideas It may be better to be comfortable with what you own for the long-term (have a few good friends), rather than always chasing the best share for the short-term (changing your friends every week).

Overnight transformations Oil exploration is one of the few sectors where it is possible – and not even all that rare – to have a large change in the fundamentals of a company overnight.

Operational and financial leverage as substitutes The oil sector is operationally leveraged, so an investor does not need much financial leverage.

Value beyond the analysts' time horizon The conventions of analyst research may mean that some types of value are under-appreciated. For example, most research focuses on a one or two year forecast horizon, so companies with a large part of their value slightly beyond this horizon may be under-valued.

Analysts' research as an index of consensus Analyst research can be viewed as an indication of the extent to which your insights are already discounted by the market.

Strategic lethargy One of the great tricks in investment is learning to be happy doing nothing.

2

NIGEL
CATCHING THE SWINGS

NIGEL: FACTS AND FIGURES

Age at interview	56
Age at leaving last full-time job	47
Background	Psychology; investment banking (shipping finance).
Style	Anticipating cyclical markets, using market psychology as well as fundamentals.
Markets and sectors	Oil and minerals (both London and overseas, especially Canada); Hong Kong residential property.
Instruments	Shares, index options, warrants, direct property.
Typical holding period	Weeks to months.
Performance indicators	Compound portfolio return over 25% per annum from 2001 to 2008, net of all living expenses and tax.
Quote	"Everyone is a genius in a bull market – so find a bull market!"
Phrases	Overlapping long and short cycles; bipolar markets; cross-market intelligence.

I nvestment success is largely a matter of timing. One makes money by being one step ahead of the market; being three steps ahead can lead to trouble, even if you are ultimately right.

Different investing approaches can be seen as different criteria for timing decisions. Some investors – the surveyors in this book – take their timing from events at individual companies. Others – the geographers in this book – take their timing from events in the overall economic and market landscape.

Nigel is an investment geographer whose timing relies on the concept of cyclicality, the idea that some investment markets – such as shipping, mining and property – can be understood as a sequence of overlapping long-term and short-term cycles. He tries to catch these markets early in their cyclical upswings, and sell before the downswings. Or as he puts it: "Everyone is a genius in a bull market – so find a bull market!"

Apart from the idea of cyclicality, another distinctive feature of Nigel's approach is the emphasis he places on monitoring market sentiment and psychology. "What other people are thinking is at least as important as what you are thinking yourself. You want to anticipate how other people's thinking is going to change before they know it themselves." This approach owes something to his early academic background as a psychology major at Harvard, and was refined over nearly three decades he spent as a banker in the fiercely cyclical world of shipping finance.

Nigel is over six foot tall with straight brown hair and an unlined face, which makes him seem younger than his actual age of 56. A slight accent still hints at his childhood in the US mid-west, but he has spent much of his career on other continents, in London, Hong Kong and Japan. Never married, he now lives in Hong Kong with a partner "whose frugality and sensibility matches my own." He visits London several times a year, where he is a non-executive director at an AIM-listed mining company. His demeanour is a slightly disorientating mixture of mid-western sincerity, cosmopolitan openness, and a leavening of cynicism borne of 25 years in banking.

Psychology and banking

Nigel started his university education at Harvard as a math major, but switched to psychology in his second year with a minor in economics. When he completed his BA in 1975, his father's Detroit engineering business was faltering, as the mid-1970s recession affected many of its auto industry clients. Eventually the company was sold for a pittance; a new business was started, but for a long time there was no income, only expenses. Conscious of the Harvard tuition fees he owed to his father, Nigel gave up his previous thoughts of law or business school, and went straight into a traineeship in New York with an international commercial bank.

For the first few years of his career he sent home a share of his income to his parents every month. Unable to keep up with the lifestyle of his free-spending colleagues, he came to see frugality as a virtue. He developed the habit of saving, even in periods when his resources were reduced by job changes or investment losses. Compared to colleagues, he found himself living in slightly less stylish neighbourhoods, taking less exotic holidays, and spending less on clothes, eating out and entertainment.

There was an excellent training programme at the bank which gave him "a strong understanding of balance sheets and credit." After the training year he joined an internal audit group, travelling around the world "looking at the bank's toughest and most troubled credits – auto companies, real estate developers in France, shipping loans in Hong Kong." His job was to look at the balance sheets, read the bank's internal memos, and give an independent view on loan recoverability. "It was a great way to learn the harder realities of banking, by focusing on loans which had gone wrong. And it encouraged independent thinking, because the function was to challenge the decisions of local management."

Capitalism on a credit card

As a bank trainee in the mid-1970s, Nigel had no money to invest, but he was able to finance his first small investments by a quirk in the bank's expenses regime. For international travel the bank provided a cash advance of $2,000 before each overseas trip, ostensibly to cover expenses, with any residual amount not covered by receipts to be returned after the trip. This overlooked the possibility of charging the actual expenses during the tour overseas to a personal credit card, thereby freeing up the $2,000 for investment. By the time the credit card bill was due, there would be another overseas trip and another $2,000 advance in hand. In effect, $2,000 was available continuously to finance investments, on an interest-free basis.

His first success was Computer Investors Group, which he still remembers in great detail more than 30 years later. High interest rates meant that computer-leasing companies were reporting losses on their lease portfolios. Studying the notes to the company's accounts, he noticed that depreciation of the computers was almost completed, so that reported profits could be expected to substantially increase in the near future. Convinced by this argument, he invested his $2,000 cash advance entirely in this one stock at just under $1. The next earnings release showed the result he expected, and he was able to sell for around $4 within less than three months.

> "Shipping is a romantic business. The romance is a magnet for excess capital."

Another source of funds for stock market investment was extracting housing equity when he sold his first studio apartment for $55,000 and moved to a one-bed in a cheaper area at only $42,000. His plans for a next move in 1980 to a duplex apartment were aborted after a surprise posting as head of ship finance by his employers to Hong Kong.

Shipping is a romantic business: a world of picturesque assets, arcane jargon, natural perils, huge fluctuations, centuries of history and global operations with a hint of geopolitical grandeur. The romance is a magnet for excess capital, so that whilst wild cyclicality showers fortunes on the lucky few, average returns to ship-owners are actually low.[1]

Nigel was in Hong Kong learning this business from 1980 to 1984; the steep learning curve in his day job left little time for personal investing. He returned to New York in 1984 and sold his apartment, before leaving for a new posting in the ship finance group in London. The weak sterling exchange rate allowed him to swap a one-bedroom apartment in Manhattan for a three-bedroom lower ground floor apartment in Kensington. In London he pioneered some new non-lending products, including the first currency option ever transacted by his bank in Europe. He also started writing articles for publication. One of these articles formed the basis of his subsequent investment philosophy.

Shipping cycles

One of Nigel's frustrations in his day job was that the bank was too reactive to current market conditions, and did not anticipate changes in the market. They would lend aggressively at low margins and high loan-to-value ratios when shipping freight rates were high, but be reluctant to lend even at high margins and conservative loan-to-value ratios when freight rates were low. Whilst this made sense from a short-term cash-flow perspective, risk would be better managed if the bank acted contra-cyclically, lending less aggressively when asset values were high.

Developing this idea, in 1986 he wrote a magazine article about cycles in the shipping industry, subsequently expanded into a book. This became a minor publishing phenomenon: he was asked to speak at conferences in London, New York, Norway and Greece, and the work is still occasionally cited by academic researchers 25 years later.

The 1986 article suggested that the history of shipping markets could be understood as a combination of short cycles lasting approximately 3-5 years, long cycles lasting approximately 16-24 years, and very long Kondratieff cycles lasting 40-60 years. The short cycle is driven by interest rate changes and the broader four year business and political cycle in the United States; the long cycle is an investment cycle, driven by variations in shipbuilding and scrapping orders, and in shipbuilding capacity; the Kondratieff cycle is a broader macroeconomic phenomenon, supposedly applying to all sectors of the economy, although both its existence and its causes are much disputed by economic historians. A few years later, he wrote an article applying the concept in the oil market, suggesting cycles lasting approximately two years, eight years and 30 years, driven respectively by inventory levels, politics and investment in oil production.

This concept of nested cycles – a long-run major cycle incorporating several short-run minor cycles – has formed the basis of his subsequent investment approach. "I start at a macro level, looking for cyclical markets, and I try to catch the swings – buying into the upswing and selling into the downswing."

Cyclicality does not necessarily imply regularity – the length of any market cycle is uncertain and variable – but nevertheless the concept of nested cycles can help understanding of many investment sectors. Apart from the insight it provides into shipping markets, the approach of monitoring and anticipating market cycles led him to sell his London property in 2001 to buy gold mining shares; and then to switch over 2007-08 into residential property in Hong Kong; and then to sell much of that property in early 2010.

But if the length of any market cycle is "uncertain and variable", does the concept really give the investor any actionable insight? Nigel's answer is that the concept of periodic cycles needs to be combined with the concept of monitoring market sentiment. This will often give an early warning that a cycle's length is about to stretch or contract. He likens the process to reading a familiar book: if the print size is changed, a chapter can be printed on fewer or more pages, but the story remains the same. It is the development of the underlying cyclical narrative, rather than a uniform time period, that defines the cycle. Monitoring changes in market psychology helps in understanding where you are in the cycle. "A market doesn't peak until the majority is convinced it is going to move higher, and it doesn't bottom until the majority believes it must go lower."

The publicity generated by the shipping cycle articles helped Nigel's career. He took on a broader role developing new products for the bank, and in 1986 they sold their first oil swap using a transaction structure he had designed: an oil producer on one side, an airline on the other, and a price margin for the bank in the middle. Over the next two years the oil swaps business grew rapidly in

> "He was the archetypal part-time trader, for whom the supposedly mercenary business of trading is often more about entertainment, or perhaps a sense of identity."

Europe, eventually leading to the bank centralising the business, with a new head in New York. A disagreement on accounting for future profits led to a falling out with his new boss and hence redundancy. But with his high industry profile he quickly found a new job with a large Swiss bank, doubling his base salary. With his much higher income he started dabbling in options more actively in his personal account, but with little success. At this stage he was the archetypal part-time trader, for whom the supposedly mercenary business of trading is often more about entertainment, or perhaps a sense of identity. "I rather fancied myself as a trader. I lost money rather consistently. But because I could afford it, I didn't mind too much."

His new job with the Swiss bank involved developing a business plan for their nascent commodity derivatives business. The plan was successfully developed but implementation proved difficult, with the bank unwilling to deploy sufficient marketing resources to develop the new business. After three years Nigel left with another redundancy payoff, which he used to redeem most of the mortgage on his London flat.

Commodity boutique

By this time he had "had enough of the politics of large organisations", so for his next job he joined a boutique bank. Initially his new employer hoped to sell commodity derivative deals to large companies and small sovereign states in Africa, but this market was dominated by larger banks. Small exploration companies were more realistic target clients, but they needed simple equity fundraisings rather than exotic derivatives. His first successful fundraising was a small mining company for which $1m was raised in a private placing, including $100,000 of his own money raised from re-mortgaging his apartment. The company floated on AIM a couple of years later, valuing the shares at more than six times the price of the earlier fundraising.

This success focused Nigel's interest as an investor on mining companies. His employer established a small mining fund, which pooled the resources of colleagues and friends to invest in small company mining shares. In the mid-1990s, mining enjoyed one of its periodic booms. Apart from the rise in gold and other commodity prices, two other factors driving the boom were discoveries and acquisitions.

When a small mining exploration company makes a big mineral discovery in the ground, it will often be possible for a large company to acquire it at a premium to the market capitalisation, but still enhance the per-share mineral reserves of the bidder. Reserves held in a large company tend to be valued more highly than reserves in a small company. This is for three reasons:

- greater liquidity means more demand for large company shares
- small companies often do not have the expertise to develop a mine
- small companies are distrusted by many investors because of their weaker corporate governance.

Nigel's fund therefore focused on "finding the next hot junior explorer which was drilling a large potential resource". Some of these situations produced spectacular gains: he particularly remembered one he missed, Diamond Fields, which discovered a large nickel deposit and went from C$0.13 in 1994 to a takeover price of C$41 in 1996. The small mining fund was initially a great success, with the net asset value rising more than 50% in a few months, but a bear market in mining followed in the second half of the 1990s. The scandal of Bre-X Minerals, a Canadian explorer which claimed to have made a massive gold discovery in Indonesia in 1995 but was exposed as a fraud in 1997, was particularly damaging to sentiment in the sector.

Nigel and his colleagues closed the fund, retaining just a few illiquid holdings. Their next exotic venture was a shipping derivatives hedge fund, exploiting arbitrage opportunities between the new exchange-traded shipping futures contract and portfolios of individual shipbrokers' forward freight agreements for specific sea routes; this produced good profits for a while, but as with most such technical opportunities in new markets, the arbitrages were competed away as the market matured.

A ten bagger and time out

Nigel did not have enough free capital to take an extended sabbatical, let alone contemplate becoming a full-time investor, until a lucky break at the end of 1999. One of the illiquid holdings that had been retained in the earlier mining fund was a small exploration company called Toucan Gold. In August 1999, Toucan changed its name to Authoriszor, and announced its intention to make an internet-related acquisition.

Nigel was no longer following the stock price day-to-day, relying on written broker statements to check the value. "When the December 1999 statement arrived, and I saw the price of $6.75 up from under $2, my first reaction was: there must have been a reverse stock split. But the number of shares was the same. I nervously called the broker, and he told me it was now trading over $20! I said sell. He said sorry, your account documentation is out of date. After that was sorted, I finally sold for $26, more than ten times what I had paid."

This windfall meant that Nigel now had the means to take an extended break. He also felt that stock market valuations were becoming irrational, especially in the technology sector, and that "it would be a good idea to get away from the investment world until sanity was restored." So he spent most of the year 2000 on a creative writing sabbatical, writing two plays and working with a theatre group. One of these plays came close to being staged, missing the

"freedom is like income that cannot be taxed"

theatre company's selection by one vote; he took this disappointment as "a sign that I was not going to be a successful playwright".

Although his creative aspirations were frustrated, he learned some important lessons in this year. "I found that it was possible to live a satisfying life on far less money than a banker's salary. Some of the actors seemed to live on fresh air, occasional part-time work, and the generosity of friends and family. It opened my eyes to the fact that a frugal lifestyle can be creative and dignified. I realised that freedom is like income that cannot be taxed."

Nigel was now 47. He did not want to live quite as frugally as his actor friends, but nor did he want to go back to banking. So he decided to see if he could support himself by his activities as an independent investor.

For the past 17 years home had been his three-bedroom apartment in Kensington, on which the mortgage had been redeemed from his second redundancy payoff. "It was on the lower ground floor, rather dark, and gloomy to work in all day. So I decided to raise capital by selling it off, and reinvest in gold and gold stocks. I moved into rented accommodation at the top of a four-floor walk-up. I felt much more cheerful about my life, even though I had no proper job."

Junior miners

Although Nigel had worked for two decades in banking, his chequered career path meant that he had not accumulated great wealth. His free capital in late 2000 was modest by investment banking standards, "probably rather less than £1 million".

Following his paradigm of identifying markets starting a cyclical upswing, he formed the view that the 2000s would see a bull market in hard assets such as gold and other commodities. He focused on researching small mining companies, using skills that he had developed running the mining fund at the boutique bank. He also began to attend mining conferences run by Minesite and Proactive Investors and similar conferences internationally, networking with investor relations firms and brokers, and attending fundraising presentations by mining companies from the UK, Canada and Australia which wanted to raise money from individual investors.

He found that his participation in fundraising was usually welcomed, even though his investments were small by institutional standards. "Always above $10,000 but only occasionally above $100,000. My largest single investment to date in a fundraising has been $400,000, and that came in 2005, after some large profits on earlier investments."

Nigel particularly favours secondary fundraisings, where an already quoted company raises more money by placing shares with new or existing investors. He sees secondary fundraisings in Canadian mining companies as having two structural advantages: they are usually priced at a discount to the current share price, and they often come with 'free' warrants attached. A warrant is similar to an option; it gives the right, but not the obligation, to buy more shares at the 'strike price' of the warrant, either at a fixed maturity date or over a period of some years. Typically, on deals involving Canadian junior miners, the secondary fundraising would be done at a discount of 10-15% to the prevailing share price, and with 'half warrants', that is for every two shares bought the subscriber would also receive one 'free' warrant. The 'price' of this 'free' warrant is that the investor in a secondary fundraising will typically be locked in, that is not permitted to sell any of his placing shares, for a period of say 120 days from the fundraising.

Because of his focus on Canadian miners, and his predominance of investments outside the UK, Nigel uses a Canadian firm as his main broker. The firm is a 'full service' operation, which caters to institutional and corporate clients as well as private clients, so that the latter can be offered participation in fundraisings. The London office of the same firm focuses solely on institutional business, but after befriending one of the institutional salesmen in London, Nigel was often invited to sit in on presentations of foreign companies marketing fundraisings in London, in which he would then participate through the Canadian office. His willingness to participate in Canadian fundraisings, and travel internationally to mining conferences, has given him a wider range of investment opportunities than those who focus solely on the UK. Over the first half of the 2000s he gradually spent less and less of his time in the UK, and eventually relocated to live permanently with his girlfriend in Hong Kong.

Portfolio management: "when it doubles, sell half"

Nigel will invest up to 5% of his total funds in a single company at the time of investment. He then follows a simple core rule: when a share doubles, sell half. He sees this as eliminating the original risk of the investment, by retrieving his capital for investment elsewhere, whilst retaining 50% of any further upside. In fundraisings where he has also received warrants – usually covering half as many shares as he bought in the fundraising – selling 50% of the shares leaves him with larger upside.

Apart from the price doubling, he also pays attention to trading volume. "If volume is still strong, I might hold on even when a share has doubled. But if a stock is hitting new highs and volume is falling, I will often reduce my position."

Listing some successes in recent years, Nigel named Canadian-listed companies which would be unfamiliar to most UK investors. "Growing mining companies such as Wheaton River and Silver Standard…then some more obscure ones…Ariane Gold, Battle Mountain Gold, Roca Mines…and Laramide Resources, that was a ten-bagger for me."

Laramide Resources was one of the most spectacular stocks on the Canadian exchange over the last decade, rising to a high in 2007 of more than 200 times its lowest price in 2003. Nigel sold far too soon, but given his normal rule of "when it doubles, sell half", making ten times his money was enough to trigger selling all the holding. He does not lose any sleep over the profit foregone. "In a junior mining bull market, you should not worry about the trades you miss, because exciting new opportunities are coming all the time."

Nigel does not use debt or spread betting or CFDs for leverage, for the same reason as Luke uses no leverage on oil explorers: "Junior mining shares are volatile anyway, and you get extra gearing through the warrants with many fundraisings. So you don't need other forms of leverage." He does not use stop-loss orders. "I think most of these shares are far too illiquid and thinly traded to use stops effectively. In my early days of trading I tried stops a few times, and I would see my stop loss orders hit, and then the stock would move higher. It was almost as if a market maker was targeting my stops as a source of supply."

Although the 2000s saw a long-term bull market in gold mining shares, it was a volatile market. The so-called Amex Gold Bugs Index fell more than 60% during 2008; a large rebound then followed and by late 2010, the index was well above its early 2008 highs. Many private investors would find this volatility intolerable, particularly if investing was their livelihood. Nigel was able to live with it for two reasons.

First, from selling his flat to invest in gold shares in 2001 until the peak in the first half of 2008, he increased his free capital more than five times after all living expenses, a compound growth rate over 25% per annum.

Second, he took about one third of his capital out of shares in late 2007 and early 2008 to buy several apartments in Hong Kong, with some gearing from mortgage debt. Although Hong Kong property fell along with almost every other asset class in the second half of 2008, it returned to near its previous highs in 2009.

AMEX Gold Bugs Index from January 2001 to December 2010

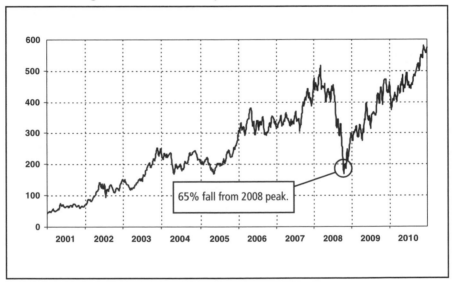

Source: data from ADVFN

Whilst the reallocation from gold shares to property was a good decision with hindsight, Nigel admits it involved an element of luck. "I definitely did not see the slump in gold shares coming. I expected trouble in general stock indices, which I avoided. I expected gold to outperform the stock indices, which it did. But I expected gold mining shares to hold up along with gold, whereas in fact they fell sharply with the broader stock market. I didn't anticipate the dynamics of deleveraging, which left some hedge funds scrambling to sell everything, including gold mining shares."

As a top-down investor, Nigel adjusts his overall market exposure according to his macro view. Apart from moving part of his portfolio between equities and other asset classes, he also uses put options on the S&P500 index and calls on bear exchange-traded funds as further means of hedging overall market risk. For example, in late 2009 his index puts were hedging around 20% of the value of his portfolio on a delta-adjusted basis ('delta-adjusted' is explained in an endnote[2]).

Exploiting cross-market intelligence

Nigel's concept of catching cyclical markets at the right point in the cycle can be enhanced by a cross-market perspective. He often compares markets which share similar economic drivers, expecting them to move in tandem. For example, shipping company shares would normally be expected to rise when shipping freight rates are rising; and oil company shares should be rising when oil prices are rising.

If markets with similar economic drivers are not moving in tandem, this non-confirmation may be a warning that a reversal is imminent. Alternatively, the lagging market may contain undervalued opportunities. Nigel cites several examples of cross-market anomalies giving early warning of price moves:

- in the late 1990s shipping freight rates turned up several weeks before shipping shares came off their lows

- in October 2002, semiconductor shares made a four-year cycle bottom a few days before broad market indices

- a few months later, the FTSE100 and Hong Kong's Hang Seng Index made new lows, while the S&P500 index only reached its previous low, and tech stocks and Nasdaq stayed over 10% above the October 2002 lows; he regarded this non-confirmation of the new low as a sign that the cycle had turned

- from January 2007, UK house-building shares started falling while house prices were making new highs, and then house prices duly turned down a few months later

- in June 2008, a fall in copper prices gave a warning that other commodity prices might turn down soon; oil reached a peak a few weeks later above $140 in late July 2008.

Nigel also noted the increasing synchronisation of commodities, shares and property prices in recent years, which he attributed to the role of the dollar as a principal "carry currency" for

"The market rewards humility and punishes hubris."

borrowing. "When dollar interest rates are low, investors borrow in dollars to invest in other assets, and all other assets tend to rise together, as borrowed funds flood in. When dollar interest rates rise, the rising cost of debt forces marginal leveraged investors to sell other assets and repay their dollar loans. So all non-dollar assets fall together, and the repatriation of dollars drives up the currency."

He sees this dynamic as a cause of increasing swings in the dollar and other asset prices, and more booms and crashes: "The market is bipolar, swinging back and forth from a focus on inflation and deflation. Bet on swings, and stay flexible."

Bulletin boards

Because Nigel lives mainly in Hong Kong, but trades western markets including Canada, most of his dealing is done in the late evening, from 9.30pm to 1am. During the day he is free to research investments, or manage his local property investments in Hong Kong. He writes occasional articles for online publications, and sometimes produces investment podcasts. He is also a very active bulletin board poster: like Luke he has around 30,000 posts on one board alone, and many more elsewhere. "I find it isolating working on my own all day. The market rewards humility and punishes hubris. Participating on a bulletin board can help with humility, if you approach it in the right way."

As an extension of his focus on mining and resource stocks, he has also developed an interest in the alternative energy sector. He was unable to find a dedicated bulletin board for the sector, so in 2006 he started Green Energy Investors (**www.gei.com**) himself. The focus on alternative energy proved too narrow to attract a critical mass of posters, but after he broadened the focus to allow other investment topics, the board grew by 2010 to an active community with over 2000 members.

Compared to mass-market boards such as ADVFN, the discussion on his niche board is less focused on gossip or news on individual stocks, and more on macro themes; the membership is unusually international, with regular posters in all the main continents. It also provides him with another insight into market sentiment: "skimming active threads on the board shows me irrational exuberance or irrational pessimism at first hand."

Nigel's enthusiasms as revealed in over 30,000 posts on his board are idiosyncratic and diverse. His macroeconomic views are Austrian, positing "mal-investment" and unsustainable consumption as the main causes of the 2007-09 global financial crisis; he is vehemently opposed to Keynesian demand stimulus as a response. These views tend to be associated with right-wing or libertarian economists. But he often writes about the ecological absurdity of American suburbia, with its wasteful consumption and unsustainable dependence on cheap oil, and the need for government policy to drastically reduce resource consumption and promote recycling; he also rails against "financial speculation encouraged by Fed monetary policy, and Wall Street trickery." His cosmopolitan range of interests makes it hard to guess his views.

Conclusion

Nigel's approach of anticipating cyclical behaviour in markets is similar to Luke's focus on the big picture. Both use top-down thinking, focusing on broad themes and trends before thinking about individual shares. Both found that top-down thinking drew them towards natural resources sectors in the 2000s – Luke to the oil sector, and Nigel to the mining and alternative energy sectors, mainly outside of the UK. Both read and post extensively on bulletin boards, whereas some of our surveyors (the bottom-up type of investors) read boards but seldom post, and others never even look at bulletin boards.

This variation is in part a matter of individual personalities and different routes to becoming a full-time investor. But it also reflects a basic difference in thinking between geographers and surveyors. Bottom-up surveyors focus on hard financial facts about particular companies, which can best be obtained directly from company accounts and news announcements. Top-down geographers, on the other hand, focus on changes in market sentiment, which cannot be discerned from company accounts or news announcements. For this reason, insights into sentiment from bulletin boards are probably a more important input for geographers than for surveyors.

NIGEL: INSIGHTS AND ADVICE

Long and short cycles   Markets can be understood as a sequence of overlapping long and short cycles.

Variable length cycles   Cycles need not have a fixed time length. If the print size in a book is changed, each chapter can be printed on fewer or more pages, but the story remains the same. It is the development of the underlying cyclical narrative, rather than a uniform time period, that defines the cycle.

Find a bull market   Look for markets in a cyclical upswing. Everyone is a genius in a bull market – so find a bull market!

Bipolar markets   Markets are bipolar, swinging back and forth between different concerns, for example a focus on inflation or deflation. Bet on swings, and stay flexible.

Double and sell   When a stock doubles, consider selling half (especially if volume is falling).

Cross-market intelligence   For clues that a cycle may be about to turn, watch for moves in markets with similar economic drivers. If you hold shipping shares, watch shipping freight rates; if you hold building companies, watch land and house prices; and so on.

Bulletin boards as sentiment indicators   Bulletin board sentiment gives an insight into market sentiment: one can often see irrational exuberance or irrational pessimism on the boards. Such insights into market sentiment are probably more important for top-down geographers than bottom-up surveyors.

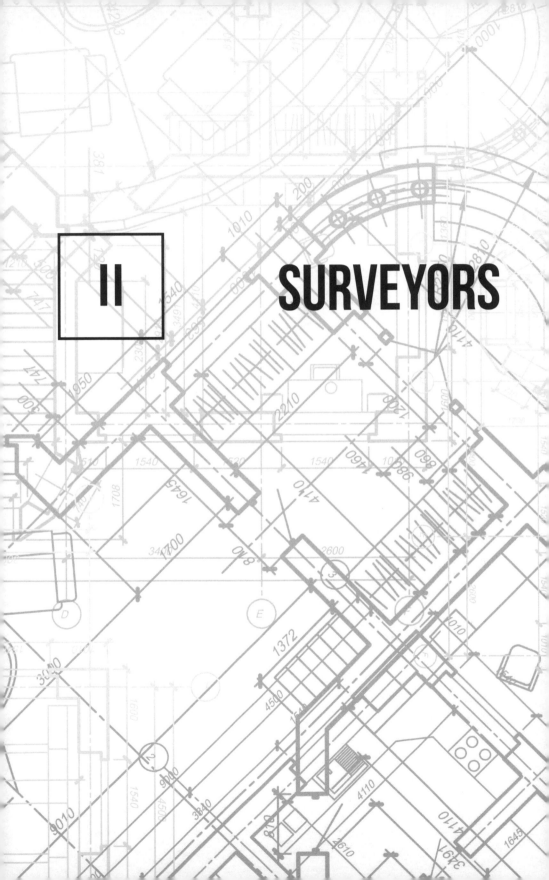

II | SURVEYORS

Surveyors start from the small picture, the individual elements of the investment landscape. They take a bottom-up approach, thinking first about the attributes of individual companies, such as market position and quality of management, and only then noting any relevant macroeconomic trends which affect individual companies.

BILL
JUST THE FACTS

BILL: FACTS AND FIGURES

Age at interview	48
Age at leaving last full-time job	41
Background	Physics, electronic engineering.
Style	Bottom-up company analysis, focusing on the few most salient facts in any situation.
Markets and sectors	All UK sectors; focus on smaller companies, but sometimes larger ones.
Instruments	Shares, spread bets.
Typical holding period	Weeks to months.
Performance indicators	Compound portfolio return over 30% per annum from 2001 to 2009.
Quote	"The art of being wise is knowing what to overlook."
Phrases	Wisdom as neglect; defensive pessimism; value spider; bulletin board tail-coating.

Portfolio investment is a zero-sum game in which the winners are the players with an informational or analytical edge. Some investors – the archetype is Eric in Chapter 8 of this book – seek an edge through the quantity and quality of their relationships and contacts. Others seek an edge not through cultivating warm relationships, but by avoiding them, and concentrating instead on hard financial facts. They focus on the few most salient concepts or metrics in each particular situation and place little weight on 'soft' factors. Bill is an example of the latter type of investor. "I never visit companies, hardly ever go to an AGM, and speak to hardly anyone. I'm not looking for soft information. I'm looking for shares where the raw numbers scream at me to buy."

Focusing on raw numbers has been very effective for Bill. In the eight years since leaving his last full-time job, he multiplied his free capital ten times over, a compound return of over 30% per annum.

Bill is a bearded, dark-haired man in his late 40s, with little trace in his voice of his childhood in rural north Wales. A former electronics engineer, he speaks and writes crisply, always polite but with little small talk. He reminded me of software engineer Paul Graham's (complimentary) definition of a nerd: a person who focuses on substance, and expends no effort on marketing himself. Never married, he lives with his girlfriend in a modest modern house in the suburbs of an English university town. The interview took place over the kitchen table, with a brief detour to a small upstairs office.

Although Bill has done well as an investor, his lifestyle has not expanded much with his capital. "The point of investment is that it has given me independence. I have ten times my original capital, but I still love shopping at Aldi."

A difficult child

Bill grew up on a smallholding in North Wales, the son of a "good farmer but poor businessman", and he remembers feeling resentful and embarrassed for much of his childhood about the family's relative poverty. He was an intellectually independent child, more influenced by numbers and facts than by appeals to authority. "I would never believe anything just on an adult's say-so. It had to make sense and fit in with my existing knowledge or model. This probably made me difficult, but it meant I was very good at science and maths."

From the local comprehensive school he won a place to study Natural Sciences at Cambridge, where he switched to electronic engineering and graduated in 1982. Finding a job was difficult in the early 1980s recession. His insistence on wearing casual dress to interviews – "I thought they should hire for quality of work, not quality of wardrobe" – probably did not help. Eventually he found work with one of the many small home computer companies which sprang up in the early 1980s around Cambridge. But it soon went bust, and so did a second similar firm he joined.

Despite the ultimate failures of these two firms, he enjoyed working for small companies. "I was given lots of autonomy, which I thought was normal. Only later did I find that working for large companies, it wasn't normal at all!" Wearing casual dress to interviews was an early indication of his focus on substance over form, a trait which is common to most people in this book. It is an effective trait for a self-directed investor, but not helpful to career advancement in most large organisations.

Privatisations: political profits

As a consequence of his financially straitened childhood, the adult Bill was "hard-wired to save and accumulate capital – it was almost instinct for me: not for spending, but for self-protection."

Like many who started in the 1980s and 1990s, his first investments were staging privatisation shares – that is, making large applications for shares in a company being newly listed on the stock exchange and selling at a profit soon after the float. The first issue Bill stagged was the Rolls Royce privatisation in 1987. "I made 14% on Rolls Royce – not much, but having never bought shares before it seemed like easy money."

He missed the next few privatisation issues because the old-economy companies involved, such as British Steel, didn't seem appealing. "Initially I didn't see that the privatisations were rigged. But eventually I understood: the issues were priced to give an initial profit for the small investor. If a privatisation started trading at a discount, that would mean the government had made a mistake." Having realised this he bought every privatisation throughout the 1990s, recycling the proceeds from each issue to the next.

> "If a privatisation started trading at a discount, that would mean the government had made a mistake."

He took some interest in other financial news, but only at a casual level: "I would read the business pages, and buy the *Financial Times* on a Saturday, but not subscribe to *Investors Chronicle* or anything like that." He did not dislike his job as an engineer and at this time had no thoughts of becoming a full-time investor.

The tech boom: knowledge doesn't always help

Several investors in this book benefited from one or more spectacular investments in the late 1990s boom in technology shares, and one might expect a geek such as Bill to have shared in this bonanza. But as an electronics engineer, he was always acutely aware that most technical projects over-run and many new technologies are not commercially successful, so he was initially cautious about investing in technology.

By 1997, he felt "fed up of missing out on these huge profits…so I cracked". In July 1997, he bought shares in the flotation of alternative telecom network Ionica, taking advantage of a friend's preferential employee share allocation to stag the issue.

When the shares fell to a discount on some bad news shortly after the float, the employee friend reported that insiders were buying more, so Bill added more shares himself. This was not a success: he eventually sold Ionica at very low prices, and the company called in administrators in October 1998; he lost half his accumulated savings on this one share. "It was an expensive lesson. Privatisations are rigged to ensure a profit for the small investor for political reasons. Stagging other new issues often gives a profit, but the political underpin is not there."

Although chastened by this disaster Bill persevered with his shrunken portfolio. He made desultory purchases of other technology, media and telecom companies, stagged one or two technology flotations, and punted a few other recommendations from industry friends. None of these was particularly successful. "I chose some good growth companies, but you can lose money on a growing company with good prospects if you pay too much for the growth. It took me a long time to understand that."

Leaving the day job

Bill became a full-time investor almost by accident, with relatively little capital and expertise. In 2001 he started a short-lived engineering job at a telecoms company; within weeks of joining he realised that his employer was likely to go bust. Finding himself idle at work and with internet access now available on his desk, he started researching investments online and reading investment books to fill the time in an otherwise increasingly empty day.

In his own words: "I read Ben Graham's book *The Intelligent Investor*, and that was my epiphany: I became a value investor. I finally understood that rather than paying a high price for the hope of high growth, it might be better to pay a lower price for the certainty of value."[1]

After a few months of spending unoccupied time at work on his investment hobby he was made redundant. He was 41 years old and at this point expected that he would eventually find another job. "I had little capital but I did get three months' salary as redundancy, and the company had paid me a golden hello just a few months earlier. I had 20 years of modest savings and no family. So I could afford to take my time finding another job."

Bill began studying the *Financial Times* more intently, hoping that with more time he could now improve on his so far indifferent investment results. His method was initially simple, even naïve. "I looked down the price-earnings column on the prices page and found a few companies on price-earnings ratios of around five, mainly retailers and other old economy businesses. Within a week I had sold all my technology shares and switched into shares on low price-earnings ratios. It seems quite naïve now. But it worked, and the lesson I drew was that focusing on a few simple metrics worked." With enthusiasm for his investment hobby renewed and plenty of time available, he was soon spending all day online. "I probably learned more in that first few months as a full-time investor than I had in the previous 15 years of dabbling."

The increasing ease of access to information online made a crucial difference to Bill's ability to survive as an independent investor. He suspects that without this change he would probably have gone back to his engineering career. Another important factor was the new facility to spread bet on individual shares for tax-free gains (see panel). He opened his first spread betting account in early 2002, using it mainly as a proxy for direct medium-term holdings in shares, with no day-trading or other short-term trades. "Within a few months I was doing so well that I gave up any thoughts of finding another engineering job."

BACKGROUND: A PRIMER ON SPREAD BETTING

Spread betting offers significant advantages when the investor wishes to take a view which is expected to be held for only a few weeks or months. Spread bets avoid stamp duty of 0.5% on share purchases. Spread bet winnings are not taxable (and correspondingly there is no relief for losses). Bets are available on many liquid assets, including a wide range of quoted shares. The custom adopted by all UK spread betting firms is that share spread bets expire quarterly, on the Tuesday prior to the third Wednesday on any of the quarter months (March, June, September or December).

Example

Suppose it is now 1 May, the LIBOR interest rate is 1.75% per annum, and the bookmaker's interest margin on funding provided to clients is 2.25% per annum, giving a total interest rate of 4% per annum. The bid-ask spread for a share is 70-72p in the market, and the share is expected to go ex-div with a dividend of 2p on 14 May. The spread bet middle price for the September contract will be

$$71p \times (1.04)^{199/365} - 2p = 70.5p$$

where interest on the 2p dividend has been ignored. The bookmaker applies the market spread of 2p and an additional bookmaker's spread of say 0.3% (~0.2p) either side around this price, and makes a September bid-ask quote of say 69.3-71.7 to the client. Bets are expressed in pounds per penny on this price. A client who wants an economic exposure equivalent to owning 10,000 shares would "buy £100 of September at 71.7."

After the bet has been opened, the client's position is 'marked to market' in real time. A client with a position of size £100 gains or loses £100 for every penny that the price moves. If a large price movement against the client occurs, the client may be required to pay a margin call; that is, deposit funds with the bookmaker to cover the marked-to-market losses.

When the client wishes to close the position, she gives an equivalent but opposite order to the original opening order. In the example above, suppose that 30 days later the quote for the share in the market is now 80-83p, and the share has now gone ex-dividend. The spread bet middle price for September will be

$$81\tfrac{1}{2}\text{p} \times (1.04)^{169/365} = 83.0\text{p}.$$

After applying market spread and the bookmaker's spread (assumed at 0.3% either side), the September bid-ask quote would be say 81.8-84.2. To close her position, the client would sell £100 of September at 81.8. The client's profit on the trade is (81.8-71.7) x £100 = £1,010.

Bookmakers will typically quote for at least the next three quarterly expiries, that is up to nine months ahead. Although it is uncommon, positions can in practice be maintained for longer than this, because bets which are close to expiry can be rolled over into the next contract. On a rollover the funding cost to the next expiry will be charged, plus a bookmaker's spread; but typically the spread would be charged on only one side (e.g. on the opening of the new contract, but not on the closing of the expiring one), and at a reduced rate compared to the normal spread for a new trade.

Spread betting, shorting and over-confidence

Apart from tax-free gains, another advantage of spread betting is the facility to short sell individual shares – to bet that the price will fall. Within a few weeks of opening his spread bet account Bill had made his first short, on the now defunct telecom company KPNQwest.

This drew on both his industry knowledge of telecoms, and his negative experience as an investor in Ionica. "There were too many alternative telecom networks. I happened to get hold of a detailed broker note which predicted several of them would go bust, and I thought the analysis was compelling. I chose the one with the most pressing debts. I started shorting it at six euros and kept adding to the position all the way down to 40 cents. I made a crazy amount of money on that in just a few months."

When the shares fell further to only a few cents, there was probably no remaining value to shareholders, and Bill thought the company's statements to the markets said as much. The share price nevertheless became very volatile, sometimes doubling and halving again within a few hours. Simon Cawkwell, the famously bearish trader and market commentator, calls this a "past particle": the company is finished but the share price bounces around like a dust particle. With a large short position, Bill felt he needed to watch the price in real time. The need for close attention to large positions was another factor in his decision not to return to his engineering career.

As with many new spread bettors, Bill's initial success with short selling quickly led to over-confidence and excessive leverage. Within months he was down 25% of his equity on a single long position, although he wasn't forced to close the position, and about half the loss was subsequently recovered. He even had to sell directly-held shares to meet margin calls – a sure sign of mismanaged leverage.

His nemesis in short selling came a few years later on the estate agent Countrywide. He had previously made money from his bullish view on the housing market by spread betting on the Halifax House Price index. "At one point I owned three virtual houses, in addition to my bricks-and-mortar house." Emboldened by this success, and having turned bearish on the housing market, he had a bearish view of estate agents such as Countrywide. When the company announced a one-third fall in its sales pipeline in the autumn of 2004 he felt confident about short selling the shares. "Because I was so sure I was right, I kept adding to the position as the price went against me." After a couple of years he closed the short 75% above his entry price, crystallising a loss of 20% of his now much larger portfolio. "It was an expensive lesson that all fundamental investors have to learn: the market can remain irrational longer than you can remain solvent. It was also the last time I over-traded."

Bill has continued spread betting on individual shares, often including short positions. At the time of the interview he was net short in his spread bet accounts – that is, his total short positions (bets on shares to fall) exceeded his total long positions (bets on shares to rise). Despite the bad experience with Countrywide, he still does not use pre-defined stop-loss orders (see panel). If a share price falls after an initial purchase, he will usually buy more shares, *provided the story has not changed*.

Like many experienced spread bettors, he has sometimes been inconvenienced by sudden drastic reductions in spread betting firms' credit limits for clients, which were a feature of the bear market in 2007-09. But with relatively low leverage, he has had no further large drawdowns.

BACKGROUND: SHOULD AN INVESTOR USE STOP-LOSS ORDERS?

A stop-loss order or 'stop' is an instruction left by the investor with a broker (or spread bet or CFD provider) to close a position as soon as possible once a certain size of loss is reached. For example, having bought shares at 100p, an investor might set a stop at 90p. If the share price falls to this level the broker will immediately attempt to sell the shares; if the price of 90p is actually achieved the investor's loss limited to 10%. An important caveat with stop-loss orders is that in general, selling at the stated stop-loss price is on a 'best endeavours' basis, and is *not* guaranteed if the price crashes. For example, if the company releases some bad news, the share price might immediately 'gap' down from 100p to 80p or below. The stop-loss order would then be executed by the broker, but at the lower price, giving the investor a larger loss than envisaged when setting the stop.[2]

The use of stop-loss orders is a controversial topic. Many people with a trading (rather than investing) background emphasise the importance of stops in preserving a trader's capital and avoiding blow-ups. For an investor who is highly leveraged this is probably correct: in the example above, if the investor is five times leveraged when the share gaps down from 100p to 80p, his entire capital would be wiped out. The stop-loss order increases the chance that the leveraged investor will live to fight another day.

But most investors in this book use little leverage. For an unleveraged investor, given a plausible probability distribution of investment returns before a stop-loss, it is not straightforward to show that adding a stop-loss statistically improves the distribution.

More intuitively, stop-loss orders represent an intention to sell based purely on price movements, with no new information or insights. They represent implicit acceptance that the market knows more than you know about the share. This acceptance seems difficult to reconcile with the expectation that you will take money out of the market over the long-term.

Stop-loss orders may be useful for reasons of psychological self-control, or as a warning flag to reassess the rationale for a position, or as a control mechanism in organisational contexts with delegated authority. But for the self-directed and self-aware investor, it is probably more reliable to control losses by limiting your leverage and position sizes, rather than taking large leveraged positions and then creating an illusion of safety and control via stop-loss orders.

Knowing what to overlook

Almost a decade after his initial successes as a value investor, Bill still favours the same facts-driven value-investing approach. The basic metric of a price-earnings ratio is his most important screen.

But he has now become aware of some scenarios where a low price-earnings ratio may not be the best metric. For recovery situations, he uses price-sales ratios, or EV/sales ratios (enterprise value divided by sales), and so on (books explaining these terms are given in an endnote).[3] For mining companies, he uses net asset values, "combined with subjective assessment of the potential of the assets from a couple of bulletin board posters I trust." For takeovers, he writes down assessments of the probabilities of various outcomes (the bid succeeding, a higher bid, the bidder withdrawing, etc). Despite these refinements, he still finds simple screens preferable to detailed discounted cash flow (DCF) or other complex calculations.

His strategy of focusing on a few essential points recalls an aphorism of 19th century American philosopher William James: "*the art of being wise is knowing what to overlook.*"[4] In further support of this preference for simple metrics Bill recalled a comment which Warren Buffett's investment partner Charlie Munger made at the 1996 Berkshire Hathaway annual meeting. In answer to a shareholder's question about sophisticated valuation methods, Munger remarked: "*Warren often talks about these DCF calculations, but I've never seen him do one.*"

Unlike many investors in this book Bill does not restrict his portfolio exclusively to smaller companies. Aren't large companies more difficult to understand? "Not necessarily. Rather than size, it depends on the type of company. The asset value of a bank is always suspect because it is the small difference between two large numbers. And the price-earning ratio of a bank is suspect because banking is so cyclical. A large bank, or even a small one, is more difficult to understand than a large manufacturing or retail company."

Whilst Bill relies heavily on metrics such as price-earnings ratios, he also considers earnings visibility; that is, the extent to which future earnings are predictable. He finds it surprising that company earnings forecasts are not published with an indication of a range or standard error. A dominant retailer of a large volume of small-ticket items – say Tesco in the UK – has highly visible earnings, and so the error band around earnings forecasts for Tesco should be a lot narrower than for a business with less visible earnings, say a currently loss-making technology start-up. But a great deal of published analysis and commentary implicitly compares single-point earnings forecasts for different types of business as if they were directly comparable.

Working methods

When Bill first left engineering he worked intensely at investing, spending 11 or 12 hours on concentrated investment work every day. As time has passed his approach has become more relaxed for a variety of reasons. "Partly because I now have enough money. Partly because of complacency. But also partly because I have become more efficient – I am a lot quicker now at recognising when I don't need to evaluate a company."

Nowadays he usually starts work between 7 and 8am each morning. He opens a web browser with several tabs – one for prices of all shares in his portfolio, one for all RNS statements, one for his main online brokers, and one for each of the main bulletin boards he follows – a few boards at Motley Fool, and all ADVFN boards via the news search function. He does not find working alone all day irksome. "I have always been an introvert. My guilty secret is that most of the time, I actually *like* being here on my own."

Bill is prepared sometimes to act quickly without much research, if he reads news or a compelling argument (for example, a bulletin board post by a poster he respects) which suggests that the price of an unfamiliar company should be much higher or lower. The willingness to act on incomplete information is driven partly by a psychological motive which he characterises as "fear of missing out – it's often the impetus to act for me," and partly by "simple laziness."

Bill keeps all his notes on specific companies in a single giant Excel spreadsheet which he has maintained for several years. As an engineer he was accustomed to keeping a general daybook, and that is effectively what he does for investments. Notes on companies he is researching are written (or often, copied and pasted from the web) into cells in the spreadsheet. Records of actual trades are written in bold. He uses the auto-filter function in Excel to select by company name, and can thus quickly display all his daybook entries for the past several years on any particular company.

He admits that a database such as Microsoft Access might be a better solution, but when he started the spreadsheet he was not familiar with databases. After making notes, in many cases he may never read them again, but nevertheless he feels that the *process* of making notes helps his thinking. Bill stressed the importance of this spreadsheet in structuring his thoughts – "it is overwhelmingly valuable to me." Because of the importance of the spreadsheet, a back-up copy is emailed every few days to a remote storage location.

Most of Bill's dealing is done online – "it's cheaper, quicker and I dislike bothering people on the phone." Many trades are done in the first hour of trading, but he does trade at other times as well, and is usually at home and at or near his desk for most of the trading day. He occasionally uses a voice broker for dealing in particularly illiquid companies.

Bill seldom speaks with company directors, and almost never attends AGMs or other company meetings. This is partly because of his focus on essential facts in any situation – "to me the numbers tell the story"; and partly because he feels he would get less out of such interactions than some investors – "I am a poor judge of character." He also thinks that attending company meetings would make him less objective and dispassionate about selling, "which is often the most difficult decision anyway". For similar reasons, he seldom reads annual reports: "most of the numbers are in the RNS, and the annual report is partly a PR exercise".

Bill's focus on key numbers is what one might expect from an electronics engineer. One might also expect some interest in highly quantitative analyses – data mining, back-testing, and other statistical approaches – applied either to prices or company accounting data. But Bill has not pursued such analyses. He gave several reasons: "partly because decent data would probably cost money, and I am too tight to pay for it; partly because I think over-fitting is an intractable problem; partly because it just hasn't been necessary: I've done fine with simpler methods, and I spend too much time on investing as it is."

But he has not entirely eschewed his technical background: he does a little programming – "just simple html and javascript" – for a shares information website he has developed, experimenting with different spreadsheet and visual presentations of investment data. One particularly original presentation he has developed is the "value spider" (see the next panel).

BACKGROUND: THE VALUE SPIDER

The value spider is a graphical representation of the financial metrics of a share compared to average metrics. Each of the spokes of the graph represents a different metric – price-earnings (p/e) ratio, yield, enterprise value to earning power (EV/EBITDA), and so on (books explaining these terms are given in an endnote).[5]

The average value of each metric across all shares in the market is normalised and plotted along each spoke, so that when a line is drawn through all these average values, it forms a smooth circle. The value of each metric for the particular share being studied is also plotted along each spoke. A line is then drawn through these plots (like a spider spinning a web) to form an irregular shape. The dimensions and geometry of this shape then characterise the share's particular strengths and weaknesses.

Basic value metrics are represented on the right-hand side spokes – starting from 12 o'clock and proceeding clockwise the spokes represent EV/EBITDA, forecast yield, price to book value, trailing and forward price-earnings ratios, EV/sales, forecast growth in earnings per share, and forecast growth in turnover. 'Quality' metrics are on the left-hand spokes – starting from 7 o'clock and proceeding clockwise the spokes represent visibility of earnings, net gearing, return on capital employed (ROCE), cash flow/EPS, dividend cover, operating margin, and directors' shareholdings.

The value spiders shown are for two shares from the *Investors Chronicle*'s annual list of bargain shares (those with unusually attractive basic value metrics) as at February 2010. Telford Homes is strong on some basic value metrics, particularly trailing price-earnings ratio and growth, but relatively weak on most quality measures. On the other hand, KBC Advanced Technologies has only moderately attractive basic value metrics, but is strong on quality measures.

Value spider for Telford Homes as at February 2010

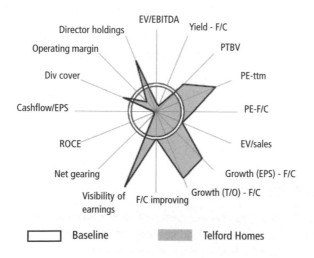

Source: original drawn by Bill

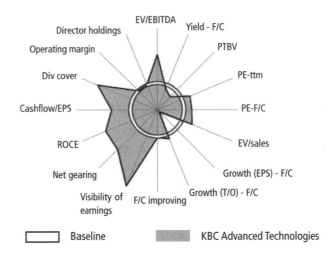

Value spider for KBC Advanced Technologies as at February 2010

Baseline | KBC Advanced Technologies

Source: original drawn by Bill

Bulletin boards and tail-coating

Despite (or perhaps because of) his intellectual independence and self-confidence, Bill is pragmatic about deferring to recognisably superior investment expertise whenever and wherever he finds it. His candid description for this technique is *tail-coating*.

"There are some private investors who are clearly more knowledgeable than me, particularly in specialist sectors like oil and gas. In these sectors I rely a lot on a few bulletin board posters whose ability I respect."

Reflecting his reliance on a few key posters he often prefers to monitor bulletin board discussions by searching on a poster's name, rather than on a company name or a topic. "For a few people, I want to read everything they write. It has taken me years to identify these people." Bill's willingness to tail-coat on others' expertise wherever it helps recalls a maxim of the professional investor Nils Taube (1925-2008): "use your eyes and plagiarise!"

He provides some ideas for others to tail-coat in return: his history on one bulletin board alone runs to more than 3000 posts. His posts tend to have a high information content and low discursiveness, summarising just a few key numbers, reflecting his usual focus on essentials.

Apart from his own posts on bulletin boards Bill also does some freelance writing for an investment site. This is primarily for ego, rather than money – "I've been a writer *manqué* for years." Rather than the usual approach tipping shares to buy, his articles have focused on idiosyncratic accounting and other features which can mean that a superficially

> "To make good decisions, you need to look actively for reasons not to buy a company."

attractive share is not a good buy. He thinks this defensive pessimism is a useful mental habit for an investor. "It is always easy to think of reasons to buy a company. That is what most tipsters do. To make good decisions, you need to look actively for reasons not to buy a company. And then invest only in those where you can live with those reasons."

Conclusion

Bill gives the impression of being an intellectually self-reliant individual, which he thinks has been important to him as an investor: "you need some inner confidence to prevent the pain of losses leading to an emotional decision to sell."

But this self-confidence is balanced by a matter-of-fact awareness of weaknesses, illustrated by observations scattered with unprompted candour throughout the interview, including:

> "Investment is a field where knowing your limitations is more important than stretching to surpass them."

not attending company meetings "because I am a poor judge of character"; sometimes making decisions too quickly with inadequate information "because of my pathological fear of missing out"; and spending less time on investment research in recent years than a few years ago because of "simple laziness". Such self-insight is especially valuable in investment, a field where knowing your limitations is more important than stretching to surpass them.

BILL: INSIGHTS AND ADVICE

Wisdom as neglect   The art of being wise is knowing what to overlook.

Selective attention   Focus on the few most salient metrics and facts in any situation. Different metrics and facts are salient for different types of company and situation.

Substance over form   A focus on substance over form is probably more effective in investing than in most organisations or in public life.

Stop-loss scepticism   It is not straightforward to show that stop-loss orders improve your expected distribution of returns. It is probably better to limit losses by taking smaller positions and diversifying, rather than taking larger positions with stop-losses.

Note-taking as mental organisation   When researching investment ideas, the *process* of making notes helps to organise your thinking, even if you never look at your notes again.

Defensive pessimism   This can be a useful habit for an investor. Look actively for reasons *not* to buy a company, and then invest only in those where you can live with those reasons.

Tail-coating on bulletin boards   Look for smart posters rather than interesting topics; read everything they write; tail-coat their best ideas.

JOHN LEE
DEFENSIVE VALUE AND DIVIDENDS

JOHN LEE: FACTS AND FIGURES

Age at interview	68
Age at leaving last full-time job	50
Background	Chartered accountant; member of parliament and minister; financial journalist.
Style	Focus on basic value metrics, especially dividends.
Markets and sectors	UK small caps, especially family-controlled 'proprietorial' companies.
Instruments	Shares
Typical holding period	Years
Performance indicators	ISA millionaire by 2003; published records in the *Financial Times* show capital return of +87% over 2001-2009, compared with -7% on the FT-Actuaries All Share Index.
Quote	"Common sense and patience are the keys to long-term investment success."
Phrases	DVD investing; 'proprietorial' companies; common sense and patience.

John Lee bought his first shares more than 50 years ago, before most people in this book were born. The straightforward investment principles which he follows – paying particular attention to dividends, and the signals conveyed by increases or cuts in dividends – have not changed much over the years. He describes his approach as 'DVD' investing: Defensive Value and Dividends. He typically buys 'Double Seven' shares – those with both a price-earnings ratio below 7, and a dividend yield above 7%. Labels like DVD and Double Seven developed through writing his monthly 'My portfolio' column in the *Financial Times*.

John's distinctive biography – a former Tory MP and minister in the 1980s who became a Liberal Democrat peer in 2006 – means that there is little point in disguising his real name. His constituency as an MP was in Lancashire, and for much of his life he has lived partly in London and partly in the northwest. At the time of the interview his role as Liberal Democrat House of Lords whip and spokesperson for various portfolios means that he is in London Mondays to Thursdays during the week when Parliament is sitting. Weekends and parliamentary recesses are spent at Altrincham in Cheshire.

The interview took place in the house on a quiet street in Chelsea which he bought in 1972. Settled in an antique armchair in the small living room, John talked genially about his investment approach and experiences, with the same obvious enjoyment that always pervades his *Financial Times* columns. The only interruption was a welcome one – the daily telephone call from one of his two stockbrokers around 4.30pm, updating him on market news on his current shareholdings.

Doctor's son

John was born in Manchester in 1942, the son of a general practitioner and a mother who was a teacher and later a child psychologist. Shortly before John left grammar school, he took a vocational guidance test which recommended a commercial or accountancy career. After five years of articles he duly qualified as a chartered accountant in 1964: "very useful, but tedious". Even before getting his final results, he joined Henry Cooke Stockbrokers in Manchester, becoming PA to the senior partner, which was a great improvement on life as a chartered accountant: "enjoyable and exciting; at the age of 22 I was being paid to practise my hobby – investing."

This hobby originated from his father, whose own father died when he was 16, forcing him to leave school early, a misfortune which John thinks probably inspired his father's lifelong thriftiness and interest in investing. He remembers his father "sitting on the floor of his study, pipe in mouth, surrounded by piles of *Investors Chronicle* and the old *Stock Exchange Gazette.*"

John remembers saving pocket money in a Post Office savings account from an early age. He made his own first share purchase at the age of 16, and still remembers the details – £45 in the one-ship company Aviation & Shipping – and the unpropitious outcome: "In due course ship, company and shareholding all foundered, but I persevered."

After two years at Henry Cooke, he left to found a regional corporate finance advisory business, Second City Securities, with a group of similarly precocious colleagues. In the early 1970s this evolved into a banking operation named Chancery Trust, which had a retainer to introduce special situations to Slater Walker – then in its heyday as a conglomerate. By 1972, at the age of 30, John was thinking seriously about a career in politics. A period of illness led to him stepping back from day-to-day involvement in the business. In 1973 he sold his interest in the business for cash, thus establishing a degree of financial independence and releasing some free capital, which became the nucleus of his investment portfolio over the next several decades.

Politics

John's interest in politics arose largely through his upbringing. His father briefly served as a Conservative county councillor (his political career was curtailed by ill health), and John himself joined the Young Conservatives as a teenager. After selling his interest in Chancery Trust he worked for the shadow chancellor Robert Carr in 1974, and subsequently contested a Labour stronghold seat in Manchester in October that year for the Conservative party, before being adopted for the marginal constituency of Nelson & Colne in Lancashire.

Over the next five years he took a day-job as an in-house corporate financier with Paterson Zachonis, subsequently to become PZ Cussons, a cornerstone of his investment portfolio. He spent evenings and weekends campaigning in the constituency, which he won from Labour by a margin of 400 votes in the 1979 election.

He served as a minister in the departments of defence and then employment, becoming minister for tourism from 1987 to 1989. He returned to the backbenches in 1989, partly in order to spend more time nursing his always precariously narrow constituency majority. Press cuttings from his years as an MP suggest that he was always on the moderate one nation and pro-European wing of the Conservative party. In 1990 he was one of five former ministers who voted with Labour against the poll tax, and he was an early and public supporter of Michael Heseltine for party leader. His majority succumbed to the national swing against the Conservatives in 1992.

He had little further involvement with the Conservative Party after 1992, and became increasingly unhappy with what he perceived as its anti-European and socially intolerant messages as the 1990s progressed, so that he eventually resigned his membership in late 1997. In the 2001 general election campaign, he joined the Liberal Democrats. In 2006 he became a working peer.

John remained an active investor throughout his years as an MP. How did his investment activities interface with his political career? "Having a second source of income was always a reassuring source of independence as an MP, especially in the light of my marginal majority. I had to avoid shares in businesses directly related to my ministerial responsibilities, but that was only a minor inconvenience. I was only 50 when I lost my seat, with no other career or business, so there was a big drop in earned income. I was glad to have my investments at that time."

Defensive value and dividends

Asked to elaborate on "defensive value and dividends", John said that the "defensive value" part meant "focusing on assets, and on avoiding losses before thinking about profits." The "dividends" part is "important not only for the obvious reason of the cash, but because it acts as a discipline – for a company to pay a dividend, the profits have to be real." He looks for companies "where I can understand the business and its philosophy, and where the management have significant shareholdings themselves." Often these criteria lead to what he calls "proprietorial" companies – those controlled by a family or families, who emphasise preserving the business rather than taking major risks, and where the presence of non-working family members who live on the income from their shareholding ensures a heavy emphasis on maintaining and increasing dividends.

"He often finds and invests in 'proprietorial' companies – those controlled by a family or families, who emphasise preserving the business rather than taking major risks."

In contrast, in larger companies directors' shareholdings are often small compared to their remuneration, and so dividend decisions may have little regard to shareholders who rely on dividend income. Another advantage of proprietorial companies is the usually reliable character of management. "They tend to be largely honest. I have had hardly any problems with knaves – I think that can be more of a problem at other types of small company, for example those which grow rapidly through acquisitions, or what I call hope-and-pray flotations."

The DVD approach excludes some types of share favoured by many private investors: 'hot tips' of speculative mining, oil and biotech stocks, 'shell' companies, and 'recovery' situations. John is content to leave all these to one side. "The value of a share is essentially the combination of the underlying profitability of the company, and the price/earnings rating the investment community applies to it. Where the profitability is unproven and based solely on hopes for the future, that is very difficult to evaluate – too difficult for most investors, and certainly for me." He does sometimes buy property companies, where net asset values rather than dividends are the primary metric. But he would only rarely contemplate buying a property share at a premium to net asset value, and is "mystified as to why other investors often do so."

As well as offering more "defensive value and dividends", small-cap companies have several other advantages: "they are less well researched, they are more likely to be takeover targets, and the directors are usually accessible to the serious private investor." But John will buy "defensive value and dividends" wherever he finds it, and has no arbitrary size limit for the market capitalisation of companies he holds.

At the time of the interview in late 2009, he had recently bought two of the largest companies in the FTSE100 index, BP and Vodafone. "I wouldn't normally invest in such large companies. But they currently have dividend yields over 6%, which is much better than cash at the moment. And because of their liquidity, I can turn the holdings into cash immediately at any time. I often cannot do that with my usual type of shares." Some investors describe this as a 'placeholder' investment – a solid and unexceptional share which holds liquid capacity in a portfolio until it can be switched into a better idea. (In view of what happened to BP following the Gulf of Mexico oil spill in April 2010, John's July 2010 *Financial Times* column gives a frank revelation of the result: his BP shares were sold at 442p for an 18% loss in May 2010, partly offset by around 3% received in dividends over the period of ownership.)

Although John is indisputably a value investor, he is a pragmatic one, concerned mainly with finding ideas which satisfy common sense rather than faithful adherence to one true creed of value. There is a more dogmatic type of value investor, the value bore, who is more concerned with Pharisaic debate on whether a share satisfies the tenets of 'true value' investing, rather than whether it should be bought or sold.

> "There is a more dogmatic type of value investor, the value bore, who is more concerned with Pharisaic debate on whether a share satisfies the tenets of 'true value' investing, rather than whether it should be bought or sold."

The relationship between dogmatism and achievement is a rare instance of close analogy between investment and John's other field of politics: the most accomplished investors and politicians tend to be flexible and pragmatic, but the ranks of second-raters include the dogmatists and bores.

Meetings: enjoying the process

John is a believer in the value of company meetings: he attends many AGMs, and also aims to visit many of his companies "in the field", at their factories or offices. Typically he might attend up to a dozen AGMs every year, as well as a few other meetings. He has visited many of his long-term holdings several times, either for AGMs or one-to-one meetings.

Although he thinks that meetings improve his investment results, he is candid that he attends them and visits companies partly because he enjoys the process. He usually finds arranging meetings with smaller companies straightforward, and thinks meetings should generally be easy to arrange for "any serious private investor", although he admits that his *Financial Times* column may make some companies keener to talk to him.

One disadvantage he recognises of establishing a relationship with companies is that "you can feel a bit of a heel about selling – sometimes you are inclined to stay aboard too long because of that." But on balance he is confident that meetings help him to make better decisions.

Portfolio management and ISAs

At any time John typically holds around 50 stocks, around half fully listed and half on AIM. In many cases the AIM holdings are long-established companies which previously had a full listing, but transferred to AIM for the lower regulation and the tax advantages for shareholders – increased capital gains taper relief (in the period 2002-08), and exemption from inheritance tax after shares have been held for at least two years.

His largest holdings tend to be in obscure companies. For example, in one of his *Financial Times* columns in 2007, he listed his ten largest holdings as Christie Group, Gooch & Housego, Pochins, PZ Cussons, Quarto, Titon, Town Centre, Treatt, Wellington Market and Windsor. As he noted in the article, nobody could accuse him of following the herd.

He does not deal every day, and approvingly quoted Warren Buffett's maxim: "*lethargy bordering on sloth remains the cornerstone of our investment style.*" But because of his focus on small companies, which tend to be relatively illiquid, he will typically need to make many purchases over a period of weeks or months to build up his desired size of holding; and similarly when selling, unless the company is taken over. Thus he places a few buy or sell orders in most weeks, but most are small increases or decreases in larger positions rather than completely new ideas. Some shares have been in his portfolio for decades. He will sometimes make marginal sales of these holdings when they advance, leaving the bulk of the holding undisturbed, and then increase the position again when the price has fallen back.

Very long holding periods in very successful companies have in a few cases led to him receiving an *annual* recurring dividend greater than the original total cost of the investment. One example is the northwest builder and property developer Pochins, which at its peak price reached around *80 times* his cost (although the shares fell and the dividend was cut in the 2008-09 building downturn).

PZ Cussons, a Manchester-based soap manufacturer which celebrated its 125th anniversary in 2009 and has extensive operations in Africa and Asia, is another large long-term holding, which John has held continuously since 1976. The longevity and growth of this business as a listed company is remarkable. It floated in 1953 with a market capitalisation of £1.2m, and over the next 57 years grew to be an international manufacturer of soaps, toiletries, cosmetics and detergents, with a market capitalisation which had multiplied more than 1000-fold to over £1bn. This growth seems stupendous, but compound interest is both compelling and counter-intuitive: 1000-fold growth over 57 years actually corresponds to a growth rate of just under 13% per annum.

As a long-term investor, John is well aware of this compelling arithmetic in tax-free personal equity plans (PEPs) since 1987, and individual savings accounts (ISAs) since 1999. He has made maximum contributions to PEPs and ISAs every year since 1987, in some years funded by selling part of his taxed portfolio. As early as 2003, his PEP and ISA contributions of £126,200 had already accumulated to more than £1m, a result which he wrote about in the *Financial Times*. "I thought for quite some time before doing that. I didn't want to appear a show-off, but I wanted to illustrate the long-term advantage of compounding regular contributions,

"His ISA portfolio published in 2003 contained 18 holdings; as of late 2009, it still held 11 of these."

because lots of people misunderstand this. High earners are often dismissive of ISAs, because the annual limits seem low to them. Many people who could afford an ISA every year are inconsistent – they buy fad funds in some years and make no contributions in others. That article showed the benefit of long-term regular contributions with a slow-motion, common-sense approach to investment." The "slow-motion" aspect can be illustrated by noting that his ISA portfolio published in 2003 contained 18 holdings; as of late 2009, it still held 11 of these; five had been taken over, and only three had been sold.

Outside of PEPs and ISAs, John has paid some capital gains tax annually for many years. Many of his gains are from passive realisations forced by takeovers, capital distributions or other corporate events: "with a portfolio of 50 stocks, there is always something happening on the corporate activity front." Because most of the 50 stocks are dividend payers, the portfolio yields a steady stream of final and interim dividends. So even if he makes no active sell decisions, there is always a flow of realisations and income available for new investments.

A difficult aspect of portfolio management is dealing decisively with stocks which turn into disappointments. John mentioned a number of early warning signs: results delayed, auditors or directors resigning, change of accounting year-end, and "too many acquisitions." He tends to give management the benefit of the doubt initially, which inevitably means some of his stocks go from bad to worse. On a number of occasions his *Financial Times* column has noted a resolution along the lines of "try to remember that my portfolio is not a joint venture with the Salvation Army!" Perhaps a little too much tolerance for the occasional serial disappointer is an inevitable corollary of the "lethargy bordering on sloth" which works well most of the time.

In a 50-year career in the stock market, John has never borrowed money to invest, not even in the early 1970s period when borrowing for any purpose was made tax-deductible. Nor has he experimented with other forms of gearing such as spread betting or contracts for difference. He has not borrowed even to buy property, except when buying his first house. He and his wife live in the same house in Cheshire that has been the family home since 1975; his London house was bought for accommodation rather than investment. "Shares are where the interest has always been for me. I have done quite well on some property companies, but that is the limit of my investment in property."

A sense of history

John's conservative investing style with no leverage and a focus on profitable, dividend-paying companies is partly a product of formative investing experiences in the secondary banking crisis of the early 1970s. In 1973-74 several secondary banks failed, and there were even rumours about the viability of Natwest Bank.

"It helps an investor to have a sense of history. Knowing the full range of what has gone wrong before makes you better prepared for what might go wrong again." In the years leading up to 2007 he often referred to this period in his *Financial Times* column, justifying his cautious approach by the likelihood of another crisis at some point. This came to pass in 2008, and the crisis was probably worse than in 1973/74, at least in the banking sector, with two of the largest clearing banks, Royal Bank of Scotland and Lloyds/HBOS, being effectively nationalised.

He also remembered the sharp turnaround in January 1975, when the FT30 index (the bellwether London market index of its day) doubled in six weeks. This made him wary of market timing the bottom in 2008. "I believe that when an individual stock seems cheap, one should buy and ignore whether general market movements might make it 10% cheaper next week." As a further argument against market timing, he noted another conundrum. "If you think Armageddon is coming, what are you actually going to do? Sell all your shares and hide under the bed with a crate of whiskey? In that scenario, if Armageddon is averted, then with hindsight shares will have been a massive bargain. And if Armageddon materialises, you would have bigger worries than your share portfolio."

A published performance record

John's activity with his 'My Portfolio' column means that he periodically gives an appraisal and review of the past calendar year in print. By collating press cuttings, I estimated the approximate long-term performance record shown in the table.

This compares actual portfolio capital return each year with the FT-Actuaries Smallcap Index capital return, which seems the most pertinent index for a portfolio invested predominantly in smaller companies. The bottom of the table gives the compound accumulation after nine years, with comparatives for the Smallcap, FTSE100, and All-Share indices. The dividend yield is about 3% per annum from the portfolio and the dividends from the indices are additional to these figures and broadly balance out. Under any reasonable comparison, performance is superb over the entire nine-year period, but the out-performance is concentrated in the earlier years.

The capital return from investing in the entire Smallcap index over the nine-year period (-13%) was much the same as that from the FTSE100 (also -13%) or the All-Share (-7%). This illustrates that the out-performance of the actual portfolio is not simply a 'size effect', but probably a combination of a 'neglect effect' and skill. Over this period, small companies in aggregate did not provide higher returns than large companies; but individual small companies were more likely to be neglected, leading to mis-pricings which a skilful stock-picker could exploit.

COMPARISON OF CAPITAL RETURNS ON JOHN'S ACTUAL PORTFOLIO AND MARKET INDICES

(a) Annual capital returns

Year	(1) John's portfolio returns	(2) FTA Smallcap Index	(3) John – benchmark (1) – (2)
2001	+5%	-19%	+24%
2002	+5%	-29%	+34%
2003	+44%	+36%	+8%
2004	+30%	+11%	+19%
2005	+20%	+20%	0%
2006	+18%	+18%	0%
2007	-14%	-12%	-2%
2008	-42%	-46%	+4%
2009	+28%	+50%	-22%

(b) Cumulative capital returns, 2001–2009

	Cumulative capital return (2001-09)
(1) John's portfolio:	+87%
(2) FTA Smallcap Index :	-13%
(3) FTSE100 Index:	-13%
(4) FTA All-Share Index:	-7%

A typical investment day

Because of John's work as an active member of the House of Lords, he is not a full-time investor in the same sense as most people in this book. But he is a serious and hands-on investor in the sense of following and thinking about markets on a daily basis.

At 8.15am every morning he speaks to one of the two brokers he uses regularly for an update on any financial results or other news affecting his 50 or so holdings. He realises that most investors now do this online, but explains that he is "technologically backward, and in any case I enjoy the human contact."

How does his broker manage to convey, in a telephone conversation, the gist of a results statement which may run to several pages? "The key thing I always want to know is the dividend decision – whether it has been increased, held or cut. That usually summarises the whole picture – the results for the past year, the directors' view of the future, and the cash position of the business."

For more important statements, the broker will fax a copy. John files these in chronological order in a single file; at the end of each year he throws out the records from six years ago. He also keeps copies of the annual report and accounts for most of his companies. Where holdings are in a nominee account (for example in the ISA), he telephones the company and asks to be added to a separate mailing list for the accounts.

For the rest of the day he is occupied with House of Lords business or other interests. But wherever possible his broker will call again towards the market close at 4.30pm with another update, and will also fax a summary of closing prices. At least once a week the broker faxes a summary of the cash positions on all the ISA and family portfolios which John manages. The daily phone calls are year-round routines, which continue even when he takes his week of salmon fishing on the Tweed in March, and a week of golf in the autumn.

As already noted, John places some emphasis on meeting with companies to inform his investment decisions. But a good deal of desk-based, or at least armchair-based, research is also required to identify companies for further investigation. He uses the Hemscott Company Guide (now owned by Morningstar), and the *Financial Times* and *Investors Chronicle*. His desk-based research involves skimming chairmen's statements and basic metrics like dividend yield and price-earnings ratios. This research is broad rather than deep.

"I regard myself as being impatient – with a low boredom threshold, hopefully masked by a fairly genial disposition! I have a broad-brush approach, and I am definitely not a fine-print man." Despite this professed broad-brush approach, John is a bottom-up rather than top-down investor: his broad-brush approach is applied at the level of individual companies, not forecasting macroeconomic events.

Stockbrokers and advisors

John uses two main stockbrokers, one of them the successor firm to Henry Cooke, his employers as a 22-year-old in 1964. The individual brokers involved have changed over the years. John is "not really looking for advice – I am just looking for them to administer and execute the business I want to do. I want them to be reliable and always ring me back, that sort of thing."

"Authorisation for investment advisors is more like a fishing licence than a driving licence."

Apart from his other main stockbroker, used for his ISA, he has not found other firms satisfactory, and regrets the decline in calibre of brokers at many firms over the years. "In the old days the broker generally had some capital of his own, and would often be investing in the shares he recommended to clients. But for many of them nowadays, it is just a job. Some of them may never have bought a share for themselves, and can only recommend stocks on a house list."

What about professional fund managers?

"Personally I would not want to give management of my assets to anyone – I think authorised investment advice is a bit of a con. Authorisation for investment advisors is more like a fishing licence than a driving licence. A fishing licence confirms that you have paid a fee, and will not be fined if you are caught fishing. It says nothing about competence."

He is not a fan of the short-term operations of some professional managers such as many hedge funds. "Without wishing to sound pompous, I believe long-term investment in growing businesses is worthwhile and in the national interest, at least in a modest way. But funds focused on leveraged positions and short selling contribute nothing to the real economy. That is anathema to me."

Apart from the social merit of a long-term approach, John has also come to think that it is usually the most profitable – a view which has been reinforced by the experiment of running parallel portfolios for his two daughters, who are now in their early 30s, since they were children. He has usually bought the same stocks for them as in his own portfolio, but with a tendency towards a lower turnover. His impression is that the portfolios with less activity have tended to do better over the years. He ruefully noted that his daughters were "pleased but not particularly impressed" with this achievement; he has not been able to impart to them his fascination with investing.

Director and trustee

With John's interest in closely following companies in which he invests over periods of several years and his background in public service, he has sometimes been offered quoted company directorships.

Apart from the listing obtained via the reverse takeover of his own corporate finance business in the early 1970s, he has at various times been on the boards of PZ Cussons, James Halstead, and JR Knowles. At the time of the interview he was chairman of OFEX-listed Wellington Market Company, the leading operator of retail street markets in the UK. This limited company was incorporated by an Act of Parliament in the 19th century, and the complete history of the business extends back to 1244, when Wellington Market was established by Royal charter. "I tend to favour businesses with a trading history!"

Over the years he has also served as a trustee and a member of investment committees for a range of charities, insurance companies and other institutions, some of them with investment portfolios as large as a few billion pounds. Most of these funds have been invested predominantly in large cap stocks.

Although he has been pleased to undertake the roles, these experiences have reinforced his belief that the more interesting area of the stock market is the small-cap end. "I didn't find endless discussions on asset allocation and benchmarks particularly enlightening. And large companies have much less human interest than small companies, where you can get to know the management."

Half a century of investment delight

More than 50 years after he bought his first share, John reflected that investing has been a more constant part of his life than any other activity. Careers and directorships have come and gone; engagement in politics and party allegiances have waxed and waned; but his most enduring interest throughout has been investment. After half a century, he thinks that there are "only two keys to long-term investment success: common sense and patience. Value will always come through in the end." His enjoyment is very obvious, both in conversation and when re-reading his *Financial Times* columns, one of which concluded as follows. "For me the stock market – particularly the small-cap sector – represents a hobby and a core activity, and I am never happier than when I am thinking, talking or writing about it."

JOHN LEE: INSIGHTS AND ADVICE

DVD investing Look for companies with "defensive value and dividends": those where a large part of the share price is covered by net assets, and with a long record of paying substantial dividends.

'Proprietorial' companies Firms controlled by a family or a few families are often sound investments. The presence of non-working family members who live off their income from the company usually leads to a strong focus on maintaining dividends.

Small companies, big returns Smaller companies offer many advantages: they are more likely to be proprietorial, less well-researched, more likely to be takeover targets, and the directors are usually more accessible to the private investor.

Investment as career diversification The back-up financial support which investment provides can be particularly reassuring to a person in an unpredictable career field, such as politics!

'Placeholder' investments These are solid, unexceptional and above all liquid shares, which hold capacity in a portfolio until you find a better idea.

Early warning signs Investments which go sour are often flagged by delayed results, auditors or directors resigning, change of accounting year-end, or making too many acquisitions.

Dividends as a signal In reading company results, pay particular attention to the dividend decision. This usually summarises the whole picture: the results for the past year, the directors' view of the future, and the cash position of the business.

Back to basics Common sense and patience are the key requirements for long-term investment success.

Investment delight Getting to know your companies through meetings and field visits can be fun. Directors and other shareholders are often interesting people. Investment need not be just a source of wealth: it can be a source of delight.

5

SUSHIL
THE APOSTATE
ECONOMIST

SUSHIL: FACTS AND FIGURES

Age at interview	45
Age at leaving last full-time job	35
Background	PhD in econometrics; business economics consultancy.
Style	Focus on what he knows and why he knows it – "investment as applied epistemology".
Markets and sectors	Exclusively UK small caps; holds around 60 shares, but with nearly half his portfolio is in the largest six holdings.
Instruments	Shares, spread bets.
Typical holding period	Months.
Performance highlights	ISA millionaire by 2003; taxable funds around 10% per annum ahead of FT-A All Small Index in eight years to April 2010.
Quote	"You don't need to know everything about a company – you just need to focus on a knowable change in state."
Phrases	Post-tax thinking; Kelly betting; reluctant punter.

Most investors believe that markets work not only for them, but for everybody: they tend to favour the free-market, laissez-faire side of political arguments about the value of markets. Despite his economics background, Sushil has rather different views.

"Markets are supposedly about resource allocation," he says, "but they sometimes don't do that very well. And from the perspective of portfolio investors, they are a zero-sum game. As Keynes put it, the object of the game is usually to outwit the crowd, rather than defeat the dark forces of time and ignorance. It has always troubled me that playing a zero-sum game is better paid than brain surgery."

This angst has not prevented him from being good at the game himself: he left his last full-time job to concentrate on investment at the age of 35, although this probably reflected 'push' as well as 'pull' factors. His publicly declared stakes of more than 3% in several small quoted companies evince an aptitude for making money. At the same time, he appears to be quite uninterested in spending it.

"There are two ways of gaining freedom: increase your assets or reduce your wants. I have always tried to use both approaches."

Sushil lives and works from two adjacent modern houses on the outskirts of a commuter town in Berkshire. In the light of the large shareholdings mentioned above, the modest scale and unimposing nature of the properties was slightly surprising. He explained that he had originally contemplated buying "a castle and acres", but then realised that his needs were actually better met by two smaller houses, one to work in and one to live in. It was a characteristically unorthodox choice, which he elaborated as follows. "The main benefit of money is freedom. There are two ways of gaining freedom:

increase your assets or reduce your wants. I have always tried to use both approaches."

Sushil speaks quickly and openly in a voice which has a slight trace of his Midlands upbringing. The interview took place in front of six large flat-screen monitors suspended over and around a large desk with electric height adjustment. Sushil sat with his back against several cushions on what he called his 'day-bed' facing the screens, with his legs outstretched along the bed under the raised desk.

This unorthodox workstation reflects his many years of orthopaedic problems, starting when he was a teenager. "I've had 15 orthopaedic operations in the past 25 years. I have to sit like this for weeks whenever I'm recovering from surgery. I don't have to today, but why not? More comfortable than an office chair. No joint pain, never any backache."

Following some "triumphs of unorthodox orthopaedic surgery" he now walks with a barely perceptible limp; but he spent many years as a young adult on crutches, and his disability largely explains why his life has drifted away from a conventional career to become focused on investing.

Getting started

Sushil grew up and went to grammar school in Birmingham. He was a keen distance runner until his orthopaedic problems started shortly before his 17th birthday. A sequence of "increasingly drastic operations by increasingly frustrated surgeons with an increasingly depressed patient" followed, and he eventually spent only two terms at school in the sixth form. He then studied economics at a redbrick university.

Summer jobs with accounting firms put him off accountancy – "it wasn't so much the work, it was the regimentation" – and having obtained a first-class degree, he went on to a PhD in econometrics. He contemplated continuing an academic career, but feeling "at that time overwhelmed by the competition, and underwhelmed by the rewards," he instead joined a business economics consulting firm as a trainee.

His career in consulting was soon overshadowed by increasing disability, which made him "very discouraged about my career – it became increasingly clear that I would have difficulty keeping any sort of job." He had previously had little financial ambition, but it now dawned on him that making some money from investment could be a source of independence despite his ill health. "For the first time, at the age of 26, I really understood money: not in terms of consumption, but in terms of freedom."

He made his first investments in shares in the autumn of 1992, soon after 'Black Wednesday', with less than £5,000 saved from salary. Following redundancy the next year he took a job as a university lecturer: "an economics post in a business school, not very prestigious. But it gave me access to a university library – very important in pre-internet days – and a lot of freedom to spend time learning about investment."

Over the next few years he slowly improved his knowledge of investing, and accumulated a modest portfolio. "Always two steps forward, one step back" is his recollection of this period. "The trend was slowly upwards, but my net worth was subject to large swings, and there were often overdrafts or credit card debt. A lot of the time I felt ashamed and unhappy about it."

He now thinks that this erratic record was partly because of the process of learning through mistakes, and partly because of his poor access to information as a private investor in the pre-internet era. "When I started, my prices literally came from rubbish bins. Every evening I would go to the railway station and pick a copy of the *Evening Standard* out of a dustbin." A newspaper bought in the evening in central London by a home-bound commuter and then binned at a suburban station would be the crucial final edition, which included closing stock exchange prices (earlier editions distributed in the suburbs included only older prices).

His learning sources were eclectic: "I remember sending a $15 international money order to Omaha in 1994 for Buffett's shareholder letters. I read a lot of academic literature in the university library. I also learnt a lot from Mike Walters in the *Daily Mail*. Academics are usually rude about the *Daily Mail*, and vice versa, but I have always been open-minded and unembarrassed about sources. If I found a good idea in *The Sun*, I would use it."

The tech bubble: "synchronised stupidity"

Sushil's investments soared in the bubble in technology shares around the turn of the century. Over 18 months, his portfolio increased more than ten-fold, and he was one of the fortunate investors who held on to most of the gains.

Asked to explain how he did this, he offered the self-deprecating phrase "synchronised stupidity", which he elaborated as follows: "Naïvety at the right moment can be a strength, if it frees you to do the right thing. I was naïve enough to invest a large part of my portfolio in technology shares from about 1995 to 1998, and to stay in the sector as it rocketed through the summer and autumn of 1999. I did well by being one step ahead of the market – much better than if I had been three steps ahead. But as time went on, I was learning. So I was not naïve enough to go on buying technology shares in the Spring of 2000."

Although Sushil used disparaging terms like "naïve enough", further discussion revealed a subtle underlying rationale. "It is clear from my notes made in 1999 that I understood there was an unjustifiable bubble in technology shares from the middle of the year onwards. But once prices become detached from the anchor of fundamentals, riding a speculative bubble can be rational. I was quite conscious of what I was doing."

He never called the top of the market in technology shares. But from mid-1999 onwards, his fundamentally-driven stock-picking increasingly meant that whenever he sold a share, reinvestment tended to be away from the technology sector. As a result he suffered only modest losses from the peak of the bubble in March 2000 to the trough of the bear market in early 2003.

Leaving the day job

Whilst he was an academic, Sushil did some moonlighting as an economics consultant, earning fees on which he could make self-invested personal pension (SIPP) contributions. The pension contributions which he made in the mid to late 1990s multiplied around 30-fold over the subsequent decade, a compound growth rate of around 40% per annum, although he stressed that a good part of this was attributable to the technology shares bubble.

Increasing success as an investor contrasted sharply with his increasing difficulty in his career as an academic. "I found my day job physically distressing. I felt acutely conscious that I probably wouldn't be able to carry on in any sort of career." He was also

"Naïvety at the right moment can be a strength, if it frees you to do the right thing."

worried that his paper fortune might prove ephemeral: "at that time half of it was a single holding, so one profit warning could make a good part of it disappear."

When a few months later it hadn't disappeared, he retired from his academic job. He was 35 years old. Although he had diversified from the single large holding, he was still not confident of hanging on to the money. But as an ascetic ex-academic he also knew his spending needs were low. "I thought I could have a better life with less pain even if I lost most of the money."

Sushil initially combined investment with some home-based economics consulting, but after about 18 months the consultancy dwindled and he was left to concentrate solely on investment. Some time later some now wealthy friends from his university days learnt about his investment record, and formed a fund to co-invest in some of his ideas. "I am not involved in investment management as a business, and I decline all enquiries on this from contacts, other friends and family. But this particular fund involves a handful of investment-savvy people whom I have known for more than 20 years, who are happy to invest in my ideas alongside me, and who understand the opportunities and the risks inherent in my style of investing."

Sushil says that on a post-tax basis this fund has outperformed the FTSE All-Small Total Return Index by around 10% per annum over the eight years to April 2010. In his PEP and ISA, where there is no drag from tax, he says the result (from a starting fund already over £1m in April 2004) was out-performance of around 15% per annum over the six years to April 2010.

He also noted that small companies had lagged large companies over this period, so that his PEP & ISA's outperformance of the FTSE100 Total Return Index was less striking, only around 9% per annum.

He is pleased with these results: "they are about the best I could have hoped for, and certainly enough to justify my carrying on with this instead of paying someone else to do it." But he also made the point that he should be able to do better than most institutional investors, because on an institutional scale his total funds would be regarded as small. "When you look at exceptional fund managers like Anthony Bolton, who achieved over 6% per annum out-performance on a fund over £1bn over a long period, an unleveraged 10% per annum out-performance does not seem absurd for an investor with funds up to a few tens of millions."

As the total funds Sushil manages have increased well into eight figures, liquidity has become a bigger issue. Liquidity is the main reason for the increasing number of stocks he holds, now around 60, up from less than ten a decade ago, albeit nearly half the portfolio is held in his six largest holdings.

Conventional financial theory explains diversification as a means of reducing idiosyncratic risk; that is reducing the risks specific to each individual company, leaving the portfolio with only 'market risk'. Sushil finds this concept unhelpful – "I *want* a portfolio with large idiosyncratic risks, provided they are mis-priced". Rather than reducing idiosyncratic risk, he finds it more helpful to think of diversification as a means of increasing liquidity in his portfolio, and hence increasing options to change his mind as prices and expectations change.

He believes that overlooking the constraint of liquidity in investment decisions can sometimes lead smaller investors to misinterpret the actions of larger investors. For example, the fact that a large investor is buying or selling does not necessarily imply that a small investor with the same information and analysis should also be buying or selling. Small investors have much higher effective liquidity for their holdings, and so can (at least in principle) look to buy near the bottom and sell near the top of the market. But larger investors like Sushil cannot do this; they need to buy and sell over a much wider range of prices. "When I buy a share, nine times out of ten I want the next move in price to be down, because I hope to buy more. And when I sell, I want the next move to be up, because I have more to sell."

> "I *want* a portfolio with large idiosyncratic risks, provided they are mis-priced."

Investment strategy: knowability

When asked to give a general description of his investment strategy, Sushil demurred: "I have no strategy, and I am suspicious of all theories. I try to be flexible and use my common sense."

But as in other areas, this half-facetious answer conceals a degree of sophistication. Pressed further, he described three ways of characterising investment decisions: buying a perpetual stream of income cheaply ("the value approach"); buying in anticipation of a change in market perception ("the Keynesian beauty contest"[1]); or buying in anticipation of what he calls a "knowable change in state". He evaluated these three approaches as follows.

"The first approach is appealing, but it can be difficult in practice. The second raises the problem of why you should have a better insight into future changes in market perception than your counterparty. The third approach –

investment as applied epistemology – is a more interesting concept. It highlights that you don't need to know everything about a company, and don't need an absolute valuation of a company – you just need to focus on a knowable change in state."

He finds this emphasis on 'knowability' a useful way of directing research effort: "Focus on things which are knowable – that is, things where research can plausibly give you superior insight – for example, the microeconomic advantages of a particular company. Ignore things which are not knowable, for example, general macroeconomic predictions."

This emphasis on knowable ideas has led him to focus largely on small companies, or situations where a seller is motivated by factors such as his tax situation or an urgent need to raise funds. "I am always conscious that when I trade, I think I have superior information, but there is usually a counterparty who thinks he does. It is not plausible that I will on average be better informed than the dozens of analysts looking at any large company. So I never even look at large companies – I hold nothing in the FTSE350. But for small companies, where there may be hardly anyone following the company, it is more plausible that I may sometimes be better informed."

Few advisors, little mathematics

Sushil places almost no reliance on advisors; the one exception is feedback and tactical suggestions from his stockbroker in response to dealing instructions. He largely avoids advice from accountants and lawyers: he prepares his own company accounts and tax returns, and has occasionally conducted his own case in tax appeals and similar tribunals. "Obviously I don't have as much technical knowledge as lawyers or accountants. But I do have full knowledge of my own facts, awareness of what I want to achieve, and an ability to change my mind quickly. So far it has usually been quicker and cheaper to research problems myself than to pay for advice."

He thinks that the concept of expert advice is generally overrated in investment. "A consensus of expert opinion is not useful in investment, because it's already discounted by current market prices. That is not true in other fields – medicine or law or even plumbing." He thinks successful investors tend not to follow the orthodox paradigm of seeking advice about unfamiliar subjects, but instead have "a psychological predilection towards figuring things out for themselves."

With a PhD in econometrics, Sushil probably has some of the strongest quantitative skills amongst our interviewees, but these skills are little used in his day-to-day decisions. "A fluent and intuitive understanding of basic probability helps. You need to be able to add, subtract, multiply, divide, and you need to understand leverage and compounding. But beyond that, I don't find more advanced mathematics helpful most of the time." The emphasis on quantitative analysis by many market participants can actually create opportunities. "The most interesting situations are often where only qualitative information suggests favourable prospects. Quantitative people – or perhaps just people who need to justify themselves to a boss – seem to shy away from these situations. That leaves more opportunity for those who can act on the qualitative information."

Tax, spread betting and leverage

Many investors pay relatively little attention to the details of tax. 'The tax tail should not wag the investment dog' summarises a commonly expressed sentiment. Sushil is unusual in this respect: he regularly factors tax into his day-to-day investment decisions.

"Most things in investment are uncertain and fluid. Tax is one of the few aspects with some certainty and stability which you can do something about." He uses no tax planning schemes –"I don't want to spend my life in a courtroom" – but he always tries to think on a post-tax basis. In the mid-2000s he contemplated relocating to a tax haven, and visited Guernsey to look at houses with his then-girlfriend, before concluding that "with ISAs, SIPPs and spread betting, the UK is quite a low-tax jurisdiction for investors anyway."

Sushil uses spread betting for only a small part of his total investments, and he has mixed feelings about it. "The absence of capital gains tax is attractive. I do a little short selling of individual stocks, and spread betting is the most convenient way of doing that. I have made money from it over the past 15 years, probably about 10% of my current net worth. But it is quite difficult to make money short selling. Markets tend to go up over time. And the dynamics are unnerving: a long position which is going wrong is a shrinking problem, but a short sale which is going wrong is an increasing problem."

Apart from short sales on individual stocks, he also occasionally uses FTSE100 futures to part-hedge his overall market exposure. "But not very often, and I have never hedged more than 30% of my portfolio. Over time the market tends to go up. I don't hedge unless I have a strong bearish view. I am a reluctant punter, using spread betting for tax reasons, but not enthused about the leverage."

Sushil seldom uses spread betting for long positions, and his only other leverage is an overdraft facility with a maximum limit less than 10% of the value of his portfolio. "Leverage can be lethal. Apart from your own mistakes, lenders can reduce or cancel the facility, and this tends to happen at the worst possible times. Leverage beyond a low level is almost always a bad idea."

He thinks that many spread betting enthusiasts may not understand the mathematical implications of leveraging a portfolio. He mentioned the theory of optimal compound growth originating from mathematicians and gambling experts such as John Kelly and Ed Thorp, and suggested that many investors would benefit from studying this, as outlined in the technical background section in this chapter.[2] "It is not so much that it gives directly applicable answers, but more that it directs attention to the right questions."

> "I am a reluctant punter, using spread betting for tax reasons, but not enthused about the leverage."

TECHNICAL BACKGROUND: OPTIMAL 'KELLY' BETTING

The key points Sushil draws from the theory of optimal or 'Kelly' betting are that investors are better off maximising expected logarithmic return, not expected return, and that this often implies lower leverage than casual intuition suggests. For example, an investment which either rises 25% or falls 20% with equal probability in each period has a positive expected return of 2.5%, but an expected logarithmic return of zero. If you then leverage this investment 2x, as would be common in spread betting, it will rise 50% or fall 40% in each period. This leverage increases the expected return to 5%, but reduces the expected logarithmic return to less than zero at -0.0527. Compounding over the long term, the negative expected logarithmic return means that the leveraged investor will almost surely go broke, despite having a positive expected return in each period.

Detailed calculations are given in an endnote.[3]

Sushil's point can be generalised as follows. If you compound a risky investment strategy over many periods, the best measure of typical results is median (not mean) compound growth. The graph of median compound growth against leverage follows an inverted-U pattern. The main features to note in the example graph shown are as follows:

■ adding some leverage initially increases median compound growth, but only up to an optimal level of leverage L^*

■ leverage above $(2L^* - 1)$ leads to lower median compound growth than the result with no leverage

■ leverage above $2L^*$ leads to negative median compound growth: the investor almost surely eventually goes broke.

Median compound growth as a function of leverage

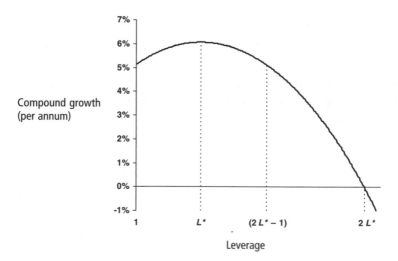

Source: assumptions and calculations in endnote.[4]

Separately from the mathematical subtleties in the panel, Sushil gave some further reasons for limiting leverage. "I already have more than enough money. Why should I take the risk of high leverage? I find it incredible when I read in the newspaper of people who already have millions getting into difficulties with leverage."

He also made the point that low leverage was psychologically helpful in making contra-cyclical investment decisions. "When the market has fallen 40% in the past year, you want to be at your boldest. That is psychologically difficult when you have already lost 40%. It is probably psychologically impossible if your leverage means that you have already lost 80%."

A typical day

Sushil's day starts sometime between 7am and 8am – he feels he should start when stock exchange news starts at seven in the morning, but he is "not a good morning person". He uses the Proquote price service, which he sets running late the night before. He checks for any news alerts on his holdings, and then compares a trades 'wish list' carried across from yesterday with today's prices.

At around 8am, he speaks to his broker to place the orders for today's wish-list of trades – sometimes anything up to a dozen orders, although typically only a subset of these may turn out to be feasible at the desired prices on a particular day. Sushil is a patient dealer who always tries to buy and sell well inside the quoted price spread. His broker will either place bids and offers on the SETS order book, or leave orders with a market maker to 'work'. This means giving the market maker the whole day to call possible counterparties, or wait and see if a counterparty spontaneously places an order during the day.

After placing the day's orders through his broker, Sushil continues working through any financial results statements or other news releases relating to his 60 or so current holdings, scribbling longhand notes on loose-leaf paper in A4 ring binders which have a separate file division for each company.

Where a company issues significant news, he re-skims at least some of his file and reviews his valuation, noting new buy and sell price levels. "I try to have buy and sell levels written down for as many companies as possible. It is important to be disciplined about this." He also looks at any new broker research which he can get hold of on his current holdings.

Having thoroughly reviewed all current holdings with news – which might take part or all of the morning – Sushil then moves on to looking for new ideas. Sources he scans regularly include lists of the largest percentage price falls on the stock exchange that day, new 52-week lows, and quantitative screens of stocks with combinations of low price-earnings ratios, high dividend yields, high net cash per share, and sometimes other metrics. He often spends several hours researching a particular company – looking at past accounts, broker research, industry websites and past bulletin board comment.

Scattered across Sushil's six screens are Level 1 or Level 2 price displays for the two dozen or so stocks where he either has uncompleted trade orders with his broker, or the price is near a level at which he intends to place an order. Also running all day are windows of the full RNS, and bid and offer prices and traded volumes for the 60 or so stocks in his current portfolio. Another 50 or so sold stocks, and about 100 others on a watchlist, are also on permanent display. He thinks a large screen area is ergonomically important. "If I have to click a mouse to see a price, I'm going to see it half as often."

At intervals throughout the day, Sushil's broker telephones to update on progress on orders and agree modified or further instructions; a dozen or more such calls through the day would not be unusual. Most calls involve only a few words, with Sushil and his broker speaking in a shorthand borne of ten years of working together. The broker may also call if a market maker offers or bids for stock in a company where Sushil currently has no orders, but the market maker knows he has dealt in recent weeks. In these cases he will spend a few minutes looking over the file to decide if he wants to deal. He seldom makes snap decisions without looking at the file, but he believes that he makes decisions more quickly than institutions, and that this is an important source of advantage for the smaller investor. "Being able to assimilate new information and act on it more quickly than institutions is a durable comparative advantage."

Sushil speaks occasionally with a handful of investing friends, and occasionally talks to further brokers, but discussions with others are not a large part of how he forms his views. "My idea of a group decision is looking in the mirror."

He skims a lot of broker research, reads various financial blogs, and dips into newspapers. He does not post much on bulletin boards, unless he wants to pose a specific question; but he does spend a great deal of time reading them. "Of course there is a lot of nonsense on bulletin boards, but there is also stuff I can't ignore: comments from industry experts, suppliers, customers, disgruntled employees. I would never buy a stock without checking what has been said about it recently on ADVFN."

He regards reading and absorbing information as the primary task of an investor. "Warren Buffett says 80% of his time is spent reading. For me, it's probably 95%." His tranquil day is not just a matter of circumstance, but also of temperament shaped by experience. "One consequence of living a difficult life for many years when I was younger, making many surgical decisions with no good options and very high stakes, is what psychologists call flattened affect. Just being pain-free now is a source of happiness, so I don't get very excited or upset about anything else. I think phlegmatism is a helpful trait for an investor."

Because Sushil works and lives alone, there is usually no prompt to stop work at a particular time, and he often works late into the evening. Overall he probably works moderately long hours, but doesn't find this at all arduous. "To call it work is a travesty – I spend all day every day learning more about the world, doing things I enjoy."

Company meetings

Many of the investors in this book are keen to meet company management, and some regard it as their principal source of 'edge' or advantage. Sushil is more ambivalent about company meetings.

In part, this is a matter of time allocation: he thinks meetings are usually useful, but they are also time-intensive. "It is fairly easy to come out of a meeting and think that was a useful hour. But the relevant question for me is whether, say, six hours spent on a meeting with one company I already own – preparation, travelling to London, notes afterwards, and following up matters arising – is more useful than, say, half an hour looking at each of 12 possible new investments."

It is also a matter of comparative advantage: he thinks that judging people in person is probably not an area where he is especially skilled. In part, it is a matter of personality: by his own account he is an introvert, happy to sit and read and think for most of the day.

Successes and mistakes

Sushil's greatest investment successes in percentage terms were in the technology stocks Trafficmaster, BATM and Advanced Power Components around the turn of the century, each of which were ten-baggers or more for him.

He says now that whilst there was some merit in buying these stocks, the extent of the successes was undeserved. He also mentioned a small engineering company (see chart) as an example of a "less spectacular but more deserved" success, where he has held a large stake for many years, selling and re-purchasing to extract a seven-figure realised gain.

"The interesting thing is that it has never looked cheap on basic metrics like price-earnings or tangible assets. But it has a lot of intellectual property, and a low risk of obsolescence. The 'change of state' is increasing regulation all over the world, which is driving the demand for its products. The business has been hit recently by the recession, but I still think it is likely to be a much bigger business in five or ten years' time."

Small engineering company: price chart from January 2001 to December 2010

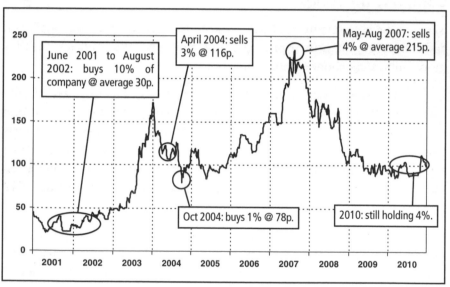

The company's name is omitted at Sushil's request.

Source: data from ADVFN

Asked about investment mistakes, Sushil laughed and said "lots". His biggest mistakes have involved outright frauds. He has occasionally taken an activist role where something has gone wrong at one of his investments. But he is not a habitual activist: his general view is that confrontation should be a last resort. "The trick is to avoid situations where activism might be necessary. There are enough nice people to interact with."

Avoiding situations where director integrity or corporate governance are suspect forms an important part of Sushil's research on possible new investments. He looks at directors' records in previous companies, their track record of promises and outcomes at the current company, and any adverse comments posted on bulletin boards. Although he often doesn't want to meet with management, he regards this 'character research' as an important part of his decisions. "One aspect of investment which nobody writes about is just figuring out if the management are crooks. For many years I have kept a little black book – actually a file on my PC – listing people who I think might be crooks."

Academia

Although he gave up his full-time academic job a decade ago, Sushil has continued to write occasional economics research articles, usually with a focus on public policy. This is partly because it provides an opportunity to be creative. "Investment is a wonderful game, but it is largely derivative. You're not building anything new. There is little original thought in investment."

He sees academic research as more of an intellectual challenge than investment. "I am always conscious of the limitations of my intellect as an academic. If I had ten more IQ points, it would make a big difference. But for anyone in the top few percent of the population, IQ points are not the limiting factor in investment – other qualities such as recognising your ignorance matter more."

He also sees academic research focused on public policy as a way of making a difference to the world. "A lot of research in economics and finance is foolish or malign; but a small part of it is far more worthwhile than being an investor, if you do it well."

Finally, he is motivated by the desire to produce at least some work which might stand the test of time. "Investment leaves no trace, it produces nothing of lasting value. Nobody will care in 50 years' time that I made money. I wish I could live usefully rather than just die rich."

In comparing investment with academia, Sushil particularly highlighted the following difference. In academia (and in many other fields) there is little credit for solving important but easy problems: kudos is gained by working on hard problems. But in investment, doing something easy can gain just as much credit as doing something complicated. Warren Buffett has summarised this point as follows: "*Investment isn't Olympic diving: there are no marks for degree of difficulty.*"

Giving it away

Sushil's low opinion of the social value of his investment activities also motivates his interest in philanthropy. "20 years ago, I didn't plan to be a philanthropist, and for many years I was just trying to survive. Having solved that problem, I am left playing a game which is interesting and lucrative, but with limited horizons and low social utility. I sometimes think I ought to do something more useful, but I don't have any specific aptitude. Investment and philanthropy are probably the highest-impact – and certainly the most congenial – ways of spending most of my time."

> "You mean economics as religion? I have left that church, and I won't be joining another. I don't want my thinking constrained by my identity."

He has established a charitable trust, to which he has donated six-figure sums, which are then allocated to operating charities. How does he choose the charities? "By the numbers. I am a compassionate misanthrope."

Sushil's motivation towards philanthropy also derives from the highs and lows of his own life trajectory. "I have experienced the comfort, self-confidence and high social regard which come with having money. I have also experienced the discomfort, anxiety and low social regard which sometimes come with disability. And neither is deserved." Perhaps his identification and empathy with these very different experiences also explains the worldviews described at the start of this chapter. When it was pointed out that someone with an economics background might be expected to have more favourable views of markets, he demurred as follows. "You mean economics as religion? I have left that church, and I won't be joining another. I don't want my thinking constrained by my identity."

SUSHIL: INSIGHTS AND ADVICE

The stock market as a game   You can make money from the stock market by treating it as a game. It is not necessary to have a high opinion of the intrinsic value of the game.

Be wise, not proud   Be eclectic and unpretentious about sources. Read academic studies and read Buffett; but also be open to good ideas on ADVFN or in the *Daily Mail*.

Post-tax thinking   Think about investment return and risk on a post-tax basis.

Synchronised stupidity   You make money by being one step ahead of the crowd. Being three steps ahead of the crowd can sometimes lose you money. Naïvety can be a strength, if it frees you to do the right thing.

Diversification for liquidity   Diversification can be thought of not as reducing risk, but rather as increasing the liquidity of your portfolio, and so increasing options to change your mind as prices and expectations change.

Focus on what is knowable   Focus your research effort on things which are knowable – that is, things where your research can plausibly give you superior insight (e.g. microeconomic advantages of unusual companies). Ignore things which are not knowable (e.g. general macroeconomic predictions).

Look for motivated sellers   Look for situations where counterparties appear to be selling for reasons unrelated to knowledge about the future prospects of the share – for example, their tax or liquidity positions.

Take your advice, not theirs   A consensus of expert opinion is often not valuable in investment, because it is already discounted by market prices. Successful investors tend to have a predilection towards figuring things out for themselves.

Look for easy problems   Doing something easy can gain just as much credit as doing something complicated. Investment isn't Olympic diving: there are no marks for degree of difficulty.

Path-independent thinking   Occupational identity can be a mental constraint. Don't let your thinking be constrained by your identity.

TAYLOR
THE AUTODIDACT

TAYLOR: FACTS AND FIGURES

Age at interview	46
Age at leaving last full-time job	31
Background	Left school at 16; worked as print estimator; long-term illness (ME) since age 31 in 1995.
Style	Puts all eggs in a very few baskets, then watches the baskets.
Markets and sectors	Mainly UK small caps; some macro trading as a hedge in the 2008-09 bear market.
Instruments	Shares, exchange-traded funds for macro trading.
Typical holding period	Months to years.
Performance indicators	Compound growth rate over 25% per annum in his SIPP from 2000 to 2010.
Quote	"Even if you are trapped by illness, investing can still be an interesting life."
Phrases	Unleveraged plunging; lack of ego; the 20-hole punch card.

I nvestment is like swimming or riding a bicycle: difficult to learn without some practical experience. But most serious investors have also had some help from formal teaching.

John Lee trained as a chartered accountant; Nigel and Sushil have degrees in economics; Luke and Vince have MBAs; Owen did the Society of Investment Analyst exams; and even the non-graduates Eric and Khalid did A-level economics. Less fortunate others may never have had the opportunity for any structured financial education. Taylor left school at 16 with almost no qualifications, and although always possessed of fluent basic numeracy, he has never worked in any investment or other professional job. His large library of investment books is testimony to the fact that he has, of necessity, been entirely self-taught as an investor.

Taylor's limited career history is partly due to long-term ill health. Since 1994 he has suffered from post-viral fatigue syndrome, also commonly known as ME. Although his condition fluctuates, for long periods he has been almost housebound. His inability to go out to work and the consequent pressure to make money from investing have led to an anxious life.

But starting with free capital of only £50,000 from the sale of a property in 1995, he managed to generate several thousand pounds of gains every year to help pay his modest living and medical expenses. In 2000 he transferred his pensions from past employment into a SIPP fund, giving free capital of around £100,000. This grew to nearly £1m by 2010, equivalent to a compound growth rate over 25% per annum.

Apart from the financial lifeline, investment has been his main window on the world from the prison of long-term illness, and the main area of progression and achievement in an otherwise restricted life. Sharing these insights with other people in analogous circumstances was one of his motivations for cooperating with the book. "I hope my story will give some hope to others that even if you are trapped by illness, investing can still be an interesting life."

Taylor lives a few minutes from the station in a medium-sized town in Yorkshire, in an old detached house split into two duplex apartments, with his mother and their Yorkshire terrier. In his mid-forties with fair hair and over six feet tall, he speaks with a slight Scottish burr. Like many people with ME, he looks untroubled on a good day. But one of the constraints which the condition imposes was illustrated by lunch – a plate of steamed broccoli, followed by live yoghurt – which he eats every day as part of a strict dietary regime to control his condition.

After lunch we moved to his bedroom-cum-office. Taylor sat on a large bed with his legs outstretched and a laptop beside him, and a large TV screen on one side of the bed. At the side of the room were several floor-to-ceiling bookcases of investment books – the most comprehensive library I saw at any of the interviews, including many esoteric titles I had heard of but never read. From time to time Taylor pulled books off the shelves to illustrate or justify particular points, so that by the end of the interview books were scattered all around him on the bed.

Teenage tearaway

Divorce and relationship breakdowns meant that Taylor moved many times as a child, attending as many as five schools in his last two years of secondary education. After leaving school in 1979 with almost no qualifications, he briefly held jobs as a builder's apprentice and warehouseman. But in those days most of his energies were directed towards youthful exuberance, and occasionally over-exuberance and minor brushes with the law. After a course at the London College of Printing, he settled down as a print estimator – a sales role requiring a basic numeracy which came easily to him, despite having paid little attention in maths classes at school.

Taylor's father took him horse and dog racing from a young age, and he started betting on the horses when he was 17, mainly for fun. He also dabbled as a small investor in the early 1990s, "mainly because the *Evening Standard* had the stock market next to the horse racing page." His investments were tiny, and his methods naïve – "£500 a time on newspaper tips, that sort of thing – and the costs when you bought them through the bank were always horrendous."

He also followed some of the stock market *causes célèbres* of the day, and particularly remembers Polly Peck, which was eventually exposed as a notorious fraud, but only after the shares had multiplied more than a hundred-fold. "Despite the later collapse, Polly Peck was actually a positive inspiration to me. I never owned the shares, but it opened my eyes to the fact that you can make a fortune in this game, if you get it right."

Getting serious

Taylor's ME symptoms started in 1994. In 1995, still unwell, he moved back to live at his mother's house in Yorkshire. Selling his London flat realised about £50,000 in free capital, and this was his starting stake as an investor.

He did not make a conscious decision to leave employment to become an investor; it was more that ME meant he could do little else. Unemployed and unwell, he thought he might as well develop his casual interest in shares.

His initial approach can best be characterised as the temperate strategy of GARP, that is 'Growth At a Reasonable Price'. He focused on fundamentals, but not necessarily the cheapest value metrics: he was prepared to pay up for companies with strong qualitative features such as recurring revenues or market dominance.

The portfolio he developed contained only a handful of shares, partly because of the relatively small amount of money he had available for investment. His first big success was Trafalgar House, which was taken over soon after he had invested a large fraction of his small portfolio in it. "That gave me slightly more confidence that I could be make a living from this, but I was still very anxious about money."

In his early years as an investor he found it difficult to access information. One vital source was the *Hemscott Company Guide* – a printed volume covering all UK quoted companies, with summaries of four companies on every page, including basic financial data and contact details for each company. "Even just having the telephone numbers for all companies to hand in one volume was a big deal in those days – you could browse through looking for interesting companies, and ring up straight away for their annual reports."

Apart from the *Hemscott Company Guide* and company annual reports, he also relied on the *Financial Times* for news and investment commentary, and even wrote to *FT* columnists such as John Train to ask for book recommendations. For several years *Hemscott* and the *FT* were his main sources of current investing information.

In 2000, encouraged by his five-year results with his own funds, he transferred his deferred pensions into a SIPP. Initially he allocated 90% of this fund to a discretionary stockbroker and only 10% to his own share selections. The stockbroker picked mainly technology shares, which in the early 2000s did poorly, whilst Taylor's own selections of small-cap shares continued to do well. Within a couple of years he had taken the whole SIPP under his own management.

Unleveraged plunging

Taylor has generally invested in a handful of shares, always less than ten at any one time, and has often 'plunged' into just one or two shares so that they represent more than half his portfolio. He explained the origins of this strategy as follows. "Reading a biography of Bernard Baruch made a strong impression on me. He was a plunger – that was how he made his fortune. [Gerald M.] Loeb's *The Battle for Investment Survival* makes the same point: put all your eggs in one basket, and watch the basket. It made sense to me: to make a large fortune from a small one, you need to be a plunger."

A very focused portfolio is easier to implement where the investor has only a small fund, like Taylor in 1995, so that there are no liquidity constraints on investing in just a few shares. And if an investor has an absolute requirement to generate a high return on a small fund to pay his living expenses, a very focused portfolio may be the only strategy with a chance of success.

For the extreme version of this argument, imagine a person in a casino with £100 who is told he will be shot at dawn if he does not then have £10,000. The best strategy for such a person may be to make a single bet (a very focused portfolio) at 100-to-1 odds. There is no point in a diversified strategy which averages out to produce reliable modest gains: despite its positive expectation, a diversified strategy has no chance of reaching the target in time.

"The pious doctrine of broad diversification guarantees positive expectation, but also mediocrity."

Fortunately an investor is never quite in this position, but the intuition holds: if you have a high return requirement on a small fund – or even if you simply want investment to make a real difference to your life – then a very few large bets (a very focused portfolio) may be an optimal strategy. The pious doctrine of broad diversification guarantees positive expectation, but also mediocrity; for the investor with a small fund and no other income, mediocrity may not be enough.

The boldness of Taylor's concentrated portfolio is attenuated by his strong aversion to debt. "I don't use leverage. Never have, never will. I am just not interested."

The combination of very few shares and no leverage gives a chance of large gains, whilst completely avoiding even a small risk of bankruptcy. Diversified investors with some leverage from spread betting or CFDs and stop-loss limits on all their positions may believe they are taking less risk than a focused investor like Taylor, and in normal conditions, they are probably right. But the use of leverage makes them vulnerable to Nassim Taleb's 'black swans' – unexpected, extreme events like the 1987 crash, or a declaration of war, or a nuclear event in a major city – which can mean that stop-losses fail, leaving them suddenly insolvent. This cannot happen to an unleveraged portfolio: it can go to zero, but it can never go negative.

Erinaceous: a lucky escape

Although Taylor's focused strategy has done well over the past 15 years, there have been some lucky escapes, like his large bet on the property and insurance services company Erinaceous. He described the attractions of the share in 2004 as follows. "Erinaceous looked great at the beginning. They put together property services and insurance broking, it was good recurring revenue, and the idea was they could cross-sell the property and insurance services. I went down to visit them in Croydon with my brother. The corporate governance looked solid – lots of heavyweights on the board for such a small company – one of the directors had actually written the *Turnbull Report*."[1]

He got to know a property trade newspaper journalist covering Erinaceous – "I often speak to trade journalists, it's easy if you email them first" – and felt he had a good understanding of the company.

One of the means by which Erinaceous grew rapidly was that it acquired dozens of companies over a few years. Rapid growth by acquisitions is a high-risk corporate strategy, because what is bought may not be fully understood. In the spring of 2006 an alleged fraud at one of the acquired companies was revealed. For Taylor this was "shocking news, enough to change my view of the company immediately."

He started to sell, but because he had several hundred thousand pounds in the stock, it took a few days to exit his holding. To his surprise, the Erinaceous share price did not fall much while he was selling. A few days later he spoke with his journalist contact at *Property Week*, and was encouraged by what he heard: the alleged fraud was limited to a single subsidiary which Erinaceous had acquired, it appeared to relate to just a single rogue office, and insurance would cover the losses.

Reassured by these views, Taylor reversed himself again, reinvesting in the company at a lower price. But soon there were more problems: in the summer of 2006 another subsidiary was affected by an alleged fraud, and a successful insurance team left to set up in competition with Erinaceous. Despite these red flags, the share price recovered in the second half of 2006.

In early 2007 Taylor spoke with his trade journalist contact, whose views on the company were still positive. But when he spoke a few weeks later with the editor of *Property Week*, which had published reassuring commentary for several months, he was shocked to learn that coverage had been circumscribed by letters from Erinaceous lawyers threatening legal actions for defamation. "That

> "From his experience with one particular company, Taylor drew a further sardonic lesson: avoid companies with silly names."

was certainly an eye-opener. The impression from talking to the editor was completely different to what I had previously understood from the articles and the journalist covering the story." This conversation and continuing bulletin board chatter about further problems at Erinaceous persuaded him to sell his entire holding. He took a five-figure loss on the reinvestment, but nevertheless had a six-figure profit on his cumulative dealings in the shares. It was fortunate that he sold when he did: Erinaceous subsequently went into administration in April 2008. Reflecting on his experience with Erinaceous, Taylor summarised the lesson he drew from it: "scuttlebutt is all very well, until it becomes spin".

The concept of 'scuttlebutt' – small items of qualitative information gained from industry insiders, which can give an investor an informational edge – was first articulated in 1957 by the American investor Philip Fisher. At that time 'spin' was less of a problem than it is today: the public relations (PR) industry was embryonic, and the concept of investor PR directed at shareholders was unknown. Like many classic investment concepts, the idea of scuttlebutt needs to be applied with a recognition of modern realities – in this case, the investor relations industry.

Taylor drew a further sardonic lesson: avoid companies with silly names. "If you look in a big enough dictionary, you will find erinaceous, it means like or relating to hedgehogs. It certainly turned into a prickly investment for investors who stayed to the end."

Erinaceous price chart from January 2004 to April 2008

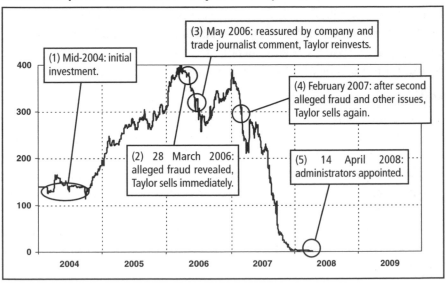

Source: data from ADVFN

Sitting tight vs. changing your mind

Taylor's investment turnover is amongst the lowest three in this book (the others are Luke and John Lee). When I asked why he preferred low turnover, he went to his bookshelves and showed me a highlighted passage in Edwin Lefèvre's 1923 classic *Reminiscences of a Stock Operator*, a lightly fictionalised account of the life and career of US stock market legend Jesse Livermore.[2]

> "After spending many years in Wall Street and after making and losing millions of dollars I want to tell you this: it was never my thinking that

made the big money for me. It was always my sitting. Got that? My sitting tight! It is no trick at all to be right on the market. You always find lots of early bulls in bull markets and early bears in bear markets. I've known many men who were right at exactly the right time, and began buying or selling stocks when prices were at the very level which should show the greatest profit. And their experience invariably matched mine – that is, they made no real money from it. Men who can be both right and sit tight are uncommon. I found it one of the hardest things to learn."

Taylor has an unusually developed ability to "sit tight", which he thinks may be partly explained by his illness. "There have been long periods when I had little energy and found it difficult to concentrate on the market, so I haven't felt like doing much." He also has a casual interest in Buddhist philosophy, and suggested that the Zen concept of calmness through meditation or concentration was helpful in developing the ability to sit tight.

Making large commitments to a very few investment ideas does not prevent Taylor from changing his mind quickly, as he did when appraised of the suppression of press criticism by legal threats from Erinaceous. This is one of the great advantages of being a one-man band: if you are wrong, you can turn on a sixpence. I observed that for many investors with a large portfolio weighting and strong belief in a particular company, negative news tends to produce cognitive dissonance; the investor responds by re-framing the negative news so as to minimise its impact, or by pushing it out of their mind. Taylor's response was immediate and incredulous: "They have got to be nuts if they do that!"

This lack of ego is perhaps his main comparative advantage as an investor. He combines Livermore's ability to "be both right and sit tight" with an ability to change his mind quickly and completely on new information. There are others in this book who have greater analytical ability or market knowledge, but none who told stories in which they appeared so completely relaxed about changing their mind.

Macro trading as a bear market defence

In early 2008, after more than a decade investing most of his funds in just a handful of shares, Taylor anticipated that this strategy might be less suited to a severe bear market. "In a period when the market falls 50%, it becomes much more difficult to find a few individual shares which you are confident will go up."

In response to this, he temporarily redirected his focus for 2008 towards shorter-term macro trading of currencies, stock market indices and bank-preference shares and bonds. To effect macro trades including short positions without leverage, he made investments in exchange-traded funds (ETFs), which can be bought and sold through a stockbroker in the same way as shares. But by late summer 2009, when the interview took place, his focus was shifting back towards larger long-term investments in single shares. "Short-term macro trading has been a good strategy to protect capital for the last 18 months, but now I'm looking for the next big idea."

In terms of the classification used in this book, he had temporarily become more of a geographer to protect capital

"It is much better to be right than to be consistent."

during the bear market, but was now reverting to his original approach as a surveyor. "When conditions change, you need to change your approach. It is much better to be right than to be consistent."

BACKGROUND: BOOKS MENTIONED IN THIS CHAPTER

Because of Taylor's self-taught investment education, mentions of books are scattered throughout this chapter. This panel gives further details of these references.

It is noticeable that most of the authors are now dead. Taylor's interest in older investment books was partly inspired by Victor Niederhoffer's *The Education of a Speculator* (1997): "I liked the book, and he said you should always look at the oldies."

My Own Story. Bernard Baruch (1870-1965) amassed a fortune from speculation by the age of 30, and thereafter became an advisor to Democratic presidents Woodrow Wilson and Franklin Roosevelt on economic matters. In his 1957 autobiography *My Own Story*, Chapter 19 on 'My investment philosophy' includes the following advice: "Don't buy too many different securities. Better have only a few investments which can be watched."

The Battle for Investment Survival. Gerald Loeb (1899-1974) was a founding partner of the brokerage EF Hutton & Company. Chapter 28 of his 1935 classic *The Battle for Investment Survival* includes the following advice: "the greatest safety lies in putting all your eggs in one basket and watching the basket." Loeb does qualify this advice as applicable mainly to expert investors, and notes that diversification may be useful for the less informed investor.

Common Stocks and Uncommon Profits. Philip Fisher (1907-2004) wrote the 1958 growth investing classic *Common Stocks and Uncommon Profits*, in which he used the term scuttlebutt to describe informal industry views and gossip about a company. The etymological origin of scuttlebutt is said to be naval slang: drinking water on a sailing ship was conventionally stored in a butt (a small barrel) which had been scuttled by making a hole in it so that water could be withdrawn. The term is thus equivalent to the modern concept of the office water cooler as a place for gossip.

Reminiscences of a Stock Operator. Edwin Lefèvre (1871-1943) was an American journalist best known as the author of the 1923 classic *Reminiscences of a Stock Operator*, a fictionalised biography of the real-life securities trader Jesse Livermore (1877-1940). Short-term traders often cite *Reminiscences* as the best book ever written about their field.

The Money Masters. John Train (1928-), the *Financial Times* columnist to whom Taylor wrote asking for book recommendations, is a US author and investment advisor best known for his books *The Money Masters* (1980) and *The New Money Masters* (1989). The format of these books is similar to *Free Capital*, except that the subjects are professional rather than private investors.

Apart from investing classics, Taylor also especially recommended some more unusual contemporary books, with a focus on trading psychology: *Zen in the Markets* by Edward Allen Toppel, *The Intuitive Trader* by Robert Koppel, and *Investor Therapy* by Richard Geist.

Conclusion: the 20-hole punch card

Taylor's strategy of investing most of his portfolio in only a handful of shares goes against a good deal of pious conventional wisdom about diversification. It is true that some exceptional investors favour a concentrated portfolio, but they know a great deal about what they buy – probably more than most private investors can hope to know.

The high-concentration, low-turnover strategy has some clear advantages: it reduces the costs of brokerage, bid-offer spreads and stamp duty, and it tends to defer crystallisation of capital gains tax. It also has a certain aesthetic appeal: sticking with a small number of wise choices seems a more elegant way of making a fortune than the grubby business of frenetic trading.

Perhaps the greatest advantage is that an investor who makes only one or two decisions a year is likely to take much greater care with each one. Warren Buffett has emphasised this idea by saying that you should think about investing as if you had a punch card with 20 spaces representing a lifetime quota of investment decisions; after every decision, one space is punched, until the card has 20 holes, and then no more decisions can be made. Taylor has adhered more closely to this old-fashioned ideal than anyone else in this book.

TAYLOR: INSIGHTS AND ADVICE

Escape from illness Many types of ill health need not be a barrier to an interesting and remunerative life as an investor.

Self-study works Reading widely can largely replace formal investment education, provided that you have basic numeracy.

Focus limited firepower If you need a high return on a small fund, a very focused portfolio may be the only strategy with a chance of success.

Listen to gossip, but remember how it's made Pay attention to scuttlebutt – that is, industry gossip about your companies; but also be alert to the pervasive influence of the modern investment PR industry.

Lose your ego A lack of ego can be helpful to an investor, because it helps you to change your mind quickly.

Better to be right than to be consistent When conditions change, change your approach.

The 20-hole punch card Strive to make your investment decisions fewer in number and higher in quality.

7

VERNON
BUYING THE GLITCH

VERNON: FACTS AND FIGURES

Age at interview	44
Age at leaving last full-time job	38
Background	PhD in computer science; management consultancy (business systems analyst).
Style	Contrarian – buys growth companies which have stumbled, usually several times, when the City is thoroughly fed up with them.
Markets and sectors	UK small caps with a focus on technology.
Instruments	Shares, index spread bets for hedging.
Typical holding period	Months.
Performance indicators	15-fold portfolio return over 1998-2000; gave back only one-third at the nadir of the 2002-03 bear market; ISA millionaire by 2005.
Quote	"The best decisions in the stock market attract no applause."
Phrases	Buying the glitch; core, secondary and hygiene factors; Pasteur luck; negative scoring v. positive scoring; heuristics.

nexperienced investors are often suckers for a good story. Announcements of new products, trading results ahead of 'market expectations', or synergistic corporate acquisitions are all examples of positive news flow which attracts buyers.

But the story is only one side of an investment decision: the other side is the price, and the price of good news is often high. Buying *bad* news might be a better strategy, if the price is low enough.

Vernon is a self-described "contrarian and misanthrope" who looks to buy companies which have recently released bad news rather than good. "My ideal company is one which has stumbled, probably more than once, so that the City is thoroughly fed up with it. I try to catch that company when nobody wants it, while it is still working through its problems."

He has a succinct phrase for this borrowed from the American investor Ken Fisher: he thinks of it as "buying the glitch".[1]

Vernon lives with his partner and their two-year-old son in the country in Kent, where they moved from a London suburb in 2006. The private wooded track down to his house ends in a forecourt with a couple of cars parked by an unremarkable brick bungalow. Entering the wide central hallway which extends the width of the building, one is drawn towards the glass wall on the opposite side. Only on approaching the glass wall does the spectacular southerly panorama from high on the hillside of the North Downs become apparent. "I have never wanted a large house, I couldn't see the point. But I could see the point of a view."

After gazing in awe at the view for a few moments, I followed Vernon into his office to one side of the hallway. One window overlooked the same view, albeit with shades drawn to enhance the visibility of five LCD monitors suspended in an arc in front of an elliptically shaped desk.

Vernon is a bearded fair-haired man in his forties, about six feet tall and of slim build. He gives the impression of thinking carefully about questions: his side of a serious conversation comprises long silences interspersed with fully formed thoughts in complete sentences. He is particularly interested in the mental processes in investing. At the time of the interview his partner, who is much younger than him, was writing up her PhD thesis based on experimental studies of decision-making.

Teenage programmer

Vernon was born in 1965 in Hampshire, the only child of an academic engineer. His father's career meant that the family spent time living in both England and the US. He describes his schooling as "privileged but disrupted": he grew up in an academic milieu, but the frequent moves meant that he was often unsettled and unhappy. He had little awareness of money as a child, having a financially secure but wholly unostentatious lifestyle, in which money was "adequate but never abundant, and therefore rather uninteresting".

As a teenager he became an enthusiastic amateur programmer, spending many hours teaching himself BASIC on the Sinclair ZX80, and selling some of the computer games he wrote via small ads in a computer magazine. He studied mathematics at a redbrick university. On graduating he stayed on for a PhD in computer science – a natural step given his father's academic background – followed by a temporary research assistant position. By now he was 26, and becoming conscious of the financial disadvantages of an academic career. "My father had never seemed to worry about money, but academic pay was much better in relative terms in the 1960s and 1970s." At the end of his research associate position he joined a large firm of management consultants as a business systems analyst.

Although his technical skills were good and superficially he progressed well in this career, he grew to dislike his job. "As you progressed into more of a consultancy role, there was an increasing emphasis on up-selling services clients didn't need. For some reason I developed the notion that trafficking in bullshit was an undignified way of making a living."

As well as more selling, a promotion after four years meant that his job grew to include internal management, another role which he did not enjoy. "I had no desire to be in charge of other people. I preferred technical work, but promotion took you away from that." There were no immediate better alternatives – he needed to make a living, and recognised that disliking his job was "more about me than my employer".

A small legacy

While he was still a PhD student Vernon had received a low five-figure sum as his share of an uncle's estate. Although the most obvious use for this might have been a deposit on a house, it was difficult to get a mortgage as a PhD student. The uncle had dabbled in investment himself, albeit unsuccessfully, a fact which created in Vernon "a notion that I should try to grow this money myself." As a result he became a "not very serious and not very successful" amateur investor in the first half of the 1990s.

"I made lots of mistakes and had no great successes. I tended to focus on software stocks, because I felt I knew something about that. I did know something about software, but I knew little about accounting and investing, and for a long time my intuition for probability was weak." Looking back, he thinks that developing this intuition may have been hindered by working in computer science. "As a numerate person I could understand probability in a formal sense, but in a casual sense my intellectual world was deterministic – in computing consequences always follow with absolute certainty from premises. The computing paradigm of certainty in a closed system was not helpful when thinking about investing."

> "The computing paradigm of certainty in a closed system was not helpful when thinking about investing."

Tech stocks boom

In late 1998, still disliking his job, he left management consultancy to become a freelance contractor, preparing and testing computer systems for the possible impact of the 'Y2K' millennial date change. This was not an unusual move for a programmer who disliked management duties and office politics. But for Vernon it had a particular advantage: more control of his own time, and hence more time to follow his investments.

Although he was happier having returned to technical work, he already envisaged that he would eventually become a full-time investor. He remembers becoming almost obsessed around this time by the stealthy power of time and compound growth. "I realised about 1998 that if I could harness that power and avoid big mistakes or bad luck, I would probably become wealthy. Specifically, if I could compound my money at 30% per annum, £1 spent foolishly now would cost me £200 in 20 years' time. So whenever I was tempted to spend £1 on something frivolous, I would ask myself: wouldn't I rather be retired in 20 years' time?"

As an investor focusing largely on technology shares in the late 1990s, Vernon remembers several 'ten-baggers' – shares where the price multiplied more than ten times during his holding period – including names such as Trafficmaster, Bookham Technology, Infobank, and Geo Interactive Media.

Whilst he thinks that he made some good decisions in 1998, he admits that the scale of the subsequent success involved a large element of luck. By March 2000, he had multiplied his free capital more than 15 times over 18 months, an unbelievable figure in normal stock market conditions, but quite plausible for a technology-focused investor in that era. By this time he had read much more widely about investing, and understood that this was a bubble of historic proportions. But he also saw no way of calling the top of a bubble. He was fortunate that some of his larger holdings were taken over in mergers near the peak. Although the merger proceeds were in the form of shares, his lack of knowledge of the acquiring companies prompted him to sell. "It was my ignorance of the acquiring companies rather than my knowledge that saved me."

By this time he had also become familiar with the idea of short selling, and opened an account with a spread bet firm to do this. His timing was again fortuitous – he first shorted the NASDAQ index in late March 2000, and maintained that position for several months. By Autumn 2002 his portfolio was down by around a third from its peak, but this still left him with a seven-figure sum, more than ten times ahead from 1998. It was a better long-term result than many who made paper fortunes in the tech boom, but lost them when technology shares collapsed.

Vernon's contracting job working on Y2K issues had been lucrative, but like many such contractors he was under-employed after January 2000. Despite his increased wealth from investment, he felt he should continue to seek contracting roles "to be on the safe side".

He did some short-term contracts, the last being in 2003 when he was 38 years old. But with the recovery in the market from March 2003 onwards, he started to think that he could make a living from investing, and so he became "increasingly picky about what contracting jobs I might accept". He never made a definite decision to stop contracting. "But by about 2004, the agencies probably surmised that I was never going to take any contract, so they stopped calling."

Buying the glitch

Although Vernon made the wealth which enabled him to become a full-time investor mainly through investments in technology shares, characterising him just as a 'tech investor' would be an incomplete description of his approach. His distinctive characteristic is buying bad news rather than good – or as he thinks of it, *buying the glitch*.

BACKGROUND: PROFIT WARNINGS

To understand profit warnings, first consider the concept of market expectations.

Investment analysts publish forecasts for the companies they follow, projecting profits and earnings per share at the company's next results (and sometimes for one or more later years). The averages of the forecasts for profits and earnings per share for the next year from all analysts following a company are regarded as 'market expectations'.

If company management sees objective information which suggests that company results will be materially different from market expectations (normally understood to mean more than about 10% different), London Stock Exchange rules require an announcement drawing attention to the discrepancy.

Analysts tend to be optimistic (this is not necessarily through misjudgement – they are paid to be optimistic). So the usual discrepancy is negative, a shortfall of actual versus expected: the so-called profit warning.

A profit warning will invariably lead to an immediate and often substantial fall in a company's share price. If the profit warning attributes the shortfall to general industry-wide conditions, investors will 'read across' the implications for other companies in the same sector, and so their prices also tend to fall.

The most common type of glitch is a *profit warning* (see panel). A profit warning often induces a dramatic change in investors' perception of a company. Some investors seem to regard any profit warning as a sign of managerial incompetence or untrustworthiness, with little regard for the particular circumstances, which might sometimes be entirely beyond management's control.

Profit warnings are also often embarrassing to stockbroking analysts, particularly if they have recently endorsed higher forecasts. To a detached observer, the discrepancy between forecasts and outcome might just as well be blamed on analysts' poor judgement as on company management. But analysts naturally tend to assign blame to company management as inept or even deceitful, rather than to their own poor forecasting skills. These negative attitudes can be hardened when, as often happens, the company issues further profit warnings some weeks or months after the first.

Within a short time a company which has issued a profit warning can go from stock market darling to pariah. Sometimes this is justified, but in many cases the change in perception is disproportionate to the change in the company's prospects. These are the cases where an investor such as Vernon, whose interest is attracted rather than repelled by bad news, can do well buying the glitch.

Another variety of glitch is the *index demotion*, when a company is demoted from a stock market index, say the FTSE100 or FTSE All-Share Index, because its market capitalisation has fallen below the lower limit for inclusion in the index. This can lead to the share being indiscriminately sold by index-tracking funds and other investors who arbitrarily restrict their investment universe to companies included in a particular index. But the reasons for the company being demoted from the index are in the past. If prospects have improved, or at least stopped getting worse, the indiscriminate selling may be an opportunity to buy a substantial volume of an unpopular share at a low price.

"Companies can be guilty of 'kitchen-sinking' their results – throwing in all the bad stuff, even the kitchen sink, to get it out of the way. The price falls needlessly – this is a buying opportunity."

Another type of glitch is the *mistaken sector read-across*, which involves not an individual profit warning but a whole market sector falling out of favour; a particular company is wrongly perceived by casual observers to be suffering problems similar to other companies in the sector. One example arose in the days and weeks after the terrorist incidents in the United States on 11 September 2001, when Lloyds insurers listed on the London Stock Exchange suffered large falls because of the fear that many had undetermined exposures to insured losses arising from the incidents. But some Lloyds insurers were able to announce within a few days that they had no exposure. Despite this, these insurers continued to fall in the following weeks, which created an opportunity for Vernon.

Another example of this type of sector glitch was the split capital trusts crisis of the early 2000s, when split capital shares were indiscriminately sold by many private client investment managers, creating an opportunity for investors who analysed the individual shares (Vernon missed this, but see Owen in Chapter 9).

Another type of glitch is the *bid failure*, where a takeover fails to complete. Typically in a takeover situation a significant fraction of the shares of the target company will be held by hedge funds and other arbitrageurs, who have bought after the bid announcement hoping to make a small near-certain 'turn' in a short time (equivalent to a high annualised rate of return). If the bid fails, the share price will usually fall sharply, so that the arbitrageurs suffer large losses *and* the original rationale of their investment has disappeared. In these circumstances the arbitrageurs will often sell without reference to the longer-term prospects of the business. If they have suffered large losses on borrowed money on the failed bid, they may be forced sellers.

Despite the shorthand description of 'buying the glitch', the strategy does not usually require immediate action when a profit warning or other glitch is announced. "People say that profit warnings tend to come in threes. I'm not sure about that, but it is true that problems often continue for some time." Although it is not necessary, nor even advantageous, always to buy quickly after a profit warning, it is important to be available when sellers appear in the weeks and months after a glitch.

The time window for buying can also be lengthened when company management, noting that the company is out of favour, shade discretionary accounting decisions so as to bring forward bad news from future periods – for example by writing down goodwill, or making full provision for doubtful debts – so that financial results in the future periods can then be unencumbered by these problems. This is known as 'kitchen-sinking' the results – throwing in all the bad stuff, even the kitchen sink. Vernon often cheerfully takes advantage of the gloom in such cases to buy cheaply. "Provided I am confident about long-term recovery, a further dose of bad news often helps me, because I accumulate more shares cheaply. That's the misanthropic part!"

Buying the glitch: QXL Ricardo

As an example of a stock bought after a glitch, Vernon quoted the example of QXL Ricardo, an internet auction business. QXL was founded by the technology journalist Tim Jackson in 1997 and floated on the London Stock Exchange in October 1999 with a valuation of £250m. The valuation multiplied more than eight-fold to around £2bn at a share price around 800p just six months later in April 2000.

Eight months after that, the share price had fallen to just 6.5p, making QXL an early member of the '99% club' (dotcom shares which lost more than 99% of their market value). In Autumn 2000 it acquired its German rival Ricardo, becoming QXL Ricardo. The share price languished for the next few years, with the stock market failing to notice quiet progress towards market dominance in some territories, in particular Poland.

This progress was clouded by a glitch – a legal dispute in 2002 in which a Polish subsidiary issued more shares, so that the UK company lost control of the business in Poland. For much of 2003 and 2004 the share price was a tiny fraction of the possible value if all or even just part of the Polish business was recovered.

Vernon bought the shares in his ISA throughout 2004. Early 2005 saw two competing takeover bids for the company, which were thwarted by a consortium of new investors, who bought shares in the market and rejected both bids. As a resolution of the legal dispute came closer, QXL Ricardo was the best performing share over 2005 on the London Stock Exchange. The more than ten-fold rise over 2005 was enough to make Vernon an ISA millionaire.

The legal dispute was resolved in 2007, and the company was eventually taken over for cash in March 2008 at a price more than 50 times Vernon's average cost. Although Vernon had sold all of his stock in 2007, he still made more than 25 times his average cost. "The key point was that the legal dispute was always likely to be resolved by a compromise, although the timescale and exact terms were unknown. In the meantime, the Polish business was growing exponentially, so even if only a modest fraction of the value was recovered, that would be many times the market capitalisation of the UK company."

QXL Ricardo price chart from January 2004 to takeover in March 2008

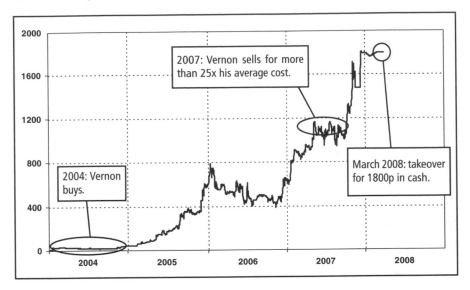

Source: data from ADVFN

Research method for glitch stocks

How does Vernon find glitch stocks? One starting point is alerts on stock market news websites for relevant phrases such as 'below market expectations'. Scanning lists of four-week and 52-week 'new lows' on sites such as the *Financial Times* (**www.ft.com**) and Digital Look (**www.digitallook.com**) is another starting point. He then reviews the shares from these lists on a case-by-case basis, to see which appear to fit the template of fast growing companies which have recently hit a glitch. Further consideration of these companies' accounts and prospects is mainly by desk-based research. He often speaks to directors on the telephone, but generally does not visit companies unless he already has a substantial holding.

Although Vernon's biggest successes have been in technology stocks, in recent years oils, minerals and emerging market property have all appeared in his portfolio. He is conscious of the trade-off between thorough knowledge of the sectors he invests in, and not missing new opportunities. Focusing on a limited number of sectors leads to "economies of scale in knowledge production" – that is, learning about one company in a sector helps you to understand others in the sector. On the other hand, if you spend all your time looking at a few sectors, you "risk getting stuck at local optima" – that is, miss

131

other sectors with much better opportunities. Moderate success in one sector can be a trap which prevents you discovering greater success somewhere else.

"make sure you spend some of your time playing offence as well as playing defence"

Another metaphor he finds helpful is to "make sure you spend some of your time playing offence as well as playing defence" – where playing defence means monitoring the companies you already own, and playing offence means scanning the other 2,500 UK quoted companies for new ideas.

Structuring investment decisions: core, secondary and hygiene factors

Describing how he thinks about the decision to buy a share, Vernon outlined a three-tier framework: a core thesis, a few secondary factors, and brief checking for problems on a larger number of "hygiene" factors.[2]

The core thesis – for example, that the market reaction to a glitch announcement appears over-done – usually occurs to him very soon after starting to look at the company, and can usually be expressed in a sentence or two.

The secondary factors are further positive reasons for buying the share, and also any important negatives. For example: cheap accounting metrics, forthcoming legislative changes which will improve demand for the company's products, recent directorial purchases of the shares, bid prospects, and so on.

"Hygiene" factors are potential catches or deal-breakers – matters that cannot provide positive reasons for buying the share, but which might put him off buying if they are sufficiently negative. For example: excessive director remuneration, the chief executive's bad record in a previous business, a sinister disclosure buried in the notes to the full accounts, credible negative comments posted on a bulletin board by a disgruntled employee, etc. Checking hygiene factors is in the nature of due diligence work – broader investigation around and beyond the core thesis and secondary factors, searching for hidden problems.

To illustrate this framework, Vernon provided me with copies of his notes on two decisions from 2008, when he was buying Haynes Publishing and Hansard International, both after substantial falls in their prices. The next section gives tidied-up versions of the summary pages from these notes.

Core, secondary and hygiene factors for two investment decisions

1. HAYNES PUBLISHING (SEPTEMBER 2008)

The Haynes name is synonymous with car repair manuals, a market which the company invented and now dominates – not just in the UK but also in the US and Australia.

Haynes Publishing price chart from January 2008 to December 2010

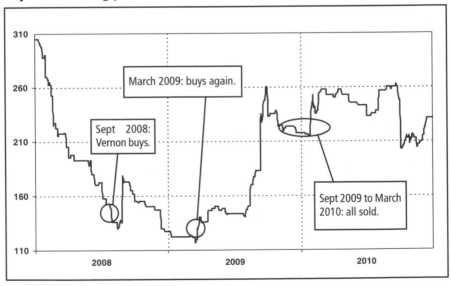

Source: data from ADVFN

Vernon's notes

Core thesis (as at September 2008):

The shares have fallen around 60% since the start of 2008, but there is no reason to think the very strong competitive position of the Haynes franchise would be affected by a credit crisis or recession. Indeed there is some evidence from past recessions that spending on DIY car maintenance actually increases in recessions.

Secondary factors:

- *Very cheap basic metrics – p/e 5x, NTAV around the share price, dividend yield 11%.*

- *Directors buying shares recently, in substantial size.*

- *The popularity of DIY maintenance on cars is in slow long-term decline, but no reason to think this has recently accelerated.*

- *Main shareholders – a number of value-oriented funds whom I respect are long-term holders of the shares.*

- *Experience of management – long track record in a market niche they created themselves.*

- *No published forecasts or broker research. To the extent this means shares are neglected, it is positive.*

Checks on hygiene factors:

- *Debt? – none.*

- *Unusual dual share structure – 'A' shares have same votes and economic interest as the Ordinaries, but can only be transferred within the Haynes family, who have control. A negative feature, but long history on stock market and outside shareholders never disadvantaged, so OK.*

- *£10m pension fund deficit on IAS19 – a negative – but OK because £7m profits before tax in each of last three years.*

- *Director remuneration is high, but OK because unusually well-defined performance related structure – key executives each receive 0.5% to 1.2% of net profits of their divisions. Yield of 11% means that shareholders are not neglected.*

- *Capitalisation of software development costs is currently increasing profits – OK, be aware that the amortisation will be a cost in future, but legitimate under IFRS.*

- *Checked bulletin boards (not many posts – good).*

- *Glanced recent years' accounts. No further issues.*

- *Glanced past two years' RNS. No further issues.*

Outcome

128,500 shares were bought by Vernon on seven days between 15 August and 6 November 2008. The range of prices paid was 130p to 170p with an average of 160p.

In March 2009 a further 50,000 shares were bought in a single purchase at 117p, giving a total of 178,500 shares bought at an average of 148p.

All 178,500 shares were sold on 12 days between 15 September 2009 and 31 March 2010. The range of prices received was 216p to 255p with an average of 232p. This represented a realised gain of around 56% over just over a year, or 66% including dividends.

With hindsight, many other companies with higher risk (e.g. higher debt) than Haynes could have been bought cheaply in autumn 2008, and enjoyed larger subsequent rises. But Haynes was an attractive purchase because of its relatively low risk.

2. HANSARD INTERNATIONAL (OCTOBER 2008)

Hansard is technically an Isle of Man life insurance company. But in reality it is largely an administration and marketing operation, with most of the life risk reinsured, and almost no investment risk because virtually all the products are unit-linked. The company has only 180 staff but sells its products in over 180 countries (not including the UK or the US), entirely via independent intermediaries.

Hansard International price chart from January 2008 to December 2010

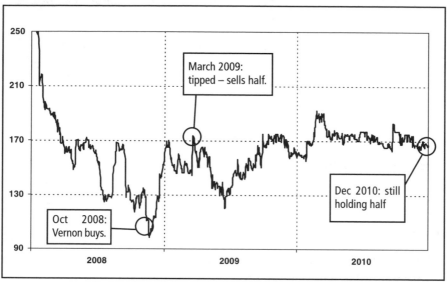

Source: data from ADVFN

Vernon's notes

Core thesis (as at October 2008):

The shares have fallen over 60% since the start of 2008, probably because of the worry that Hansard is a financial company affected by falling asset values and solvency risk. This is misconceived. The reality is that Hansard is a service company disguised in the ugly clothes of a life insurer.

Secondary factors:

- *High dividend yield – around 10% at 120p – provides reassurance that the profits are real. The company promises to pay out 70% of earnings as dividend.*

- *Other metrics (p/e, NTAV, etc) less useful because of complexity of life company accounting, which I don't understand fully. This difficulty in understanding is a negative. But around 40% of the share price is covered by cash and the minimum solvency margin is covered more than 10x, so as far as I can tell it is a strong financial position.*

- *They claim higher margins than other life insurers. Although I don't fully understand the accounting, there is probably some truth to this.*

- *Broker research – several detailed notes by analysts I respect with positive recommendations, and price targets well above current price.*

- *The CEO is 80 years old and owns around half the shares => bid possibilities in the medium term.*

- *50% of sales in dollars, so current dollar strength helps.*

Hygiene factors:

- *Debt? – none.*

- *Management remuneration – OK. CEO takes just £1 as salary => dividend may be important to him, and unlikely to be cut unless unavoidable.*

- *UK pre-budget report announced a review of Crown Dependencies – possibility of adverse tax changes in Isle of Man as result of EU/UK pressure – but general view seems to be that Isle of Man will try not to damage businesses which provide jobs and revenue for the island.*

- *Some intermediaries have a target for incremental production where the target has to be met by the end of the year to trigger a reward – slight worry that this structure could incentivise false accounting – but no evidence of any problem so far.*

- *All the business is channelled through 20 account executives – OK, but be aware that the company probably depends on quite a small group of people.*

- *Checked bulletin boards (not many posts – good).*

- *Glanced recent years' accounts. No further issues.*

- *Glanced past two years' RNS. No further issues.*

Outcome

161,632 shares were bought by Vernon on five days between 23 September and 20 November 2008 – the period when the misperception of Hansard as a financial company affected by solvency issues was at its most acute. The range of prices paid was 132p to 100p – the price fell during the period of purchases, with the lowest price achieved at latest date. The average price paid was 124p.

On 20 March 2009 the shares jumped from an opening price of 141p to a high for the day of 177p. There was no news to explain the rise, so Vernon surmised that the shares had probably been tipped somewhere, although he never traced the source.

Following his "when it's [probably] been tipped, sell some" rule, he sold 80,000 shares on six days between 20 March and 26 March 2010. The range of prices received was 161p to 177p, with an average price of 166p. This represented a realised gain of around 34% over about five months, plus a final dividend of 6% received in December 2008 on some of the earlier purchases.

The remaining shares were still held in late 2010, when the price was around 170p. Vernon noted that with the dividend yield of 8% on a low risk share with bid prospects in the medium term, he was in no great hurry to sell the remaining holding.

As with Haynes, Vernon regarded Hansard as a successful purchase not just because of the size of the gain, but because of the low perceived risk at the time of purchase.

Discussing the framework further, Vernon said that the core-secondary-hygiene categories were not sacrosanct, and it was not just a matter of checklists (although they can help), nor a rigid sequence – the core thesis might be modified as new information came to light. But you should always have a clear and concise core thesis, so you know why you hold the share; and then a hierarchy to structure other points, and to help allocate your time sensibly in investigating those points.

He also made the point that *it is not worth knowing everything about a company*: every investigation has a time opportunity cost. Your aim is not to check all possible hygiene factors, but to check enough to reduce your error rate to a time-efficient acceptable level: a low, but probably not zero, rate of error.

Asked when he sold stocks, Vernon said "when they become popular". Elaborating on this, he said that selling was conceptually a more difficult decision than buying. "In principle you should always think about selling as a switch to an alternative investment. You should sell if the prospective returns on the alternative investment – which might be a cash deposit – are sufficient to compensate for the tax and other costs of switching. But that is impossibly difficult in practice, so you need heuristics, that is rules of thumb."

One of his rules of thumb is "when it doubles, always sell some" – analogous to Nigel's rule (see Chapter 2) of "when it doubles, sell half." Another rule is "when it's tipped, sell some": he is more likely to sell than to buy a share which is tipped in a newspaper or magazine, although he may ignore this rule if he has only recently bought the stock, and still considers it cheap after the tip.

Portfolio management and leverage

Apart from bets on the FTSE100 index for occasionally hedging up to 25% of his market exposure, Vernon does not use spread betting. He thinks that leverage and limited-term products such as spread bets are probably more suited to trend-following than contrarian investors. This is because shares which are out of favour because of a recent glitch may remain out of favour for a considerable time. Sometimes a glitch will get worse before it gets better. The contrarian investor has some sense that things *will* turn around, but often has little idea *when*. Compared with other investors, contrarians are relatively insensitive to time.

> "Compared to other investors, contrarians are relatively insensitive to time."

He uses two traditional brokers, and thinks that the skill in dealing in larger size is worth the extra cost compared with an online service. Having two brokers is also helpful when dealing in illiquid small companies, because sometimes one broker can find stock when the other cannot. Given his preference for buying shares on bad news rather than good, Vernon has no interest in the brokers' offers of new issues. "A new issue is the opposite of a glitch – you have a small army of people promoting the story, and sweeping bad news under the carpet. That is not the time to be buying."

For organising his work he keeps a file on each holding, and writes lots of notes, which he keeps mainly electronically. "The notes are not important in themselves, but they help me to maintain mental consistency over time. They are a stabilising influence when some news comes out which might tempt me to trade impulsively."

Mental skills for investing

Asked what skills were important for his type of investing, Vernon's first response was "be lucky!" But he qualified this by distinguishing two different types of luck in investment, as mentioned in this book's introduction.

One type is completely random, where being in with a chance of good luck requires only trivial effort, like buying a lottery ticket. But another type is characterised by a quotation attributed to the French microbiologist Louis Pasteur: "in the fields of observation, chance favours the prepared mind". For example, only a few investors around the millennium exploited the opportunity to both make *and keep* fortunes from technology shares. These investors were lucky, but their being in with a chance of this luck arose from their interest and diligence in researching and investing in technology shares.

Vernon probably has a better technical knowledge of software than anyone else in this book. How important is this in his investing?

"Technical knowledge can help, but it is not a panacea; plenty of technical people are unsuccessful investors. Broad knowledge-gathering and being emotionally able to change your mind are more important than detailed technical knowledge." Compared to his mathematics degree and his doctoral work in computer science, he thinks investing is not technically difficult, but it does require some mental habits which are "possibly unusual, although not difficult." In particular, he highlighted the need to "keep several competing ideas or insights in your mind in parallel, accepting uncertainty for long periods, and choosing between them at the last possible moment." He calls this operating with "multiple mental models".

He also highlighted that an investor's thinking should be focused on "a search for the truth, rather than supporting prior affiliations." In many other fields – politics, business, law – truth is not important, prior affiliations largely determine opinions, and thinking is mainly about generating arguments to support those opinions. But for an investor, the question "whose side are you on?" is usually meaningless: "investment is not a team sport."

A corollary of not focusing on affiliation is an indifference to popularity. When you buy a great bargain, you are leaning against the crowd, and usually pretty much alone. It helps to be happy with being alone. "This concept of being happy alone is so culturally alien that English seems to have no positive words for it – only negative words like lonely, solitary, or isolated."

He also highlighted the particular importance for an investor of *avoiding mistakes*. He drew a distinction between activities with 'positive scoring', where success is defined by gaining wins, and activities with 'negative scoring', where success is defined by avoiding faults.

Positively scored activities include selling, leadership, and most sports. In these activities bravery, 'having a go' and risk-taking give a better chance of success than careful deliberation, and the downside of making errors is low. Negatively scored activities include driving a car, piloting an aircraft, and anaesthetics in medicine. The successful driver, pilot or anaesthetist is not the brave one who always 'has a go', but rather the meticulous one who never makes any big mistakes.

> "Learning modern portfolio theory to pick investments is like learning physics to play snooker."

The relevance of this to investing? "The ease of online dealing makes many people act as if investing was positively scored, but the arithmetic of compounding dictates that it is really negatively scored. Success in investing consists mainly of avoiding big mistakes."

Apart from focusing on avoiding mistakes yourself, he also mentioned the value of systematically studying *other people's* mistakes. "Investment books and articles have a bias towards success stories. I find it useful to read about disasters – not for *schadenfreude*, but for learning."

Because Vernon has strong mathematical skills, he has spent some time studying modern portfolio theory in the sense understood in financial economics – that is, optimising portfolios based on estimated means and variances for the universe of possible investments. But he has not found this concept helpful in practice. "Learning modern portfolio theory to pick investments is like learning physics to play snooker."

A final skill which Vernon highlighted as important for the self-directed investor was effective time allocation. "Time is a limited resource with strongly diminishing returns. The first hour you spend researching a company is much more important than the tenth hour. Some private investors are management groupies – they spend too much time on their favourite companies, posting on bulletin boards and going to AGMs and all the rest of it. They are squandering time which would be better spent looking for new ideas." To limit the time resource applied to any one company, he reminds himself of psychological research which suggests that in many contexts decisions are best made with no more than five to seven points of information. Any more information beyond that does not significantly improve decisions, and may even degrade them.

Conclusion

Although Vernon's background is in mathematics and computing, his distinctive interests compared with the other interviewees appear to be cognitive psychology and decision making: he has thought at length about his investment thought processes.

This perhaps reflects the fact that his strategy of "buying the glitch" requires a high degree of mental self-control. Most people feel good about buying shares which have positive news flow, exciting prospects, and a team of bulletin board cheerleaders. "Buying the glitch" involves shares with negative news flow, poor immediate prospects, and little popular appeal. It requires a mindset which is contrarian, and perhaps a little misanthropic. Although straightforward in theory, this is for most investors psychologically uncomfortable in practice. Most investors, consciously or subconsciously, seek the approval of their peers; but the best decisions in the stock market attract no applause.

VERNON: INSIGHTS AND ADVICE

Buy the glitch   Look to take advantage of profit warnings, demotions from indices, mistaken sector read-across, bid failures, and other temporary problems.

Core, secondary and hygiene factors   Investment decisions can be mentally structured as a core thesis (one or two sentences), a few secondary factors, and then checks on 'hygiene' factors (due diligence searching for problems). It helps to be clear what your core thesis is. After a certain point, additional inputs to a decision may not improve its quality. Basing a decision on a core thesis and five to seven secondary points may be a good guideline.

Optimal rates of error   It is not worth knowing everything about a company, because every point investigated has a time-opportunity cost. Your aim in checking hygiene factors is not to find out everything, but to reduce your error rate to an acceptable level.

Heuristics   Comprehensive analysis is often too difficult, so general rules of thumb – heuristics – can be helpful. For example, when a share doubles, sell some. When a share is tipped, sell some.

Time as a resource   Time applied to any one decision or project has strongly diminishing returns.

Balance offensive and defensive play   Monitor the time you spend playing offence (looking for new shares to buy) and the time you spend playing defence (following shares you already own).

Pasteur luck   In the fields of observation, chance favours the prepared mind.

Investment is not a team sport   Nobody cares whose side you are on. Base your judgements on facts, not prior affiliations.

Games with negative scoring   These games are won by avoiding mistakes, rather than by bravery. Study and learn from other people's mistakes.

III

ACTIVISTS

Activists attempt to influence company managers' decisions in line with their own views – by dialogue and persuasion, by using the votes on their shares, and if necessary by publicity. They are sometimes prepared to buy shares knowing that company management is in some way unsatisfactory, and that changes are needed. Most investors try to avoid such situations, that is, they do not go looking for trouble. The activists, to varying degrees, do sometimes go looking for trouble.

ERIC
THE NETWORKER

ERIC: FACTS AND FIGURES

Age at interview	51
Age at leaving last full-time job	28 (last employment), 39 (sold his own business)
Background	Sports journalism; property lettings management; Samaritans volunteer listener.
Style	Exhaustive on-the-ground observation and personal networking.
Markets and sectors	UK small caps with accessible management.
Instruments	Shares, spread bets.
Typical holding period	Months to years.
Performance indicators	Several ten-baggers or more over the past decade, including Indigovision (20x), Lo-Q (15x), and most significantly Ben Bailey (10x); large post-tax drawings (at least £10,000 per month) to support large family.
Quote	"You can't always get an inside track, but you can often find someone who lives near the stadium."
Phrases	Small-cap paradox; strategic naivety; feed the ducks when they're quacking.

At its core, private investing is an individualistic activity: one person deciding to buy or sell a share. For many investors this introversion encompasses all their investing activity: they mainly read and think, seeking to derive an edge from superior observation or financial analysis, and only occasionally speaking to anyone else. But for some investors, social interactions with company directors and other investors and contacts are the primary source of their edge.

Eric often speaks to several company directors in a day, and he attends annual general meetings almost every week. He also speaks frequently to many other investors – not just old friends, but often strangers with whom he has no prior connection other than holding shares in the same company (this was how he originally found me). Each month he cajoles a varying group of several dozen investors to attend a social dinner he organises with presentations by one or more small quoted companies. His network of investing contacts is almost certainly the largest of anyone in this book.

Eric is in his early fifties, a short rotund man with a northern accent, and straight dark hair above rimless spectacles on a rounded face. His voice, vocabulary and syntax all give the impression of an empathetic family man, with the vague benevolence of someone who started with few advantages and has been lucky in life.

Reading a sample of his bulletin board posts revealed the same amiable style, with none of the heated arguments or grandstanding which often characterise bulletin boards. It was easy to envisage how this agreeable demeanour might elicit occasionally unguarded comments not only from company directors, but also from the sales staff and regional managers whom Eric will often contact when researching a company.

Less immediately obvious was the extent to which the unthreatening demeanour hides a sharp business brain. Eric was making serious money relative to his family's circumstances by the time he was 15, and using savings from his teenage earnings for deposits on property purchases by his early 20s. He last worked as an employee at the age of 28, and built up and sold a substantial property lettings business before he was 40.

Eric lives in a large period detached house in a cul-de-sac in a London suburb. His two youngest children, a son of 11 and daughter of ten, showed me into a long high-ceilinged living room with five large sofas and a bay window overlooking the garden and swimming pool. Telling Eric's story was a family effort: the ten-year-old offered a crib sheet, a biography of dad with all the key facts and dates, previously written for a school project, and both children slipped in and out of the room throughout the afternoon, asking questions and adding their own comments. With four children and four stepchildren, Eric cannot make a fetish of frugality like some people in this book. "Most of the kids are not yet earning money, so my regular spending is at least £10,000 per month. I need either dividends or gains to cover that."

Teenage gaming for profit

Eric grew up in Blackpool. His father ran a "small – and I mean very small" business, a grocery home-deliveries service based on a single van, working very long hours for seven days a week. Eric helped in this business from a very young age, which gave him a head start in maths at school, and an early insight into the business facts of life. He was a precocious, commercially aware child, keenly interested in the economics of his father's business.

At the age of 11 he won a full-fees scholarship to a local private school. Changing schools was a culture shock: "For the first time I realised how poor we were. We didn't have a telephone or a car, only Dad's grocery van, and even my uniform was second-hand." He was a middling student, keen on sport, "good at the basics of English and Maths, which got me the scholarship, but not so good at other subjects". He passed nine O-levels, and proceeded to the then-extravagant number of five A-levels including Economics, but by this time his money-making projects were starting to crowd out academic work. One of these helps to demonstrate his distinctive approach to investment.

During the work breaks in his teenage summer job in Blackpool, he would while away the time around the arcades of the Pleasure Beach. He developed a particular adeptness for 'Elton Derby': a game of skill lasting a few minutes, involving rolling a ball past obstacles towards a target, a little like skittles or bowls, where the winner of each game received tickets which could be accumulated and redeemed for valuable prizes. Playing for about three hours in the breaks from his job throughout the day, he was soon winning far more in prizes than the modest entrance fees for the games.

Realising that the game operators might object to a consistent winner, he adopted a tactic which was later to become one of his hallmarks: developing friendly relationships which worked to his advantage. "Basically I befriended the family which operated the games, and particularly the owner's daughter, hoping to make it awkward for the father to ban me." He also sought to remain inconspicuous and inoffensive to other game patrons, sometimes tactically feigning a lack of ability, rather like a card counter at blackjack. Following a frank discussion with the owners, an acceptable *modus operandi* was agreed: he could win as often as he liked, provided that he moved frequently from one game to another, and took care not to let his winning frequency arouse indignation amongst other patrons. The fact that any game where he played was likely to be over quickly was possibly even helpful to the owners, because it facilitated a higher number of games through the day, and hence an increased throughput of paying customers.

Having reached this accommodation with the Elton Derby operators, his real job lost some of its attraction. In subsequent years Eric spent his entire summer holidays on Blackpool Pleasure Beach, playing Elton Derby for prizes, and making bulk disposals of the prizes for resale via one of his cousins – hundreds of pounds worth of digital watches and cassette recorders and other fashionable consumer items every week.

By the time he left school, Elton Derby had netted him several thousand pounds – or approaching ten times that amount in today's money. "It seems a bit of laugh now, but it was very serious at the time, and life-changing in the context of my family. My father was in his late 60s and still working all hours just scraping a living." Success on the beach was his first insight into the advantages of focusing on the most remunerative from the range of available activities, working on relationships, keeping a low profile, and sometimes appearing less skilled or sophisticated than he really was – all strategies which he carried forward to his later property and stock market activities.

Property management

Eric's A-level grades were good enough for university, but he could see that his parents, whilst reassured by his adeptness at making money, were unenthusiastic about a choice which would involve several years with no earnings. Although he already had entrepreneurial aspirations, he started his working career in London as a trainee journalist on a sports newspaper. The job was not particularly demanding, and left him with plenty of unstructured time to pursue his own business ideas.

Most of these ideas went nowhere, but using the capital earned from his teenage gaming, he established a toehold in property. From letting a spare room he progressed to taking over and completing an unfinished building project, which gave him three mortgaged flats for letting. He then branched out into lettings management for third parties, and this gradually became his main activity.

He ran the lettings business on a shoestring, with a calculated strategy of creating an informal word-of-mouth ethos amongst the tenants. "Our headquarters was always just an ordinary house. Most of our advertisements looked like those of an amateur landlord, which allowed us to get some free advertising for many years in the London free-sheets. We preferred tenants introduced by other tenants – they were less likely to default or be disruptive, because they would be letting down their friends."

The low-key presentation did not impede (and may have helped) the rapid growth of the business. Eric left his last job to concentrate solely on property management at the age of 28; he has never been employed since then. By the mid-1990s he had half a dozen staff and 800 tenants, as well as his own substantial rental portfolio.

He was now married to Belinda, who had four children from a previous marriage. Having grown up an only child with no cousins, he had always wanted a large family, and they soon had children of their own. Eric realised that his long hours running the business increasingly clashed with being a dad. "When I was a kid I used to stay up until ten o'clock, hoping my dad would finish his deliveries and get home before I went to bed. I didn't want my kids to be like that."

So when he received a good offer for the business in 1997, he was pleased to sell. He was 39 years old. He continued informally managing property for a few landlords who had become personal friends, "but only on a small scale, for 40 or 50 properties". By 2004 he had handed over even this residual business to his nephew.

Starting in shares

Throughout the 1980s and 1990s, Eric punted on privatisations and occasionally dabbled in other shares. But this was always just a hobby – the property lettings business and his own rental properties were his main priorities. Starting in the mid-1980s, he also made some business-angel type investments in small private companies, but none of these were particularly successful. His approach to share investing was always the practical one of someone involved in business himself, often focusing on his familiar sectors of property and housebuilding, rather than that of an analytical financial expert.

After selling the lettings business in 1997, he started to spend more time on shares. "Financially, if we had lived quietly I could probably have never worked again after selling the business. But I would have been bored, and there was the role model issue – it would not be a good example for the kids if Dad did nothing."

In the technology shares bubble in 1999-2000, he had one or two shares which went up more than 30 times, but these were "just punts for pin money" which made little difference to his overall wealth. In the aftermath of the bubble, he suffered big losses on the large companies Independent Energy and Marconi, both constituents of the FTSE100 index when he first invested. These disasters sharpened his focus on the advantages of investing exclusively in small companies. He recognised an important paradox about small companies: they are less well researched, and yet easier to research. Compared to larger companies, the accounts are simpler, the directors are more accessible, and the business can usually be explained in a sentence or two.

> "There is an important paradox about small companies: they are less well researched, and yet easier to research. "

The resolution of the paradox is liquidity: for most institutional investors, it is not worth researching a smaller company, because even if the research shows it is cheap, only a small investment could be made. But it is worth researching for private investors.

Ten-bagging Ben Bailey

Around the millennium Eric carried out several small property refurbishment projects. With an architect partner he developed a highly successful standard formula for converting old South London flats from one to two bedrooms, but competition from other builders gradually reduced their margins.

As the 2000s progressed, he directed more time and money towards shares rather than direct property investments. One company in particular, the northern England house-builder Ben Bailey, could be compared directly with his own refurbishment projects. To assess Ben Bailey's margins and prospects, he developed a painstaking – and perhaps unusually personal – approach to market research.

As well as studying the accounts and talking in detail with the directors, he closely monitored sales at each of the company's sites. "All the developments and the details of available units were on the internet. Across the family, we had half a dozen mobile phones. So I developed a programme of periodically ringing the sites, posing as a potential buyer in a variety of names, and gleaning what I could on sale numbers and prices, and how many units were left on each site. I knew the names of all the sales agents, and I kept detailed notes on every enquiry I made."

Ben Bailey plc: price chart from January 2001 to takeover in August 2007

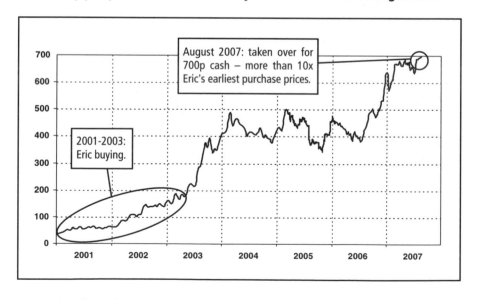

Source: data from ADVFN

Eventually the company's sales director rumbled this role-playing tactic, and rang Eric to demand that he desist. "I explained to him something of my personal background, and I said I am investing my own money, which has been earned from a lifetime of hard graft. Any information I can discover as a potential customer is publicly available, so I am not doing anything illegal. If anyone wants to stop me, they will have to persuade a court that it merits an injunction, and good luck with that!"

Given that Eric already knew a lot about the company, did continuing this elaborate programme of research really add any information? "I had a huge investment in the company – one third of my portfolio at one stage – so that justified my spending a lot of time on it. Also, I got to know many other private investors in the company and I enjoyed the social aspect of that." Ben Bailey was eventually taken over in 2007 for more than ten times Eric's first purchase price.

As with Ben Bailey, Eric's other successes have often tended to be "traditional dividend-paying family companies, often with a Yorkshire connection, or at least a Yorkshire mentality." Successes of this type in recent years included engineering company Chieftain, toy manufacturer Character Group, and lighting company FW Thorpe. On the other hand, high-tech growth companies have provided some of his largest percentage gains, albeit not always with large amounts invested. In this vein he particularly mentioned CCTV supplier Indigovision (30x gain on his lowest purchase price) and 'virtual queue' technology company Lo-Q (15x gain on his lowest purchase price).

He undertakes detailed research on current business levels at all his larger investee companies, at a level which is probably more detailed than the one or two City analysts who typically follow a small company. He often telephones sales staff seeking information as a potential customer, for a "school project", or with some similar pretext for assessing current levels of business. He summarises his objective in these calls as follows: "You can't always get an inside track, but you often find someone who lives near the stadium."

Eric's edge comes mainly from these enquiries about current trading, rather than from sophisticated financial analysis. Indeed, having never had any formal training in investment analysis, he admits that his accounting knowledge is weaker than that of some of his investor friends. Asked about failures over the years, he mentioned companies such as Mayflower, Minorplanet and SFI. On investigation I found that these were all companies with complicated accounting, and large discrepancies between profit accruals and cash flow. A process of personal enquiry can reveal a great deal of scuttlebutt about current business levels, but healthy sales activity does not preclude a cash flow problem – indeed it can *cause* a cash flow problem. Sometimes the honest optimism of staff at the front line of sales is misleading. Sometimes the accounts speak louder than any words.

Portfolio management and spread betting

Eric holds shares in around 50 small companies at any time, but the majority of his portfolio by value is usually in around a dozen companies. He keeps paper notes on all his holdings, in a separate file for each company. Although he places much greater emphasis on personal communication with companies than most people in this book, if he likes a company he will make an initial purchase before speaking to the directors. "Once I own the shares, I feel more justified in asking lots of questions and taking up their time. I find it psychologically helpful to have at least a small holding."

When he started investing Eric initially used the stockbroking arm of his high street bank, but in recent years he has used a small traditional private client broker. He also has accounts with several spread bet firms, which he uses almost exclusively for betting on single shares, usually small companies rather than indices or commodities. The choice between a spread bet and a share purchase is driven mainly by whether he anticipates a short holding period for which he will use a spread bet, or a longer one for which he will buy the share. He has never experimented with online brokers, and uses the telephone even when placing spread bets. He uses no IT systems or services more sophisticated than free real-time prices, not even Level 2 prices from the London Stock Exchange. "I might find Level 2 data interesting if I got it, but for a long-term investor I don't think it's essential."

Despite having been an investor in shares since the early 1990s, he has not had the good luck to concentrate his best returns in an ISA. Given his substantial non-discretionary family spending needs, he is also not an enthusiast for tying up funds in other tax-efficient but inaccessible wrappers, such as self-invested personal pensions.

How does he make selling decisions? "With large holdings, you can't hope to sell all at the top. You have to sell into demand when a share is still rising – feed the ducks when they're quacking. So I am a slicer – always slicing the top tenth or so off holdings which are going up." Given his substantial family outgoings, he has sometimes needed to raise cash when there is little market liquidity in his holdings, for example in Autumn 2008. In these circumstances, because many of his investee companies have substantial net cash, he has sometimes found that the company itself is willing to buy in some of his shares.

Eric also uses his spread bet accounts for short selling. At any time he will have up to a dozen or more short positions on single shares. These are generally much smaller than his long positions, and their success rate is lower. The last time he reviewed his full record he found that around 55% of his shorts had been closed at a profit, compared with 77% of his longs, with a large part of the cumulative profit coming from a few big winners amongst the longs. His bets are usually increased and reduced in small increments, for which there is no cost penalty of a fixed minimum commission in spread betting (unlike a traditional client broker). He emphasised that for him spread betting is about tax efficiency, rather than leverage. "It doesn't have to be crazy gambling. There is no reason why a portfolio in a spread bet account should be any different from one in an ISA."

In the winter 2008-09 bear market, as well as increasing his short positions on single shares, Eric did some more systemic hedging. He hedged 20% of his portfolio with a spread bet short on the FTSE100 index, and shorted oil via a spread bet as a hedge for his oil exploration shares. This was only a partial success. As the bear market ended, the FTSE100 turned up while his small-cap portfolio was still falling, so for a time he was losing money quickly on both. But the short did help him to resist the temptation to sell his portfolio of small caps. If he had sold, it would have been impossible to reverse quickly near the bottom of the market, because most of the positions were too large to accumulate quickly.

> "You have to sell into demand when a share is still rising – feed the ducks when they're quacking."

A typical day

Eric is "not a morning person" and will be up at 7am only on days when one of his investee companies is expected to release results or a trading update. He is a member of a Microsoft Network (MSN) group of about a dozen investors, and through the morning he exchanges comments and ideas on the day's news with the group.

After reading through any RNS releases from his investee companies, and skimming bulletin boards, a good deal of his day is spent on the telephone, trying to contact company directors and other staff in a company. When speaking to directors, he asks about "the real story, not just the PR spiel in the RNS…often about salaries or share options…I also ask about their competitors in the sector." The responses to these enquiries vary widely. "Some small companies are just not used to anyone ringing up. Sometimes they are irritated. Sometimes they are delighted that someone is interested." Some of the conversations are rather uncomfortable or awkward, but Eric is not discouraged by this: "I'm not trying to have difficult conversations. But in the end I think that success depends on the number of difficult conversations you are willing to have."

When directors are unresponsive or unhelpful to a private investor making such persistent enquiries, does this put him off investing in the company? "Not necessarily. I try to understand the history which has led to that. Quite often they are family companies which just happen to be listed. Directors being unhelpful to me personally doesn't always mean it's a bad company." Sometimes he finds that directors who were initially unhelpful to his enquiries become comfortable over a period as he gains their trust.

Apart from persistence in making contact and asking questions, another subtle element of Eric's technique is simply *listening* – not casually, but with unusual perception and intensity. He learnt this skill in a field completely unrelated to investment: for several years before he got married he was a volunteer with the Samaritans charity, spending several hours a week on the telephones. "It taught me a lot about tone of voice, the importance of listening without judgement, and waiting for the right moment to comment. Those skills have definitely helped me in investment research."

Eric works on investment research for much of the day. After school hours, in the late afternoon and early evening he will usually be willingly distracted by the children, but he is often back at his PC late in the evening and into the early hours. One of the benefits of being a full-time investor is freedom to participate fully in his children's lives. "When I ran the property business, even though I was the boss, I could never be sure of getting away, because I had to meet clients when they wanted to meet. But as an investor, I never miss a school or social event for any of the kids."

Tactics for annual general meetings

Eric attends around 50 AGMs every year, with a high concentration between March and July, reflecting company year-ends on 31 December and 31 March. Asked about tactics for such meetings, he said it was important to establish expectations at the start, for example by informing the directors that one has a dozen or more questions to ask. Although he usually lingers to chat after the meeting, he prefers to ask many of his questions of the board collectively, rather than in one-to-one conversations.

"It is sometimes revealing to see who answers which questions, and the dynamics of how members of the board interact: who is really in charge. You can also pick up a lot from any hesitancy and from tone of voice." If the chairman is answering all the questions, Eric will address some questions by name to other board members. The reception given to private shareholders at AGMs varies considerably, from an affable welcome and refreshments to a security cordon and demands for proof of identity, but Eric's questioning is never deflected by unhelpful directorial demeanour. A mutual friend characterises Eric's approach to questioning directors at AGMs as follows: "Asking lots of seemingly naïve questions in a seemingly naïve way, like a polite but persistent child. Other people in the room sometimes get a bit embarrassed. But Eric doesn't seem to worry about that, and the naïvety is an act, he really knows exactly what he's doing."

> "At AGMs, Eric asks lots of seemingly naïve questions ... the naïvety is an act, he really knows exactly what he's doing."

Apart from gathering information and assessing directors, attending AGMs is also a means of meeting other shareholders, analysts and company advisors, building up a network of contacts for future activism.

Keeping a low profile

Knowing that Eric has substantial investments in many small companies, I wondered why I had never seen him announce a notifiable holding of over 3% of a company. He said that this was a deliberate policy. "If I find I am approaching 3% of a company, that is definitely a reason to stop buying. I would feel uncomfortable with such a blatant display of wealth."

This reticence about obvious manifestation of success maintains a pattern of his past: the deliberately low profile as a teenager winning thousands of pounds in prizes at Blackpool Pleasure Beach, and the ordinary house he once kept as headquarters for a property business managing 800 tenants. He also maintains a low profile in his activist campaigns, acting behind the scenes rather than as a figurehead. He has engineered the appointment of other private investors as non-executive directors at several small listed companies, but has never become a listed company director himself.

Not all activism produces a successful result, and sometimes the bad guys win: the directors retain their excessive share options or bonuses, or persist with a wealth-destroying strategy. Eric is unfazed by this, because he sees activism as partly about doing the right thing. He has sometimes taken activist interest in directorial malfeasance in companies where his financial stake was relatively low. "Some directors say to me that if I don't like their actions, I should sell the shares. From their point of view, that is probably the worst thing to say to me."

Conclusion

Eric's style is the epitome of low-profile investing. He has a very wide network of personal investing contacts, and owns substantial stakes in many small companies; but Google finds almost nothing about him. He often draws journalists' attention to company stories, but his own name has never appeared in a newspaper or even in a shareholding announcement on RNS.

He would never be mistaken for a captain of industry, and few people would guess he was wealthy; rather the first impression is of a genial but unremarkable family man. But first impressions can be deceptive. Shrewdness disguised by a façade of amiable amateurism is the strategy he first developed nearly 40 summers ago, systematically winning thousands of pounds in prizes on Blackpool Pleasure Beach.

ERIC: INSIGHTS AND ADVICE

Network for information Networking widely with company directors and other investors can be a source of competitive edge.

Strategic naïvety It can help to appear less sophisticated than you really are. Asking seemingly naïve questions with a genial demeanour can help persuade directors and others to open up.

Uncomfortable conversations Do not worry if some of your conversations with directors and others are uncomfortable or awkward. Success depends to some extent on the number of uncomfortable conversations you are willing to have.

The small-cap paradox A paradox about smaller companies: they are less well researched, and yet easier to research.

The inside track Approaching a business for information as a potential customer can be a useful way of gauging current sales activity.

Feed the ducks when they're quacking You normally cannot sell all of a large holding at the top of the market. You have to sell into demand – 'feed the ducks when they're quacking'. Periodically 'top-slicing' by selling a tenth or so of your holding is a useful discipline when prices are rising.

Manage company meetings At annual general meetings, set expectations at the start of the meeting by informing the directors that you have several questions to ask. It is often interesting to observe how the board interacts in answering questions.

One mouth, two ears Learn when to shut up and listen – not casually, but with perception and intensity.

OWEN
EFFICIENCY AND OPPORTUNISM

OWEN: FACTS AND FIGURES

Age at interview	45
Age at leaving last full-time job	38
Background	Physics; investment banking (proprietary trader).
Style	Opportunistically buys closed-end funds at discount to net assets, then presses directors for action to close the discount; often holds substantial cash for long periods when there are no good activist opportunities.
Markets and sectors	Split capital investment trusts in 2002-03; listed hedge funds and private equity funds in 2008-09.
Instruments	Shares, index spread bets as hedge.
Typical holding period	Months.
Performance indicators	ISA millionaire by early 2000s; since multiplied ISA "several times".
Quote	"It is a mistake to think of cash as burning a hole in your pocket."
Phrases	Stag; arbitrage; prop trader; split-capital trusts; listed hedge funds.

One wry definition of a value investor is a person who places a high premium on having the last laugh. This often requires patience: the last laugh may be a long time coming, if you simply buy shares with cheap accounting metrics and wait passively for mean reversion.

But sometimes the last laugh can be speeded up by activism. For example, some hedge funds and other arbitrageurs specialise in buying shares in closed-end funds – investment trusts or property companies – at a discount to net asset value, and then agitating for the fund to return value to investors closer to net asset value. In his previous City career, Owen was one of these agitators, and his own investing has retained this opportunistic approach.

Owen's education, culminating in a first-class physics degree from Oxford, combined with his many years in a directly relevant career as an investment bank proprietary trader, make him one of the more obviously sophisticated investors in this book. Large shareholdings of up to 10% in investment trusts and similar companies, which he announces from time to time, suggest that this sophistication has a payoff in terms of investment success.

Slightly less obviously, sophistication also appears to have a payoff in terms of efficiency, limiting the time he needs to spend on investing. Compared with some others in this book, he appears to spend less time working on his investments, and he is less tied to being in front of a screen. "I don't have a typical day," he explains. "In the school holidays, when the kids are here, I'm doing things with them. I will go through market news late at night or sometimes early in the morning. But I don't feel an obligation to be at my desk at regular hours every day, and I'm certainly not watching markets all day."

Growing up young

Owen's father owned and operated several low-budget hotels in West London. He was an altruistic man, deeply involved in the Anglican church and various local philanthropic interests. Owen remembers accompanying him as a young child on visits to local nursing homes and hospitals. He also has memories of a stream of temporary residents in their home, apparently people down on their luck for one reason or another.

His father had a strong interest in investment, and particularly in 'stagging' new share issues. Owen understood only a little of this as a young child, but already had the impression that "Dad always seemed to make most of his money from stagging new issues, rather than the hotels, which were almost part of his philanthropy."

Tragically, when Owen was 11 years old, his father committed suicide. "Dad suffered from depression and he had some aggravation from squatters in his hotels, but it was a terrible shock." There was little practical support from his father's church for the young widow and her children, an experience which left Owen with a lasting antipathy to organised religion. "It made me conscious of being on my own in the world, and that if I was going to get anywhere, it would be by myself. It meant I grew up young."

The year after his father's death, Owen started as a boarder at the well-known boy's public school which was a family tradition. Although a family trust paid basic school fees, so that the cost was not an overwhelming problem, he was nevertheless conscious of his relatively straitened social and financial circumstances as the son of a young widow, compared with the more expansive home backgrounds of many of his peers. "You do get treated differently at school if you're a widow's son, compared with the son of a captain of industry – I suppose teachers and others just find those families more interesting." Conscious of this status difference at school, the teenage Owen already thought of investment as a possible route to freedom and independence.

Owen read Physics at Oxford, which he found "a real shock intellectually at first – you went from being top at school to having lots of very smart people around you." He gained a first and an exhibition in his first year exams, "although the others who gained firsts were smarter than me". Asked if he knew what these people were doing now, he mentioned academics including professors at both Oxford and Cambridge, and that one had just become a

Fellow of the Royal Society – a useful frame of reference for the self-deprecating claim that some of these peers might have been smarter than him.

Schoolboy stag

After Owen's father died, his mother continued some of her husband's investment activities, including the stagging of new issues. When Owen was 16 he inherited £2,000, which allowed him to start playing the new issues game for himself. By the time he went to university, he had turned the £2,000 into £20,000.

Nowadays most new share issues are made solely to institutions, but in earlier times a London Stock Exchange rule required part of all larger issues to be offered to the general public. The practice of stagging new issues tended to be profitable, because new issues were priced by the sponsoring broker with the aim of a strong after-market, and hence a small initial profit for anyone who had bought the issue.

New issues were often substantially over-subscribed, and hence applications were 'scaled back' – for example, an application for 10,000 shares might be satisfied only to the extent of 2,000 shares – and so stags would normally apply for more shares than they actually wanted, to the limits of their bank resources and often beyond. Smaller applications tended to be treated preferentially, and so to maximise allocations stags would habitually arrange applications for several family members.

> "Share applications from all members of a family, including children, were legal; those from perspicacious cats or dogs were not."

Share applications from all members of a family, including children, were legal; those from perspicacious cats or dogs were not, but in the exuberant market of the 1980s these niceties were sometimes overlooked by adventurous stags. Sometimes applications up to a certain number of shares (announced only after the issue closed) would be partly satisfied, with larger applications entirely rejected. A family's optimal application strategy might involve different members of the family each applying for different numbers of shares.

Owen's schoolboy activities as a new issues stag in the early 1980s involved "reading prospectuses, reading the newsletter *New Issue Share Guide*, talking to brokers, and forming a view on how over-subscribed the issue might be."

He would then make his applications in what he judged to be the optimal sizes, taking account of his available resources. "I could usually cover all the cheques I wrote – or if I couldn't, I never got caught out!" Once the new issue started trading, he would usually sell promptly. "I always needed the cash for the next good new issue opportunity."

Why is little heard of stags nowadays, either schoolboys like Owen in the 1980s or semi-professionals like his father in the 1960s and 1970s? The main reason is that in 1995 the London Stock Exchange abolished the rule which required all new issues over a certain size to include an offering to the general public. Even the government now shuts out private investors, with recent privatisation issues open only to institutions. And so there are now few public offers, and no more schoolboy stags.

Into the City: prop trader

Towards the end of his time at Oxford, Owen thought about going into the City. But he also interviewed for other careers, and eventually joined a management consultancy, because the starting pay offer was particularly good. But he did not enjoy management consultancy. "I thought the bullshit factor was off the scale…the whole business model was to find what the client wanted to hear and dress it up for delivery."

Realising that he definitely wanted to use his investing knowledge, he switched to a risk management trainee position in the equity market-making division of an investment bank. He studied for the Society of Investment Analysts qualification, and won a prize for the best performance in examinations at the end of his first year.

After about 18 months he moved to another investment bank, in a back-up role in the equity market-making team, working on Black-Scholes modelling to help with pricing and monitoring the book of equity options. His employer was a pioneer in equity index arbitrage: buying or selling the FTSE100 futures contract, whilst making offsetting trades in the constituent shares of the FTSE100, so as to lock in certain profits. Owen wrote and maintained the programs to generate the appropriate buy and sell orders for the equity market-making book to implement the arbitrage. This was a very profitable business in the early days, when there were few competitors, especially in times of market dislocation like the 1987 stock market crash. "We did very well during the crash – the arbitrage of futures against cash was incredible, as much as 400 basis points."

Building on this success, Owen and his boss in equity options extended their activities to investing their employer's funds into other special situations; that is, they became proprietary ('prop') traders. The special situations included arbitrages or near-arbitrages involving mergers, options, closed-end funds, and capital structure arbitrage (details of these strategies are outlined in the next panel). It was an opportunistic strategy, with positions typically held for just a few weeks or months, and no notion of investing long-term in exceptional businesses as in the earlier chapters of this book. Many were high risk, and the gross positions Owen and his colleagues ran were much larger than the capital notionally allocated by the bank to support the activity, so they were in effect using substantial leverage.

He particularly remembered one nail-biting takeover where the outcome was "very uncertain and very binary – if the bid had failed we would all have been fired – but in the end there were 58% acceptances, so it went through." He also noted that many of these opportunistic strategies became less profitable over the years because so much more hedge fund money and other investment capital was directed towards them. "I no longer do merger arbitrage, because the margins are far too thin these days. On the deals which fall apart, you have a double whammy – both your long on the target and your short on the acquirer get hit. All those deep out-of-the-money puts you have sold come back and kick you very hard!"

BACKGROUND: ARBITRAGE

Merger arbitrage

The investor buys shares in the (cheaper) company subject to a takeover bid, and shorts the (more expensive) acquiring company's shares. The investor expects to make a gain as the difference in valuations is eliminated when the takeover bid completes (but may make a large loss if the bid fails).

Option arbitrage

The investor takes a position in traded share options, with an offsetting position in the underlying shares. The investor expects to make a gain as the difference in valuations is eliminated when the options mature.

Closed-end fund arbitrage

Closed-end funds (also known as investment trusts in the UK) are listed companies whose sole purpose is to hold shares in other companies, hedge funds or property assets. The share price of the closed-end fund often trades at a discount to the net asset value of the underlying assets held by the fund. An investor can buy the closed-end fund shares, and go short of the underlying shares or a proxy such as index future. The investor then agitates for closed-end fund to realise its assets at the net asset value and return cash to shareholders, or take other action to reduce the discount.

Capital structure arbitrage

Where a company has more than one class of share capital, for example ordinary shares and convertible preference shares, the two classes sometimes trade for a time at inconsistent prices. An arbitrageur can buy the cheap class, sell the expensive class, and profit as the inconsistency disappears.

After four years, Owen's employer lost some of its appetite for taking principal risk, so he and his boss moved on to another bank, in a similar proprietary and opportunistic risk-taking role. "We started off running a total book of about £50m gross in long and short positions, broadly market-neutral overall. We made money every year, so that the bank allocated us larger limits, until we were eventually running a book of as much as £2bn."

They also started to take positions where they would seek to influence management, by talking to them, by using the votes on their shares, and by talking to other shareholders. This was the start of Owen's experience as an activist.

Often this involved investment trusts or other closed-end funds trading at discounts to net asset value of 30% or more. In these situations actions to reduce the discount, such as share buybacks or winding up the fund, will invariably benefit shareholders. This often led to a conflict of interest for the trust's boards of directors, if they had formal or informal links with the fund managers who were charging fees on the assets of trust, and so stood to lose management fee income if buybacks or winding-up were pursued. Owen has come to favour a decisive approach in these situations: "We learnt through bitter experience that it was usually unwise to give the directors a second chance."

These activities were conducted all across Europe and later extended into Russia, using ideas found by their local broker contacts in each country and Owen's desk-based research. Sometimes the culture clash between activist shareholders and imperialistic management made for comedy: for example, a French chief executive who spoke perfect English, but nevertheless insisted on answering every question asked by visiting English shareholders in French. Even in such difficult cases, management would eventually do something to placate the activist shareholders: a share buyback, a merger or some other action to close the shares' discount to net asset value.

Owen's entire career in banking from the age of about 24 had been focused on essentially the same role in prop trading. This meant that whilst his pay increased rapidly based on the returns his team made for the bank, he was disengaged from the organisational politics which dominates the working lives of many people in large organisations. "We didn't think about climbing the ladder, because there was no ladder to climb." Even in the 1990s, when suits and ties were still *de rigeur* at all times throughout the City, Owen usually dressed casually for work. "I used to keep an emergency suit in the office in case we had to go and see someone!"

As for any employee in a regulated firm, compliance rules constrained Owen's personal account or 'PA' trading: he was not allowed to invest in the same ideas as he was implementing for his employers. But he was allowed to make other investments, and these tended to have a similar rationale to the investments he made in his day job: opportunistic investments of a few weeks or months in situations involving discounts to net assets or some other short-term valuation anomaly. During the 1999-2000 technology boom, one of these situations produced an astonishing return.

Moonshot: Horace Small

When Owen first came across the archaic-sounding Horace Small as a potential personal investment, the company was a moribund manufacturer of uniforms and other work wear, with its shares trading at 28p, when the business had net cash of 40p per share.

"There was a possible environmental liability relating to a property in the US, but I didn't think it was significant. I knew some of the large shareholders, at least by reputation, and thought they might be looking to use it as a cash shell for an internet venture. So I loaded up."

Shortly thereafter, in December 1999, the shares were suspended pending a reverse takeover of Redbus Interhouse, an internet co-location company. When the shares resumed trading in March 2000, they opened around *15 times* higher than Owen's purchase price. "I didn't believe in the internet business at that price, so I sold straight away. It was the top of the tech boom, almost to the day. That was my moonshot: I cleared over a million pounds on that single trade, and a lot of it was in my ISA."

> "That was my moonshot: I cleared over a million pounds on that single trade."

Owen admitted that this multiple of 15 times his cost after a holding period of just a few months was exceptionally lucky, particularly given his overall approach to investing. "Generally I am looking for something at a knowable discount to assets, and once the discount narrows, I will move on. I don't buy 'story' stocks with blue-sky promises of massive gains. Horace Small was a discount story. I was lucky that it turned into a blue-sky story."

Because he didn't believe in the sustainability of the tech boom, he had also taken a hedge while Horace Small was suspended, shorting the American NASDAQ technology shares index via a spread bet. This was very expensive at first, because the index continued to run up, rising around 25% in a week; but he managed to hold on until it turned in March 2000, and ended up making several hundred thousand pounds on his short as well.

As well as this moonshot in his personal account, 2000 was a great year for his employer's proprietary account: they made around seven times their largest profit in any previous year. With large gains on both his personal account investing and from bonuses, Owen's wealth had multiplied many times from a few years earlier. He was now tiring of the intensity of his high-pressure job, and for a time he was also preoccupied with his divorce.

He had enough money to be reasonably confident of a future as a personal investor: "I could afford to lose an awful lot without needing to go back to work. And I wanted to get away from having a boss." So in the spring of 2002, he resigned from his job. He was 38 years old.

Split capital trusts

After leaving his job, Owen continued investing his own money in special situations, with the same opportunistic philosophy that he had followed as a prop trader. The most lucrative theme in his early years as a full-time private investor was the split capital trusts sector during 2002-03.

BACKGROUND: SPLIT CAPITAL TRUSTS

A split capital trust is an investment trust which has issued more than one class of shares, with the separate classes having different rights to the trust's income and capital. The first split capital trust was Dualvest, launched in 1965, but they became popular only in the 1990s.

Typically, there might be *income shares* which receive all the trust's income as dividends, but have only a limited capital entitlement on a winding-up of the trust; *capital shares* which carry most of the capital entitlement, but receive no dividends; and *zero dividend preference shares*, which receive no dividends, but promise a modest and low-risk return via capital payment at the end of their term (subject to the sufficiency of the fund's assets).

The split capital structure was devised to satisfy the differing risk preferences of different types of private investor, and their differing preferences for income or capital returns. For example, retired people living on the income from their investments like the apparently high dividend yields on income shares; adventurous higher-rate taxpayers like the apparently high returns on capital shares, combined with lower tax rates on capital gains and tax deferral until the investment is sold; cautious higher-rate taxpayers like the apparently certain returns on zeros, again with tax advantages.

The repeated *apparently* in the previous sentence highlights that the split capital structure does not create a free lunch: the promised dividend yields or capital returns are all subject to risks. These risks are subtle, and often difficult for the non-technical investor or financial advisor to evaluate. In the 2002-03 bear market, many of the risks materialised, with the value of some split capital shares falling more than 90%. The lack of understanding by many shareholders and advisors then led to indiscriminate selling of *all* split capital shares, and hence some large anomalies in prices.

The obscurity and small size of the split capital sector meant that few hedge funds or other institutional 'smart money' actors paid attention. The valuation anomalies which arose during the 2002-03 bear market therefore remained substantially available to sophisticated private investors.

In principle, the multiple share classes of split capital trusts can be analysed as combinations of options. For example, the zero dividend preference shareholders are short a put option at the redemption price of the zero, and also long a put option at the level of any 'prior charges' such as the trust's bank debt. But although he understood this type of analysis, Owen found its sophistication unnecessary in 2002-03. "The anomalies were so large and obvious that you didn't need sophisticated calculations. If a decision requires detailed calculations, you should pass, because it's probably too close. It is better to look for easy decisions." By way of example of an easy decision, he cited income shares trading at 2p "which would probably pay out 2p of dividend that year, and then 2p a year for the next five years."

When an investment trust (or one of its share classes) is trading at a large discount to net asset value, the best action for shareholders is usually to wind up the trust or share class. Owen's long experience of closed-end funds activism in his previous job as a prop trader was a helpful background in dealing assertively with such situations. Normally the value of a share is related to its prospective cash flows, but Owen has occasionally seen situations where the value was more in a share's vote. "There was one case where I held income shares standing at a large discount, but the board proposed to extend the life of the trust rather than wind it up. This was clearly in the interests of the managers, not the shareholders. The capital shares were worthless in terms of future cash flows, but they carried votes. So I and a couple of other holders of the income shares each spent £5,000 buying ten million capital shares at 0.05p per share, so that we could vote against the continuation of the trust."

Following the exceptional opportunities at the nadir of the split capital trusts sector in 2002-03, Owen continued making some new investments in the sector over the next few years. But the opportunities gradually dried up, and by 2005-06 he was holding a substantial amount of cash. He spent some time supervising the development of two large modern houses (one of which became his home), but found property development time-consuming and relatively unremunerative compared with his stock market activities. He made some poor investments in 2007 and 2008 – "I should have been doing less, the opportunities were not good enough." But over the winter of 2008-09, the bear market produced a greater flow of closed-end fund opportunities.

In particular, heavy redemptions in the hedge fund sector led to many listed funds of funds, which had traded at negligible discounts for many years, falling to trade at discounts of 40% or more. This was similar to the splits fiasco a few years earlier – indiscriminate redemptions by panicking, uninformed or liquidity-constrained investors, creating opportunities for discerning investors with cash firepower and good understanding of the funds.

Portfolio management and leverage

Owen runs a concentrated portfolio, usually with no more than a dozen holdings. He is also happy to hold large amounts of cash while waiting for the right opportunity. "It is a mistake to think of cash as burning a hole in your pocket. When there aren't any good situations, I may be entirely in cash." He is focused almost entirely on idiosyncratic opportunities which tie up his capital for only a few months: he does not trade like a geographer on macroeconomic factors such as currencies or bond yields, nor does he search like most surveyors for businesses with strong long-term prospects.

Owen was fortunate that his Horace Small investment was made largely in his ISA. With this moonshot compounded by many further successes since then, he has accumulated a substantial seven-figure sum in the ISA. He therefore has less use than some of our investors for other tax-free investment vehicles such as spread betting. He does sometimes use spread betting for part-hedging his portfolio, by shorting stock index futures, and occasionally for bets on large company shares such as banks. Overall he uses virtually no leverage. Whilst he is prepared to short index futures as a hedge, he has never shorted an individual share. This risk-averse combination of negligible leverage and no shorting was interesting in the light of his previous career as a prop trader, which implies a deep knowledge and experience of leverage and short selling.

Activism in action

Owen keeps most of his notes in electronic files. In terms of information sources, he looks at the RNS and annual accounts for the companies which attract his interest. For closed-end funds, he checks the listing documents and the company's articles of association, taking particular note of the management fee, any discount protection mechanism, and winding-up provisions. He spends no time reading bulletin boards, and only a little discussing possible investments with other investors. He rarely meets with company management. All this probably makes him unusually efficient compared to other investors in this book.

A distinctive feature of closed-end funds is that non-executive directors, rather than executive directors, tend to have a larger role in governance than at other types of company. Owen often therefore needs to press his views on non-executive directors. Does his status as a private rather than institutional investor make this difficult? "Directors often initially don't want to speak to me, but I always persevere. I find it helps to put something in writing. I get the company secretary's email from the advisors, then I get the directors' contact details from the secretary and I write to the directors. I express my views, I refer to the directors' fiduciary duties and I ask them to call me. Once there is a paper trail, the directors can get into trouble if anything goes wrong, so they have little option but to communicate with you."

He keeps notes of all conversations with non-executive directors. "Apart from factual answers, you pick up nuances such as whether the non-executives are really independent, or whether they are just puppets of the management company. If they are unresponsive to reasonable shareholder concerns, knowing that is valuable information. You can also sometimes pick up any whiff of fraud around the company."

"successful activism sometimes leads to a sense of personal agency distinct from any financial benefit"

Owen seldom attends AGMs or other meetings, despite his convenient base near London; asking specific questions on the telephone is a more efficient use of his time. He does sometimes speak to institutions which hold shares in his investee companies, and emphasised the importance of tracing the right contact, by networking with the company's advisors and other shareholders. "You need to speak to the right person for a particular situation at an institution, otherwise you will get nowhere."

Although persuading directors with conflicts of interest to act in shareholders' interests is often a war of attrition, successful activism sometimes leads to a sense of personal agency distinct from any financial benefit. "It is satisfying to see directors doing the right thing for all shareholders as a direct result of your own actions." Except on one occasion, he has managed to influence events without formally requisitioning company general meetings or taking other actions which require consultations with lawyers. "It usually doesn't come to that!"

Father and athlete

Owen's efficient working methods mean he probably has more time for non-investment activities than some people in this book, despite managing a larger fund than most. In term-time his elder son lives with his ex-wife, and his younger son with an ex-girlfriend; but both sons live mainly with him during school holidays, when he spends a lot of time "either doing things with them or acting as a taxi service." The elder son is now 12, old enough to understand that his father is wealthy and does not have a conventional job. "I hope he understands that although I don't have a job like other dads, I am working. And I tell him that he needs to start contributing soon to the family economics!"

Owen plays golf (off a single-figure handicap) most weeks, although this may not mean he switches off entirely – a mutual friend reported that he has been known to trade or conduct investment conversations from the golf course. At the time of the interview, he and his girlfriend had just returned from a weekend in Scotland to take part in a five-hour orienteering-style race which involved running, cycling, and kayaking. A couple of weeks earlier, he had taken part in the London duathlon. In response to the observation that none of these interests or pursuits seemed expensive, he had an immediate riposte: "Divorce is expensive!" More seriously, he agreed that he does not have expensive tastes like yachts or art or French villas – "don't do second homes, that's an incredible money drain" was his sardonic comment on that concept. Apart from his architect-designed contemporary house, he identified only one extravagance: "I'm taking delivery of one of the first Tesla electric cars in the country next week."

Conclusion

Owen's strong academic background and long experience as a prop trader make him one of the most obviously sophisticated investors in this book. He is also one of the most risk-averse, prepared to hold large amounts of cash for considerable periods, never shorting single shares, and using almost no leverage.

His approach is focused and opportunistic, concentrating on situations where activism can release value in a time frame of a few months. This focus helps him to be unusually efficient. Because of this economical use of time, his approach is the one in this book which I most wish I could emulate.

A profound psychological effect of increasing wealth is to change the relative importance you place on money and time. For a successful investor, practical worries about money must eventually recede: no matter how high your spending needs, passive income will eventually outrun them, once you have accumulated a large enough fund. But time is not like this: time is a universally depleting resource, at the same rate for the wealthy as for the poor. This gives one way of defining a successful investor: a person for whom time has become a more binding constraint than money.

OWEN: INSIGHTS AND ADVICE

The last laugh A value investor is a person who places a high premium on having the last laugh.

Look for obscure niches A sophisticated private investor can do well in an obscure niche which is too small for most hedge funds and other 'smart money'. Stagging new issues up until the mid-1990s was one example; the split capital sector in 2002-03 was another.

Look for easy decisions If an investment decision requires detailed calculations, you should pass, because it's probably too close.

Focus your enquiries If you are efficient and focused, meeting management is often not necessary. Most of the information you need can be obtained online or on the telephone.

Create a paper trail Communicating with non-executive directors in writing, perhaps referring to their fiduciary duties, makes it harder for them to ignore you.

Take no prisoners As a shareholder activist, it is usually unwise to give errant management a second chance.

If there are no good opportunities, stay in cash Be disciplined about waiting for the right opportunity. Cash never burns a hole in your pocket.

Time efficiency You will know you have become a successful investor when time has become a more binding constraint than money.

10

PETER GYLLENHAMMAR
THE CORPORATE ENGINEER

PETER GYLLENHAMMAR: FACTS AND FIGURES

Age at interview	56
Age at leaving last full-time job	43
Background	Dropped out of business school aged 20 to co-found investment management business; later worked as stockbroking analyst and corporate financier.
Style	Buy bombed-out companies trading at discounts to net assets; obtain 'negative control' through a shareholding approaching 25%; instigate corporate re-engineering to release value.
Markets and sectors	UK small caps with 'open' ownership – large institutional shareholders who are open to selling their stakes.
Instruments	Shares, 100% ownership of de-listed companies.
Typical holding period	Months to years.
Performance indicators	Grew an initial investment in UK small caps of around £50,000 in 1996 to tens of millions of equity by the early 2000s (but supported by credit lines guaranteed by a wealthy business partner).
Quote	"I have never felt that investing is like working. It is more like playing ten parallel games of poker or chess."
Phrases	Negative control; negative working capital; judicious disregard for advice.

F or the activists profiled in the preceding chapters, activism is the exercise of persuasion rather than power. This reflects the fact that they usually control only a small fraction of a company's shares – almost always less than 10%, and often less than 1% – and so generally do not have the 5% voting power required to requisition a company general meeting.[1]

By holding a larger fraction of a company, you can influence events more decisively. You can change corporate strategy, change the management, or negotiate mergers or asset disposals yourself, thus directly creating value rather than passively awaiting events. Peter is a proponent of this type of corporate engineering. He is the most substantial investor in this book, with publicly visible total holdings in AIM companies running into many tens of millions of pounds. He is also the only interviewee to have gone bust, not once but twice in his earlier career.

Peter is based in Sweden, with a small office in Stockholm with two executives reporting to him: Martin Hansson who manages a portfolio of around 25 rental properties, and Jan Holmström who spends a substantial part of his time in England acting as a director at several of Peter's investee companies. In earlier years Peter himself was a director of several AIM companies, but at the time of the interview he had reduced this to one directorship, and was visiting the UK perhaps half a dozen times a year. He spends several weeks in the summer aboard his yacht in the Baltic, with full satellite broadband connectivity to enable him to keep following the markets.

Peter was approached cold for an interview via the finance director of a company in which we both held shares. He readily agreed to take part, saying that the reflection required by an interview might be helpful to his own thinking. The scale of his activities and distinctive details such as his Swedish background make anonymity less practical for this chapter than for others, so he agreed to his real name being used.

The interview was conducted in four telephone conversations of between one and three hours each, extending across a couple of weeks; I also drew on a profile previously published in Swedish in a business magazine.[2] Bearing in mind that this interview was conducted with a person whom I had never met, and in his second language, I was prepared for a stilted conversation. In fact Peter's flawless unaccented English and frankness about every phase of his investing career made interviewing him particularly easy and enjoyable.

"Noble without land"

Peter was born in Djursholm in Sweden in 1953, the youngest of three brothers. His father was 50 when he was born, married to a much younger French wife, and was "adel utan land" which literally translates as "noble without land". This originated from the exploits of an ancestor in the service of the king of Sweden in the 17th century, which earned the family a degree of nobility, but no land or other wealth. The Gyllenhammar family name remains distinctive in Sweden; Peter's distant relative Pehr Gyllenhammar is well known as the former chief executive of Skandia and then Volvo, and subsequently of the UK insurance company Aviva. Peter's father was originally an army officer, but after marriage he became property manager for a large retail group in Sweden.

Growing up in socialist Sweden – in Peter's words, "a banana republic in those days" – it is remarkable that he became seriously interested in investing from a young age. He had no family connection with the investment world, and today he finds it difficult to identify reasons for his precocious interest, except a facility at maths and a small legacy, including a few shares, which he received from his grandmother when he was 14.

He soon made his own small first investments with the legacy, and still remembers the two shares he bought: Svea, a shipping line, and Bofors, a defence company. "I bought both for their high dividend yields, and both scrapped the dividend soon afterwards. That was my first lesson." He knew nobody who had any interest in investment, with one exception: his school woodwork teacher, whom he would encounter every Tuesday when he went to the public library for the latest business magazines. "Both fairly unlikely investors – the elderly social democrat and the precocious teenager – but he was amused by my interest, and we kept in touch until he died in his 90s a few years ago."

At the age of 18 Peter started a business degree at the Stockholm School of Economics. By this time he had already accumulated several years of practical experience as an investor. When he was 19 he led a shareholder revolt in a takeover battle involving two retail companies, cajoling shareholders in the target company to hold out for an improved offer from the bidder – which happened to be the employer of his bemused father. He found his degree studies theoretical and remote from the practical reality of his investing activities, and took to spending part of every day at the nearby Stockholm Stock Exchange. In his second year, he dropped out of his degree course to spend more time on investing. "I was not patient enough to study anything not directly related to the stock market. And I was absolutely sure I could make money. I never questioned my brilliance in those days – that came later!"

He still remembers his first big idea for corporate engineering: Göta Kanalbölag, the company which controlled the 120-mile Göta Canal connecting Gothenburg and Stockholm. As a quasi-utility, the canal's operating costs were subsidised by the government, but it remained privately owned. Studying the financial statements, he realised that the forest land around the canal was worth vastly more than the entire company's market capitalisation, so that value could potentially be released by breaking up the company. "I approached a holding company of the controlling family and asked if they were interested in selling some shares. They just laughed at me. Although the market didn't understand the hidden value of the land, the family understood it perfectly well."

Return to Go

Peter had been discussing ideas such as Göta Kanalbölag with a friend, Sven-Olof Johansson. Sven-Olof knew another mathematics graduate and his economics lecturer father, who were both interested in investment. The four of them joined forces to form an investment company called Trend Invest. They rented an office and established a private client investment management business, doing "fundamental analysis, share charts, all the standard techniques."

One of their ideas for activism was that the Swedish special steel industry could be made more efficient by consolidation. Seeking to engineer this consolidation, they invested a large part of their own funds, client funds and further borrowed money in Fagersta Group, a steel company which also owned hydro-electric power plants, eventually acquiring nearly 50% of the company. They also acquired interests in other steel and forest companies, with the intention of merging all the steel interests on the one hand and the forest interests on the other.

But before they could implement their plans, Fagersta issued more shares in a large rights issue: that is, existing shareholders were given rights to buy newly created shares directly from the company in proportion to their existing holdings, at a discount to the market price, and any rights which existing shareholders did not exercise were allocated to third parties. Trend Invest did not have funds to take up its rights, and so its near-50% interest in Fagersta was greatly diluted.

The issue of the new shares at a discount caused a substantial fall in the price of Fagersta, ultimately leading to the bankruptcy of Trend Invest. "Our commercial logic was absolutely right – the special steel industry did consolidate over the next few years as we had foreseen – but we were naïve about the politics. We thought that if we could show a way to make 1+1=3, everyone would accept the logic. What we didn't understand was that if there was a way to make 1+1=1.5, and get rid of us, the incumbent management would prefer that."

Peter had borrowed money personally to increase his investment in Trend Invest. He now owed around £200,000 to the stockbrokers Häglöff, a substantial sum in 1976, especially for a young man of 23. In Monopoly terms (and in the famous title phrase of Jim Slater's 1977 autobiography), it was a case of 'Return to Go'.[3]

"Our commercial logic was absolutely right – but we were naïve about the politics."

He set about restoring his fortune with remarkable panache. "I made an appointment to see the Häglöff senior partner. He started by noting that my account was £200,000 in deficit, and what was I going to do about it? He probably expected me to ask my father to bail me out. But my father didn't have much money, and anyway, I would never have asked him. So I told the senior partner: "Clearly someone has lost £200,000. It can't be me, because I never *had* £200,000. *You've* lost £200,000!" He pondered this for a few moments, and then he started to laugh. He conceded that in practical terms I was right, but did I have any more constructive proposals? I offered to work for the firm for free as an analyst to pay off my debt. He agreed to this, but said that he wanted to pay me a small salary, because otherwise I would end up moonlighting elsewhere."

Over the next three years Peter worked very hard as an analyst for Häglöff. His reputation had been tarnished by the Fagersta debacle, but he still had a great deal of self-belief, and his family remained supportive. He also gratefully remembers Pehr Gyllenhammar inviting him to a formal dinner at his home, thus publicly welcoming and endorsing his young cousin in front of a large group of prominent Swedish businessmen.

A much later *Financial Times* article, reviewing Peter's career when he first started to attract attention as an investor in the UK, said that his activities at Häglöff in the late 1970s and early 1980s attracted "a brilliant reputation for identifying undervalued companies and building large stakes in them…many disagree with his aggressive investment style, but all recognise his skill at picking opportunities."

At the end of three years, the Häglöff senior partner invited him to a meeting to review their arrangement. "He started the meeting by tearing up the documentation for my remaining debt to the firm, and said I was now free to leave if I wished. I told him that I had always wanted to be a partner in a stockbroking firm. I walked out of that meeting with a 5% share of the firm's equity." At the age of 26, it was a remarkable comeback from a 'Return to Go' with debts of £200,000 only three years earlier.

"A Swedish Goldman Sachs"

Peter spent another three years as a Häglöff partner, working as an analyst and corporate financier. In 1983, at the age of 30, he sold his interest in Häglöff for around £400,000 and left to form a new company, Proventus, with Robert Weil, whom he had met some years earlier.

After about a year the differing risk appetite of the two partners (Peter being the more adventurous investor) led Peter to de-merge his activities into a new entity, Gyllenhammar and Partners. One of the backers of Gyllenhammar and Partners was Ulf Lindén (1937-2009), a one-time sea captain and entrepreneur who had got to know Peter at Häglöff, and was to become the most important supporter of his subsequent career.

The dream was that Gyllenhammar and Partners would be a corporate finance and trading house, a "Swedish Goldman Sachs". The firm grew to around 40 people in the mid-1980s, and obtained a listing on the Stockholm exchange. But within a few years the success of Peter's debt-funded investing activities as principal overshadowed the corporate finance advisory activities. In 1987 he merged his personal investing activities with Gyllenhammar and Partners to form Mercurius, an investment company, in which Peter himself held around a 35% stake.

Apart from corporate investments, Mercurius also had substantial property, ship-owning, and oil and gas production interests. Bank credit was easy to obtain in Sweden in the late 1980s, and Mercurius was always substantially leveraged. By the late 1980s Peter had been looking at UK micro-caps through the *Financial Times* and *Investors Chronicle* for some years. At the turn of the decade Mercurius was starting to attract attention in the UK. British press cuttings from 1990 refer to large investments in companies such as the battery manufacturers Chloride, the transport company TDG, and the timber company Phoenix Timber.

Return to Go – again!

Mercurius relied on banking facilities which were renewed on a rolling 12-month basis each December, and Peter had also borrowed around £10m personally to participate in a rights issue by the company. During 1990, early signs of worsening conditions in the property market foreshadowed what became a crisis of the Swedish banking system. In December 1990, the main lender to Mercurius called in the company's loans. Peter suspects that loans to Mercurius were called in before loans to other similarly leveraged companies because most of its assets were overseas, and therefore the sale of these assets would not depress the prices of other assets held by the bank as security for other Swedish loans.

Forced sales of assets into a falling market rendered Mercurius insolvent. Peter himself was left with a personal deficit of around £10m. He was 38 years old.

What did he learn from this second and more spectacular failure? "First, I learnt who my friends were. Some people never called again, and others called more often. Second, it wasn't the end of the world not to have to go to the office every morning. And third, the sun shines even on the poor man." Peter's self-belief in his own abilities reinforced this equanimity. "I had made some misjudgements about leverage, but I was still confident about my ability as an analyst."

One of the friends who did call was Ulf Lindén. He had a crisis of his own at Lindén Group, which had around £600m of debt and *minus* £30m Swedish Kroner of equity, and was under pressure from the banks to realise assets. Peter offered to do the corporate finance work on asset disposals for Lindén Group, as an in-house corporate financier. Ulf offered a salary, but Peter preferred to work for free: "I wanted to be able to give Ulf frank advice, and anyway my debts at the time seemed so overwhelming that the salary wouldn't make much difference after tax."

Over the next three years around 75% of his time was spent on Lindén Group, and 25% on other fee-charging corporate finance consultancy. The confidence which a prominent businessman like Ulf demonstrated in him, and the success of the Lindén Group workout, allowed Peter to rebuild his reputation. Although he was resigned to personal bankruptcy, and "expected the debt collector to turn up and turf me out of my flat any day", the bank never pursued this course, "possibly because, unlike some entrepreneurs in Sweden in the late 1980s, I hadn't done anything dishonest or reckless." Initially the bank was suspicious that he must be hiding assets offshore, but after a couple of years, when it was clear that he was not, the bank wrote off 80% of his debt.

After three years Ulf Lindén offered to make a retrospective payment for the corporate finance work, which Peter declined. Instead he suggested a joint investing venture, with Peter supplying the ideas and doing the work and Ulf guaranteeing a credit line. Ulf made an initial investment of around £50,000 into a new company Browallia AB, and also guaranteed a credit line of £2m. Peter had an option to acquire an interest in Browallia at a later date, which he exercised in 2002. After some initial property investments in Sweden, in 1996 he re-entered the UK micro-cap market.

Attractions of UK micro-caps

In Peter's view, micro-caps in the UK were and still are particularly attractive investments for two reasons.

First, many UK institutional investors refuse to consider new investments in companies below an arbitrary lower market capitalisation threshold (the actual threshold varies for different institutions, such as £10m, £50m or even £100m). Some institutions will even sell an investment they already hold if it falls below their lower market capitalisation threshold, irrespective of the fundamental merits of the company.

Second, the ownership structures of many small UK quoted companies are relatively open: the substantial shareholders usually include several institutions which regard their entire stakes as marketable holdings, which they are potentially willing to sell to anybody. This contrasts with the position in Sweden, where family control of quoted companies is more common, often via devices such as shares with special voting rights which can be held only by family members.

Peter wonders if the lower prevalence of family ownership and control reflects different attitudes to spending entrepreneurial wealth in the UK as compared with Sweden. "In the UK, the aim of many entrepreneurs seems to be sell or float their company, and so crystallise a cash fortune to spend. Spending the cash on country estates and yachts and other consumption seems quite accepted and unremarkable. In Sweden, there is more disapproval of conspicuous displays of wealth, although that is gradually changing."

> "I find troubled companies intellectually more interesting. I enjoy restructuring and creating value."

Whatever the reason for the difference, the typical open ownership structure in the UK gives more opportunity for a corporate engineer to acquire a substantial shareholding and implement value-creating changes.

Corporate engineering in bombed-out shares

Peter summarises his basic strategy for UK micro-caps as follows. "Pick up bombed-out shares trading at a large discount to net asset value. If they are badly managed or not managed in the best interests of all shareholders, then implement change. This typically takes you into operationally risky situations and some of the investments go bad, but the risk/reward in aggregate is attractive."

Some investors in this book regard direct involvement in activism as a last resort; take, for example, Sushil's remark: "The trick is to avoid situations where activism is necessary." Peter has a different view: "I find troubled companies intellectually more interesting. I enjoy restructuring and creating value." He emphasised that "I don't try to construct a portfolio of shares around an index benchmark. I am always looking at the underlying businesses, and thinking what can be done to create value in them."

To implement corporate engineering a shareholder needs a degree of influence over a company. Generally speaking, a larger percentage shareholding means greater influence. Peter regards a 25% shareholding as a particularly important threshold. This is because the Companies Act requires major corporate actions such as new issues of shares to be approved by 75% of the votes cast at a company meeting. A 25% shareholding therefore guarantees 'negative control' in the sense that one can veto these decisions. In practice, because some shareholders (particularly those with nominee holdings) neglect to cast their votes at company meetings, a somewhat lower percentage than 25% is often sufficient to give effective negative control.

In his early career, when Peter was attempting to build wealth, he always concentrated and leveraged his investments, often investing a large part of his portfolio in his single best idea. This was a double-edged sword: potentially a way of building wealth quickly, but also the route to being wiped out twice. Now that he is securely wealthy, he has become more concerned with wealth preservation: he is no longer leveraged, and his investments are widely diversified. But he admits that greater diversification has not been a carefully planned strategy. "It's partly curiosity and hip-shooting – I love getting involved in business areas that are new to me. I am never happier than when I have a new industry to research."

Britannia Group

Britannia Group was Peter's first corporate engineering project at a UK company. In this case, he did not have to do much himself, because a capable management already had plans for exactly the restructuring he had in mind. "The net tangible assets were about 80p. The shares were trading at 20p. Studying the accounts, I realised that the construction contracting side had a negative working capital requirement [see the next panel for explanation]. The house-building side had a positive working capital requirement. So if the house-building side was sold off, the negative working capital requirement of the contracting side could finance investment in other under-valued situations."

Over a few days in April 1996, he acquired around 20% of the shares. He then travelled to England to meet with the chairman Michael Nelmes-Crocker, who nervously remarked that he hoped Peter would not object to the company's advanced plans to sell the house-building division. "That was exactly what I wanted, and it worked out just as I had planned. It was a very positive first deal in England – a great management team to work with."

BACKGROUND: POSITIVE AND NEGATIVE WORKING CAPITAL REQUIREMENTS

The concept of a working capital requirement arises from the staggered timing of receipts and payments in a business, and can be explained as follows.

Positive working capital. Most businesses need to maintain a stock of finished products ready for sale, or pay employees for their work before the business invoices clients. For example, a house-builder needs to maintain a stock of completed or near-completed houses for marketing to potential house-buyers. The house-builder has to pay all the costs of building the houses many months before any sale proceeds are received. The house-builder needs capital to bridge the time gap between payments and receipts – that is, the business has a positive working capital requirement.

Negative working capital. In contrast, a construction contractor does not need to maintain a stock of finished products. Furthermore, a contractor will typically receive up-front payments on contracts some months in advance of actually paying for supplies and labour to fulfil the contracts. The contractor therefore has a negative working capital requirement. A contractor in receipt of a succession of up-front payments may be able to use the negative working capital to finance other investments in the time interval between payments and disbursements on contracts.

Another common example of a business with negative working capital requirement is retailing, where customers pay in cash at the shop till, but suppliers are often on 30-day or 60-day payment terms. Provided that the turnover of goods is high, the retailer may consistently receive cash (which it can potentially then immediately deploy to finance investments) many weeks before suppliers need to be paid.

An extreme variant of the negative working capital concept is insurance: an insurer receives premiums up-front, but the cost of claims falls many months or years later. One of the insights on which Warren Buffett's fortune has been built is the availability of this so-called 'float' of premiums to support other investments. (However, with insurance there is a catch: the cost of claims is an unknown and highly variable quantity.)

YJ Lovell

YJ Lovell was a construction company with a turnover of £254m in the year ended 30 September 1996. The balance sheet suggested that the ordinary shares were worthless, because of a large prior claim of convertible preference shares, which had been issued to several banks in a debt-to-equity swap several years earlier and were due to be redeemed in the year 2000.

When Peter started buying the shares in 1997, the market capitalisation of just £2m (less than 1% of turnover) was effectively 'option money' – that is, it reflected only a remote chance that the ordinary shares might be worth something. But as at Britannia, he knew that a construction company like YJ Lovell probably had negative working capital of around 5-10% of turnover, that is up to £20m. If he could restructure the business to release that amount for investment elsewhere, the ordinary shares would have substantial value.

> "I told the banks that if the company had £20m in late 1999, I would take the cash to Monte Carlo and bet it all on one spin of the roulette wheel."

Having accumulated around 25% of the ordinary shares, in the autumn of 1997 Peter went to see the banks which held the preference shares, and set out the position as he saw it as follows. "The face value of the preference shares held by the banks was £40m. Crucially, the preference shares were non-voting, so they had no control over how the company was managed. I said that with my shareholding of around 25%, I could re-engineer the company's operations to release £20m of negative working capital by late 1999, but I had no chance of releasing the £40m required to redeem the preference shares. With a little poetic licence, I told the banks that if the company had £20m in late 1999, I would take the cash to Monte Carlo and bet it all on one spin of the roulette wheel. If we won the gamble, we would be able to redeem the preference shares and have several hundred million of surplus cash left over; and if we lost, we were no worse off. Alternatively, if the banks didn't want the £20m sent to Monte Carlo, they might prefer to do a deal with us now."

Faced with these propositions, some of the banks agreed to convert their preference shares into ordinary shares; the others agreed to take 12p in the pound to redeem their preference shares. Having thus solved the problem of the preference shares, Peter implemented his plans to release negative working capital and reinvest the funds in other special situations elsewhere. This was a spectacular success, returning more than ten times his initial investment. "It was an interesting example of how corporate finance activity can sometimes create substantial value almost overnight."

Full bids

In the early 2000s, Peter made full bids for several small quoted companies, including British Mohair, Union Discount and Yorklyde. In several cases he recovered the purchase price by asset sales soon after the purchase, leaving substantial operating businesses which had effectively cost him nothing. In the case of Union Discount – formerly one of the important 'discount houses' in the City, but by then reduced to a small asset management business – the £25m bid price was entirely covered by cash within the company, so that only a short-term bridging loan was required to finance the bid.

Why does an extreme under-valuation like this arise? Usually because of a distressed seller, combined with institutional neglect of small-cap companies. In Union Discount's case, a Greek investment company had bought a stake intending to make a full bid, but had run into difficulties with unrelated internet investments and so had become a distressed seller.

What about the time commitment involved in mounting a full bid? In the early years of his UK micro-cap investing, Peter spent a substantial amount of time in the UK, acting as a director and negotiating asset sales at the companies he controlled. He would also visit property sites held by quoted companies in which he invested, talking to estate agents and evaluating options for redevelopment.

In more recent years he has preferred to nominate trusted associates as directors, for example his executive Jan Holmström and other people who have impressed him as directors in previous investee companies, rather than taking on these roles himself. This partly reflects Peter's involvement in a larger number of companies, but it also represents an increased focus on his own area of comparative advantage. "I am good at looking at lots of companies and working out the concept of what needs to do be done. I am not so good at implementation, and I am certainly not a good manager of people. I am happy to have only two executives, Jan and Martin, reporting to me, and leave all the implementation and administration to them."

Not taking advice

Discussing a small company with which we were both familiar, Peter remarked that the management had "a typical big-company mentality – they spend heavily on professional advisors and they do what the advisors tell them to do." Peter himself uses advisors as little as possible, usually only when regulation obliges him to do so. "As well as advisors for takeover bids, we are obliged to use advisors when we implement investment strategies for pension funds, publish audited accounts, and so on. But often the advice is box-ticking and rubber-stamping of what we have already decided to do, rather than a real input to our decision. And in some situations the best course is judicious disregard for the advice."

He habitually attends negotiations about possible corporate mergers or sale of assets unaccompanied by advisors. "Having an advisor adds little to an initial discussion. It is certainly not a guarantee of avoiding mistakes. I am always being asked by counterparties where are my advisors? I often have to answer simply that I have none."

> "I am always being asked by counterparties, where are my advisors? I often have to answer simply that I have none."

He had a similar experience at the Takeover Panel. "They asked me to come in to discuss Leeds Group, so I went along and presented myself. They asked where were my lawyers? How could I come to see the Takeover Panel without lawyers? Did I realise this was a serious matter? I had to tell them that I personally didn't consider it a serious matter!"

Successes and mistakes

What have been Peter's results from buying bombed-out micro-caps at large discounts to net asset value? In the late 1990s and early 2000s he had several big successes; the renegotiation of preference shares at YJ Lovell was the most spectacular.

On the most optimistic view, it could be said that he turned an initial investment of only around £50,000 equity in 1996 into tens of millions of equity by the early 2000s. But this spectacular result cannot fairly be compared with other investors in this book, because it depended on credit lines guaranteed by Ulf Lindén.

There have been no further home runs since about 2003. This is partly because market conditions have not been so favourable – the AIM All-Share Total Return Index in mid-2010 was still below the levels it reached in 2003.

With Peter's strategy of deliberately seeking out bombed-out shares and operationally risky situations, it is to be expected that some investments will fail. He was particularly frank in discussing mistakes, which he divided into the following categories, which are not mutually exclusive.

- *Poor research.* Sometimes most of the blame for an investment going sour is fairly allocated to Peter's own errors of understanding or analysis of the company's market position. For example, the DVD retailer Choice UK entered administration in August 2007, losing him several million pounds. "I didn't recognise the full extent of their problem with internet downloading and piracy."

- *Poor management or supervision.* This is where management makes poor decisions after Peter has invested. For example, Yorkshire Group made some poor acquisitions in the US and Greece. One lesson which Peter has drawn from such cases is that where he accumulates a stake of 20% or more, he will always seek a direct involvement in the company's strategy, typically via board representation. "I have learnt that it is not sensible to have a large stake and leave yourself entirely in the hands of management."

- *Too much debt.* Buying bombed-out stocks trading at large discounts to net asset value often involves companies with a high level of debt, which in some cases has ultimately proved overwhelming. Following changes in pension regulation from 2003 onwards (discussed further below), rapid increases in pension fund deficits have come to represent another form of debt. In recent years, Peter's tolerance for high levels of debt in his investee companies has reduced, primarily because he has seen that "the banks have become increasingly brutal in pulling the plug on companies in any trouble." On a personal level, he has de-geared completely: "I don't need debt any more, now that I am already wealthy." His Swedish property portfolio still has some debt, but it is secured only on the properties, with no recourse to the rest of his assets.

Policy issues for the UK

Because of Peter's experience in corporate activity, he had some views which he wished to share on corporate governance and market structure in the UK. Some of these were also touched on by other investors, but Peter's frequent involvement as a principal in takeovers, placings and other corporate transactions made them more salient in his interview.

CHOOSING COMPANY DIRECTORS

Peter seldom talks to company management before making an initial investment, and often first makes contact when he exceeds the 3% shareholding level which UK regulations require to be notified to the company. He often carries on buying until he is just below the 30% shareholding level at which a full bid for the company becomes mandatory under Takeover Panel rules.

Once he has finished buying, he requests board representation, either through the appointment of a candidate suggested by him, or by joining the board himself. Companies' responses to these requests vary. "Some companies welcome active and engaged shareholders. But I have also met some astonishing attitudes – at some companies I am the largest shareholder with 29%, and yet the directors strongly resist my having any influence over their strategy." In some cases directors have explicitly told him that they "don't want shareholders on the board," and he has had to force the issue by calling a general meeting to remove the incumbent and appoint a new chairman.

Unless shareholders take exceptional action such as calling a general meeting to propose new directors, the UK system is that new directors are normally selected by a nomination committee comprised of a sub-set of the existing directors – a procedure which in Peter's view often leads to a "back-scratching gang of insiders." From a shareholder perspective this compares poorly with the procedure in Sweden, where nomination committees are always comprised of major shareholders rather than directors.[4] In the UK, the appointment of representatives of major shareholders as directors often seems to be frowned upon: the UK Corporate Governance Code implicitly deprecates such directors as "non-independent". In Peter's view "it is absurd to say that a non-executive director who holds no shares at all is better positioned and motivated to advance the interests of all shareholders than a 29% shareholder." This issue is particularly acute in smaller quoted companies, where the typical calibre of independent non-executive directors may be lower than at larger companies, and an 'independent' director may often be a synonym for an uninformed director.

One reason for the different Swedish system may be the greater prevalence of concentrated ownership structures in Sweden as compared with the UK. That is, in Sweden, many quoted companies are controlled by a small number of large shareholders with long-term commitment to the company; but in the UK, at least in larger companies, widely dispersed ownership by owners who have no long-term commitment (and may not wish to have board representation) is more common. However, when Peter is seeking board representation at a UK company, it will invariably have a concentrated shareholder structure, simply by virtue of the fact that Peter himself is holding 20% to 30% of the shares. Therefore the Swedish approach seems more suited to the circumstances in which he usually finds himself.

More generally, he feels that the culture of corporate governance in the UK is aligned to serving the interests of advisors, rather than major shareholders. "The UK rules are good at creating work for the advisors. They are less good at empowering shareholders to influence corporate decisions."

COMPANY PENSION SCHEMES

In recent years the law surrounding UK final salary company pension schemes has changed substantially, turning the liability of the sponsoring employer from a best-endeavours 'promise' into a debt with high legal priority.

The previous pensions watchdog, OPRA, was widely seen as a poodle, but the new Pensions Regulator is a veritable Alsatian. Starting in 2003, the Regulator was granted wide anti-avoidance powers to issue 'contribution notices' to anyone involved in corporate transactions which had the effect of avoiding pension liabilities. A contribution notice requires the party to whom it is addressed to make up some or all of any pension fund deficit. These powers were introduced as a result of inadequacies in the previous regulations under the Pensions Act 1995, which led to a number of scandals where long-standing employees lost all their pension rights in questionable circumstances.

However, from Peter's viewpoint the new regulations have sometimes been a significant impediment to the restructuring needed to allow a business to survive. The stringency of the new regime is unique to the UK, making cross-border mergers and consolidation more difficult. Apart from the inhibition of value-creating corporate transactions, Peter also highlighted the high costs of the mandatory actuarial and legal advisors required to navigate the UK regulatory regime. These costs do not reduce proportionately with reducing fund sizes, so they can often be excessive for the small funds associated with small companies. He cited an example where a pension top-up payment of £1.25m incurred £700k of actuarial and legal costs.

Given the UK's legacy of generous pension promises, the costs of which have been increased by secular increases in longevity and reductions in interest rates, these issues are difficult to resolve. Jarvis Porter, Gaskell and Bulloughs are all companies in which Peter held a substantial shareholding and which foundered largely because of their increasing pension debts. At British Mohair, 100% owned by Peter, a deal was made to buy out the pension liability with the specialist insurance company Paternoster. At Pittards, a voluntary creditors' arrangement allowed pensions to be transferred with the Regulator's agreement to the Pensions Protection Fund, a default fund for schemes where the employer has effectively failed.

Peter noted that in Sweden none of these dilemmas arise, because most pension assets are invested in seven centrally managed pension funds, which because of their size achieve significant economies of scale.

MARKET-MAKING IN UK SMALL CAPS

Peter carries out his share dealing through two Swedish banks, which place his orders with London brokers. This introduces a degree of remoteness from the market, which he admits is "probably a weak link" in his operations. He feels that the large spreads which UK market makers can extract when dealing in micro-cap companies are very disadvantageous to investors. He prefers the Swedish system, where even small companies trade on an order-driven electronic trading system (similar to the SETS and SETSmm systems for larger stocks in the UK). "I have occasionally tested the UK system by placing buy and sell orders at the same price through different brokers. You don't always get offered both sides of the deal at similar prices when you do that."

Notwithstanding his specific criticisms of some aspects of UK corporate governance law and practice, Peter was also keen to stress that he has had good experiences in the UK, and indeed most of his quoted investments are in this country. "25 years ago the image of the City was amateurish, but that has gone. Most people in finance in the UK are very hard-working, with a high level of education."

Working days and sailing days

Peter leads a quite relaxed working life. He usually spends the morning working at home, then takes the 15-minute walk to his office around lunchtime. "I can do most of my work just as well at home, and often don't really need to go to the office."

Whether at home or at the office, he spends much of his day just reading and digesting information. Sources he uses regularly include the bulletin board ADVFN, CNBC television, several UK and Swedish newspapers, and the Thomson Reuters databank for quantitative screening for new ideas. He generally finds ideas himself rather than having them brought to him by brokers. In the early evening he walks home, cooks for himself most evenings, and then often returns to investment research later in the evening.

"When the sun shines, we go sailing if we feel like it."

Management of the Swedish portfolio of around 25 commercial and industrial properties is delegated to Martin Hansson and his administrative assistants. Jan Holmström also has a desk in the Stockholm office, although he spends much of his time in London. They have a relaxed attitude to working hours: "when the sun shines, we go sailing if we feel like it", and indeed in the past couple of summers Peter has spent several weeks cruising the Baltic aboard his 70-foot yacht.

Apart from the yacht, Peter's other indulgence is buying and restoring antiques. As well as the pleasure of ownership, this interest inevitably has a financial angle: "I am always delighted when I buy something for a good price. It is also interesting that value enhancement from restoration can often be many times its cost." But these indulgences are small relative to his wealth. From his experience in the early 1990s, when he was massively in debt for several years, he knows that having money to spend extravagantly is actually unimportant to his happiness. He has not yet thought seriously about people or organisations who might inherit his fortune. "After my up-and-down financial history, I have only started to feel secure again in the past three or four years."

Conclusion

Peter's strategy of corporate engineering depends on holding a sufficiently large stake in a company to exert meaningful influence over strategy, together with a proactive, hands-on approach to mergers, divestments and other corporate deals. But apart from these corporate governance activities, he spends his day in similar ways to other people in this book: no set routine, few meetings or telephone calls, and much of his time spent just reading and thinking. This may not sound much like work. The wonderful truth is that to Peter, it is not. "I have never felt that investing is like working. It is more like playing ten parallel games of poker or chess."

PETER GYLLENHAMMAR: INSIGHTS AND ADVICE

Experience trumps education If you are already sufficiently interested and involved in practical investment, formal business education may be less worthwhile.

Buy troubled companies and sort them out Buy bombed-out shares trading at a large discount to net asset value. If they are badly managed or not managed in the best interests of all shareholders, then implement change. Some will fail, but the risk/reward in aggregate is attractive.

Negative control Company law requires some important decisions, such as issuing new shares, to be approved by a special resolution at a general meeting. To pass a special resolution requires 75% of the votes cast to be in favour of the resolution. A 25% shareholding therefore gives an effective power of veto.

Small is beautiful Micro-cap companies in the UK can be attractive investments for two reasons:

1. indiscriminate institutional selling: some institutional shareholders appear to sell regardless of a company's merits if market capitalisation falls below an arbitrary threshold (say £10m or £50m or even £100m)

2. open ownership structure: the ownership of many micro-cap companies is open, with no controlling interest, and large blocks held by institutions which are prepared to sell. This means that a new investor can quickly build up a stake which gives meaningful influence over corporate policy.

Release negative working capital Businesses with a negative working capital requirement, such as construction contractors, can sometimes be re-engineered to release capital for other investments.

Use advisors sparingly Initial negotiations of company sales and other transactions are often better conducted without advisors. Generally, use advisors only in situations where it is unavoidable, for example because regulation requires you to do so.

Choose your own directors In Peter's view directors of smaller companies should be selected or at least approved by their larger shareholders, not (as usually happens in the UK at present) by the existing directors.

Beware pension pitfalls The onerous regulation of company pension schemes in the UK can be a trap for the unwary value investor.

IV ECLECTICS

Eclectics are the residual category. They cannot be clearly identified as top-down geographers or bottom-up surveyors, nor are they obvious activists. One eclectic is a fundamental investor who draws on both top-down and bottom-up analysis, with no clear predilection for either. The other is a day trader who trades partly on short-term news flow, and partly on technical analysis (that is, charts of recent share price histories).

KHALID
THE DAY TRADER

KHALID: FACTS AND FIGURES

Age at interview	45
Age at leaving last full-time job	37
Background	Left school at 18 to join the family retail business (originally clothing and knitwear, latterly furniture).
Style	30 to 40 trades every day on short-term news flow and technical indicators.
Markets and sectors	FTSE350 companies only (mainly FTSE100).
Instruments	Contracts for difference (CFDs).
Typical holding period	Minutes to hours.
Performance indicators	Pre-tax compound return in excess of 40% per annum from 2004 to 2010 (with leverage).
Quote	"I don't care much what a company does, and I usually know little about fundamentals. I rely more on upgrades and downgrades, price charts and technical indicators."
Phrases	Bloomberg; direct market access; Relative Strength Indicator (RSI); TD indicators.

mongst long-term investors, day traders do not have a good reputation. They tend to be thought of as people with short attention spans and short survival periods. Khalid fulfils the first of these expectations: he makes 30 to 40 trades in contracts for difference (CFDs) every day and almost all of his positions are closed within a few hours. He carries few positions forward at 4.30pm, ending each day largely flat and holding mainly cash overnight. Although his wealth is comparable to several people in this book, his dealing turnover is vastly larger – he trades over £30m worth of shares every month. After nearly a decade of full-time trading, he appears to be an example of a phenomenon which many long-term investors doubt can exist: a day trader who has demonstrated long-term survival, and in recent years enviable success.

Khalid is a man of Indian descent in his mid-40s with a short wiry physique and an aquiline face. He speaks in the quick-fire patter of a trader, in an accent which gives a hint of his location. He lives in a detached three-storey Victorian house on a hill on the outskirts of Sheffield, a few minutes from open countryside.

On the day I visited builders were working on a refurbishment of the house, but we were able to talk uninterrupted for several hours in the windowless sky-lighted office on the top floor. Khalid sat on a swivel chair in front of an L-shaped desk, with three large screens displaying news and charts from his Bloomberg market data service. The telephone rang a couple of times – a call from his broker, a proprietary trader at a City bank wanting a chat – but this was a quiet day. Although the markets were open, he was able to concentrate fully on our conversation, because he had already closed off all his positions for the day before my arrival in the early afternoon. His wife appeared a couple of times, but only when called for cups of tea: "she knows not to disturb me during the trading day".

The rag trade

Khalid's family were originally from Kashmir, the disputed territory in the northwest of India bordering Pakistan. His father emigrated in the 1950s, and settled in Sheffield, where he developed a clothing retail business in which the whole family helped. Khalid was born in 1964 in the family home, the house in which he still lives today, and grew up in a family of six brothers. He attended local state schools, and studied Economics and History at A-level. "My grades were good enough to go to university, but I chose not to. That was partly because of the lure of business and making money."

Most of the brothers helped in the family clothing business, in which management roles were shared after their father died when Khalid was eight years old. On leaving school aged 18 in 1983, he joined the business, working on buying, pricing and general management.

The brothers prospered for another decade until increasing competition forced a switch from clothing to furniture retailing in 1993. Khalid felt less enthusiasm and affinity for the new business: "as the youngest and shortest brother, I wasn't suited to lugging furniture around." By the late 1990s increasing competition from a new out-of-town shopping development and the continuing weakness in the Sheffield economy led to a decline in trading. It was at this time that Khalid decided to see if he could develop his hobby of share trading into a full-time activity.

Ratners

Khalid remembers participating in some stock market trading games in Economics classes at school, but first bought shares for real when he was 25. Because of his own involvement in retailing, his interest was piqued by newspaper reports of the Ratners fiasco.

Gerald Ratner was the chairman of the eponymous jewellery company, which had made a big success of retailing inexpensive jewellery in the 1980s until a notorious event of self-sabotage at the Institute of Directors on 23 April 2001. Giving a light-hearted speech about his business which he did not expect to be reported, Ratner remarked: "People say, how can you sell this for such a low price? I say, because it's total crap," adding that earrings sold by Ratners were "cheaper than an M&S prawn sandwich, but probably won't last as long".

Khalid: The Day Trader | **Chapter 11**

This mockery of his customers achieved instant press notoriety, and in the following days the stock market value of Ratners fell by around £500 million. Ratners was Khalid's first ever purchase of shares. "I didn't catch them at the bottom, but I put £3,000 on them at 15p. I can still remember filling in the form at the bank and pushing it across the counter to place the order." Within three months he sold the shares for more than £6,000, "a lot of money to me at the time."

Trading the account

Encouraged by this success, he opened an account with the discount broker Sharelink (now long since defunct) and started to "trade the account". Under the old stock exchange settlement system, the trading calendar was divided into account periods, usually a fortnight, or three weeks around bank holidays. All trades within any account period were netted against each other, with the net balance due to or from one's stockbroker payable on the single settlement day after the end of the account. This made it possible to buy shares during an account period – possibly without having the money to pay for them – and then sell them before the end of the account, so that only the net gain or loss was due on settlement day. Account trading effectively offered an informal line of credit for share dealing. It was the forerunner of more formalised forms of credit for share dealing such as CFDs and spread betting.

"He continued along the erratic path characteristic of many amateur investors – neither consistently making money, nor losing enough to put him out of the game."

Since he was working full-time in this period, Khalid was never able to focus fully on trading and "never made any real money from it". After three years of desultory trading he was cold-called in late 1993 by Financial Management International Limited, a grandiose yet anodyne name which might have been a warning flag to a more experienced investor. He signed up as an advisory client and began following their recommendations. Within a few months he had lost more than his modest profits from the previous three years, and was even starting to get into credit card debt.

Over the next few years he continued along the erratic path characteristic of many amateur investors – neither consistently making money, nor losing enough to put him out of the game. His credit card debt gradually increased to around £15,000. In 1997 the poor standard of advice offered by Financial

Management International attracted the attention of the regulatory authorities, leading ultimately to the firm's closure. He received a letter from the regulators asking for details of his dealings with the firm. About a year after replying, he recovered all but a small amount of his losses as compensation. "With hindsight that was probably lucky, because my losses were due to bad advice rather than fraud."

After receiving the compensation in 1998, Khalid decided to start trading again, but resolved not to act on other people's advice. At this point, he had been involved in investment for over seven years, and had made no money from it. This prolonged period of early failure was a common experience of several of our interviewees, reminiscent of the journalist Malcolm Gladwell's idea that the key to success in any field is to practise for around 10,000 hours.[1] "I was young and single, so whilst it wasn't great, it wasn't really a problem. Even now that I am married, I have few major commitments. The variable income of a trader could be more difficult if you have children."

The old stock exchange settlement calendar which facilitated account trading ended in 1996. Thereafter every day became a settlement day, with settlement initially due T+5 (that is, five trading days after the day of the trade); later the standard was reduced to T+3. It remained possible to deal for extended settlement, say T+20, and then close the position before the 20 trading days expired. But in the late 1990s CFDs (see the next panel) became popular as a more formalised yet flexible means of dealing on credit.

BACKGROUND: CONTRACTS FOR DIFFERENCE (CFDs)

A CFD is a substitute for directly buying or short-selling a share. The CFD provider and client agree that an amount based on the difference between the share price at the opening and closing of the contract will be payable between them. If the client takes a long position, the equivalent of buying the share, and the price rises, payment will flow from the CFD provider to the client; and conversely if the client takes a short position, the equivalent of selling the share.

Example CFD long position

Opening a long: Suppose the bid-ask spread for a share is 69-70p. The client opens a long CFD position over 100,000 shares at 70p. The opening contract total is £70,000 plus say 0.1% commission.

The client does not actually pay the opening contract total of £70,000. Instead the CFD provider funds the position, charging interest daily to the client's account. If the LIBOR interest rate is 3% per annum and the CFD provider's interest margin on funding provided to clients is 2% per annum, then:

Daily debit interest paid by trader = 70,000 x (0.03+0.02)/365 = £9.59 per day

The client is required to hold sufficient cash in his CFD account to cover the initial margin on the position, as a demonstration of good faith and ability to cover losses. In this example, the initial margin might be 10% of the contract total; that is, £7,000. We assume the client holds £10,000 cash in his CFD account, more than covering the required initial margin.

A margin call: Now suppose that the shares fall to 65-66p by the end of the day the CFD was opened. The position is now worth £65,000, and the client's mark-to-market loss on the open position is £5,000. The client needs enough cash in his CFD account to cover a variation margin to reflect this loss. The initial margin (£7,000) plus the variation margin (£5,000) exceed the total of £10,000 cash in the client's account. The next morning, he will receive a margin call for the deficit of £2,000. If the client fails to pay the margin call promptly, the CFD provider will close the position (and then pursue the client for any unpaid loss – ultimately through the courts, if necessary).

Closing a long: Now suppose that at a later date the share price rises to 80-81p. The client closes his position at 80p for a contract total of £80,000 less 0.1% commission. The difference between the opening and closing contract totals payable to the investor is:

80,000 x 0.999 - 70,000 x 1.001 = £9,850

Example CFD short position

Opening a short: Using the initial share price of 69-70p as in the previous example, the client who wishes to open a short CFD position over 100,000 shares sells at 69p, for a contract total of £69,000 less commission. Because funds are raised by a sale, a short position has no funding requirement. The CFD provider therefore pays daily interest to the client, say at the 3% LIBOR rate less a 1% credit interest margin:

Daily interest paid to trader = 69,000 x (0.03 – 0.01)/365 = £3.78

As in the long CFD example, cash in the client's account needs to cover initial margin plus variation margin.

Closing a short: Suppose the client closes the position when the price has fallen to 60-61p. The contract total will be £61,000 plus 0.1% commission. The difference between the opening and closing contract totals payable to the client is:

69,000 x 0.999 - 61,000 x 1.001 = £7,870

Dividend payments on the share during the life of the CFD are accounted for by crediting the payment to the client if he has a long position, and debiting the payment if he has a short position.

Advantages of CFDs over direct shares purchases include the availability of leverage, and the legal avoidance of the 0.5% stamp duty payable on real share purchases. This point is critical for day traders such as Khalid, who aim to profit from a large number of trades on small movements in share prices – a strategy which would be unviable if 0.5% stamp duty had to be paid on every trade.

COMPARISON OF CFDs WITH SPREAD BETS

The main differences between spread bets and CFDs are as follows (for examples of spread betting see Bill, Chapter 3):

- bookmakers charge wider price spreads, and these are usually considerably more expensive than CFD commissions

- there is no capital gains tax on spread bet winnings (and no relief for losses); the bookmaker pays a small betting tax, which is effectively funded by the wider price spreads

- interest and expected dividend payments are allowed for in the opening prices of a spread bet, rather than being credited or debited on a daily basis as with CFDs.

Starting in CFDs

Khalid's first exposure to CFDs was an advertisement from Deal4free in the *Financial Times* in 1999. Deal4free offered CFDs at market or near-market prices with no commission. For example, if a share was quoted at 100-101p bid-offer in the market, Deal4free would quote 100-101p as the buy-sell spread for opening the CFD, or sometimes a slightly wider spread.

Deal4free derived their profit from three slightly opaque subtleties of pricing, which were probably not well understood by many of their clients:

- the interest margin charged on the leverage provided to clients

- matching client buy and sell orders against each other and 'earning the spread'

■ sometimes quoting a slightly wider spread to customers than the underlying market spreads at which their hedging was executed.

Also in 1999, Khalid subscribed to the Updata share price data service, which in those days was delivered over the TV signal. The Updata service included good charting facilities for its time, which stimulated his interest in technical analysis. But he was still dabbling in several strategies, and his overall results, although improved, still had the same erratic pattern as in the 1990s: the best that could be said was that he never had a setback big enough to make him quit.

Only in 2002, when he homed in on two successful strategies, did his trading become generally profitable. The two successful strategies were trading broker upgrades and downgrades, and following a small number of technical indicators.

Broker upgrades and downgrades

A broker upgrade refers to a new research note on a company from a stockbroking analyst, raising the earnings forecast or target price for the share. The converse reduction is known as a downgrade.

At its simplest, Khalid's strategy is to be the first buyer of an upgrade as soon as it is released, and then sell within a few hours into the demand generated as news of the upgrade is disseminated to other market players. Conversely, for a downgrade he wants to be the first seller.

This is not a purely mechanical approach: he also takes into account soft information, such as his knowledge of which brokers' upgrades and downgrades are more or less influential, the reputation of individual analysts, general market conditions (if he is bearish, he will be more wary about buying upgrades), and also technical analysis. He also skims the narrative of the analysts' notes. "I try to read between the lines. For example, if it is a strong upgrade, say from sell to strong buy, I will usually take a larger position."

He doesn't analyse accounts or research a company's business himself. "I don't care much what a company does, and I usually know little about the fundamentals. I rely more on upgrades and downgrades, price charts and technical indicators."

By 2004, Khalid was trading 20 or more times a day, and his trading was becoming more consistently successful. He was also becoming more aware of the drawbacks of dealing via a commission-free service such as Deal4free for a substantial trader. Because a commission-free service makes its profit from the price spreads, it needs to prevent astute clients from picking off any anomalies in the spreads.

For example, suppose the market quote for a share is 100-101p. The CFD provider quotes a spread of 100-101p, good for a standard size of say 10,000 shares to buy or sell. Suppose a CFD client opens a short position over 10,000 shares at 100p. The CFD provider immediately attempts to hedge the position by selling 10,000 shares in the market at 100p. But the bid of 100p in the market at that moment may be for only a smaller number of shares, say 1000 shares. The CFD provider would then be faced with executing its hedge over the remaining 9000 shares at a lower (worse) price. To avoid this, the CFD provider is likely to re-quote the client, that is, the client's attempt to deal at 100p will be rejected, and a slightly lower price will be quoted to open a short position over 10,000 shares. From the client's viewpoint, frequent re-quotes produce a frustrating dealing experience, with a lack of transparency as to the extent to which price quotes are really actionable.

With his trading increasingly disrupted by re-quotes, Khalid was receptive when propositioned as a potential client by MF Global, which provides a trading platform for CFDs known as GNI Touch. This provides 'direct market access', meaning that clients can place their own bids and offers on the London Stock Exchange electronic order book, or act directly on bids and offers already on the order book. In the example of the previous paragraph, rather than the client seeing a Deal4free price of 100-101p and then being frustrated by a re-quote when he tries to execute against the 100p bid, the client would be able to see the actual market order of only 1,000 shares bid at 100p, and so be fully informed about the small size of the bid before deciding on his trading tactics and placing an order.

Although MF Global charge commissions, Khalid's turnover of over £30m in equities every month has enabled him to negotiate exceptionally low commission rates. Apart from the excellent trading platform, he also values his good working relationship with his dealer at MF Global, with whom he speaks several times most days. "He has a trading mentality himself, and one of the best in the business. If he left MF Global, I would probably go with him."

As well as upgrading his brokers, in 2004 Khalid also upgraded his data service from Updata to Proquote, a more sophisticated service also used by

Sushil (see Chapter 5). But for Khalid this was only an intermediate step towards the ultimate in market data services, a Bloomberg terminal, which he has used since 2005. Home-based private traders rarely have a Bloomberg – not least because of the cost, over £20,000 per annum for a single terminal in early 2010. Khalid regards it as money well spent. "There is an enormous depth to Bloomberg – data sources, market news, obscure technical indicators. I am always finding new features on the service."

Apart from data, the Bloomberg terminal also provides an Execution Management System (EMS) which allows users to execute trades directly against multiple sources of liquidity, with their own broker providing clearing and settlement. This means that as well as the official London Stock Exchange electronic order book, Bloomberg users can also execute trades in the 'dark pools' to which institutional dealing in larger companies is increasingly migrating. This is particularly helpful to someone who deals very frequently and in large volumes.

Khalid has encouraged Bloomberg to improve features which he felt would be helpful in his own trading. "When I started with Bloomberg, they were quite lethargic in collating lists of broker upgrades and downgrades, which they often published only in late morning. If I see the upgrade or downgrade before the market opens, I will often buy or sell the stock in the opening auction. Earlier rather than late publicity on Bloomberg then helps those positions, so I prodded them to be more efficient in publicising upgrades and downgrades."

BACKGROUND: THE ACADEMIC VERDICT

If asked for a casual opinion of the strategies in this chapter, most finance academics would probably be derisive. Technical analysis traditionally has a terrible reputation in the academic world, and following analyst recommendations is not much better. But in giving casual opinions, academics suffer from over-confidence like everyone else: the recent academic literature is actually ambivalent, and it is not hard to find some degree of support for both technical analysis and the economic value of broker upgrades and downgrades.

On technical analysis, a study published in 2000 in the *Journal of Finance*, the premier academic finance journal worldwide, found that several technical indicators may have some practical value.[2] More recently, an exhaustive survey in the *Journal of Economic Surveys* of 95 academic studies indicates that 56 report positive results from trading

---

strategies using technical analysis, 20 report negative results, and 19 report mixed results.[3]

On upgrades and downgrades, a paper in the *Journal of Financial and Quantitative Analysis* in 2006 found that on NASDAQ, trading on new recommendations issued on First Call (loosely, a competitor to Bloomberg) before the market opens results in average two-day returns of 1% for buys and 1.5% for sells.[4] Another 2006 paper found that stock prices react significantly to analyst recommendations in all G7 countries except Italy.

These findings contrast with earlier papers which found that following recommendations reported over general newswires[5] or on television[6] is not worthwhile. To profit from recommendations you probably need to access them early in their dissemination, on premium services such as Bloomberg or First Call, rather than via websites or newspapers.

Favourite technical indicators

Khalid's primary technical indicator is the relative strength indicator or RSI (see the next panel). His uses of RSI include monitoring 'spread ratios', that is the ratio of prices of two companies in the same sector. For example, he may monitor an RSI of the ratio of the share price of two banks, say Barclays to HSBC; when the ratio moves to an extreme, he will go long the cheap stock and short the expensive stock. He finds focusing on spreads of prices rather than absolute prices is particularly useful in periods when the market as a whole is trending.

He also uses some more obscure technical indicators, including several of the 'TD' proprietary indicators developed by Tom DeMark, a technical analyst who has worked with trading luminaries such as George Soros and Paul Tudor Jones. Calculation of the TD indicators is another example of a resource which Bloomberg provides and which is not readily available from cheaper sources. The TD indicators are based on the concept of price exhaustion; that is, they seek to identify turning points. This objective is reminiscent of RSI, and stands in contrast to the trend-following approach of many other technical analysis systems.

It can be difficult to continually monitor the price action on a large number of stocks. Khalid relies partly on price alerts set on all the FTSE350 stocks.

When a price alert on a stock indicates that a key technical indicator has been breached – for example, RSI below 25 or above 75 – he calls up the chart and looks at recent news on the stock. He also has news alerts for broker upgrades and downgrades on every stock in the FTSE350.

Most of the other interviewees in this book are fundamental investors: they select shares based on metrics and characteristics relating to underlying businesses and the broader economy, rather than the recent history of the share price. Any success achieved through technical analysis can be irritating to fundamental investors, because it implicitly treats prices as having elastic, physical or graphical qualities – an 'over-stretched' RSI, a TD indicator of 'price exhaustion', a 'trending' price or other chart pattern – which seem to have no connection to the underlying business.

To fundamental investors, technical analysis concepts all seem false metaphors: prices do not actually have the imputed properties, they are just the equilibrating numbers which balance buyers and sellers. But to technical analysts, false metaphors can be fertile; and if the metaphors make money, why not use them?

BACKGROUND: RELATIVE STRENGTH INDICATORS (RSI)

Relative strength indicators (RSI) were first popularised by the American engineer J. Welles Wilder in his 1978 book *New Concepts in Technical Trading Systems*.[7] Relative strength is based on the notion that a share which is trending upwards over several days will tend to have larger price changes on the days it rises than on the days it falls. The relative size (or 'strength') of the average moves on 'up days' and on 'down days' is then seen as an indication of whether 'up' forces or 'down' forces are dominant. The definition of relative strength is:

$$\text{Relative Strength (RS)} = \frac{\text{Average price change on up days}}{\text{Average price change on down days}}$$

It is convenient to normalise to a range of 0 to 100. The relative strength indicator (RSI) is calculated as follows:

$$\text{Relative Strength Indicator (RSI)} = 100 - \frac{100}{(1 + \text{RS})}$$

so that RSI = 50 indicates a neutral position, with RSI above 50 suggesting 'up moves' have been dominant in recent days, and conversely for RSI less than 50.

Typically the RSI is calculated using a period of the last nine, 14, 20 or 25 days. Technical analysts believe that when a share's RSI reaches a high or low value, the price has

---

become 'over-extended' in that direction and is likely to retrace. As with many notions in technical analysis, this has no theoretical justification – it is simply an observation which some technical analysts regard as supported by experience. An RSI below 30 is generally considered 'over-sold' (a buy signal), and an RSI above 70 is generally considered 'over-bought' (a sell signal). Khalid prefers to use the levels 25 and 75. The chart of Vodafone plc for the first six months of 2010 and its 20-day RSI illustrates the concept.

Vodafone plc: price chart and 20-day RSI, January 2010 – June 2010

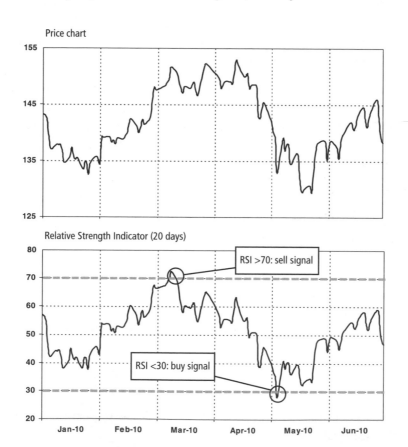

Source: data from ADVFN

A typical day

Khalid's working day starts at six in the morning. He looks at news from the Far East, and skims anything up to 30 new research notes on individual FTSE350 companies from broking analysts. These notes are not generally available to private investors, but over the years Khalid has developed friendly contacts at several City firms who help him with access to research. "Although I am up here in Sheffield, quite a lot of traders in the City know me. Newswires like Reuters or Bloomberg are always looking for a pithy comment on market news; sometimes they ring me, and if they quote me, that gets my name known."

For Khalid the value of analyst reports is not so much the underlying fundamental analysis, but rather the early clues they provide on market flow – that is, how clients of major firms may be seeking to trade. "Suppose my technical indicators are starting to suggest a share might be over-sold. If a big bank is also saying it is a buying opportunity, they are likely to have clients ready to pile in, which will tend to support the price. So a bullish note from a big house might tip the balance in my own decision to buy the stock."

By 7.45am, Khalid usually has "a fair idea of what I am going to be doing in the opening auction." The opening auction and first hour of trading are the busiest part of his day. From 7.50am onwards, he uses direct market access to enter bids or offers on stocks with broker upgrades or downgrades which he has decided to trade in the opening auction. Typically each order will be for at least £50,000, and he will take perhaps a dozen positions on any one day. For the first hour or so after the market opening he watches all these trades intently, and will generally look to close for a profit of 1% or 2%, or sometimes a small loss.

> "The value of analyst reports is not so much the underlying fundamental analysis, but rather the early clues they provide on market flow."

He has an aggressive dealing style which favours immediacy rather than earning the bid-offer spread. For example, if the best bid and offer prices on the screen are currently 100p and 101p, and he wants to sell, he would usually use direct market access to hit the bid of 100p immediately, rather than to offer his stock at 100.75p and wait in the hope that a buyer willing to pay that price will come along. For spread trades on pairs of related stocks (e.g. long Barclays, short HSBC), he does not trade in the opening auction, but prefers to get another reading on the spread at 8.30am to 9am after prices have settled down.

For the rest of the day he reads more news, investigating stocks flagged by his technical indicators on Bloomberg, and monitoring any spread trades or other positions which he is running past the first hour of the day. He does not trade on bid rumours. He keeps an eye on commodity prices and currencies, but only as inputs to his decisions on shares (e.g. a rising oil price is generally good for oil shares) rather than for direct commodity or forex trading. A small window on his screen displays the CNBC business television channel with the sound muted for most of the day.

Khalid does not act on every positive-expectation opportunity that he finds, preferring to restrict his portfolio to a small number of positions with strongly positive expectations. "I don't aim to have 50 positions and make money on 30 of them. I would prefer to have ten positions and make money on eight of them." He will trade anything in the FTSE350, but most of his trading is in FTSE100 stocks.

He does not read or post on public bulletin boards. He communicates throughout the day with his broker and other professional traders at banks and hedge funds, on the telephone, via Bloomberg chat or by email. He emphasised the importance of two qualities in such interaction: a lack of ego, and a degree of reciprocity. "Some people seem to post on public bulletin boards to show off how clever they are. I don't see the point of that. I try to speak to people who are cleverer or more sophisticated than me. I try to give them something useful and I hope they will give something back to me."

A few years ago, anomalies sometimes arose in the London Stock Exchange closing auction at 4.30pm. For example, on the evening a stock was to be added to a market index such as the FTSE100, index-tracker funds might place market orders to buy the stock at any price in the closing auction; astute traders could then make a killing by entering matching orders into the auction at anomalously high prices. But the index-tracker funds have become more careful, and such anomalies seldom occur nowadays. Khalid now uses the 4.30pm auction mainly to close out existing positions. He goes into each evening largely flat, holding mainly cash. He does hold some positions overnight, sometimes for several days or even weeks, but these longer-term positions are not a large part of his total trading.

After the market close, he looks at more research for an hour or two. He also keeps an eye on trading in the US, but only for its read-across implications for London; he does not deal in US shares. He leaves his top floor office around 6pm. Around 9pm he comes back to the office, checks the closing levels of US indices and any major news in the US, and spends half an hour or so preparing for the next start at six the following morning.

Khalid habitually operates far inside the maximum leverage offered by his CFD provider – "my positions are typically only 50% of the maximum MF Global would allow" – and very seldom pays a margin call: "never in four years with MF Global, and only once with Deal4free." If he comes close to a margin call, he prefers to reduce his positions. He feels that the advertisements of many CFD providers emphasising the high leverage on offer "give completely the wrong idea to new traders". He does not use pre-set formal stop losses, favouring instead a discretionary "pain threshold method – when the pain is too much, you get out!" He monitors his overall exposure and margins in a spreadsheet which he developed himself.

Day trading in difficult markets: 2007 onwards

Asked about his worst trades, Khalid was open that 2008 had been a difficult year. "In fact 2007 was a bit tricky as well!" In 2007 he was caught with a large long position of over £1m exposure in the real estate company Hammerson. "I bought on a broker upgrade, but the whole real estate sector was coming under pressure, especially leveraged stocks like Hammerson. The loss kept increasing for several weeks, but I was in denial. I eventually sold it in an opening auction, on the day when I would otherwise have been liable for a margin call to MF Global. It was the worst price of the day, on the worst day of the year. That was my largest ever loss – nearly a quarter of a million pounds on that one trade."

In the frantic days of September 2008, with many financial institutions apparently in trouble, he took part of his funds out of MF Global for a time. He looked around for alternative CFD brokers, and contemplated switching to the Icelandic-owned Kaupthing Singer and Friedlander, but in the end did not – a lucky escape, because Kaupthing itself went into administration on 8 October 2008. He concluded that he "could not find anyone more substantial than MF Global who would take me on." He still does not have a good solution to this dilemma. "I am classified as an eligible counterparty, not a retail customer, so if MF Global ever gets into trouble I will be at the back of the queue for compensation. You just have to get your money out at the first sign of trouble."

Had these difficult periods ever led Khalid to consider retuning to employment? "It never looked quite as bad as that!" He added that the difficult periods were made easier by the fact that apart from long holidays abroad, he and his wife do not have expensive tastes. "I could afford to retire – just buy a few investment properties and live off the income – but what would I do then? I'm sure I'd be bored." Although he expects to go on trading, he highlighted the conundrum that a business which happens largely in one person's mind can be difficult to scale up. "I have thought about employing an assistant, but I think it is difficult to delegate much as a trader. It is a dead-end job in that respect."

Conclusion

Khalid's strategy of making tiny percentage profits from a high turnover on short-term trades depends on innovations in dealing services over the past decade. In particular, CFDs offer leverage, the ability to go short, and avoidance of the 0.5% stamp duty on share purchases; and fierce competition between CFD providers has led to very low commission rates. Without these innovations, profitable day trading by the private investor would probably not be feasible at all. This is another example of how the environment for private investors has improved over the past 15 years.

> "To a fundamental analyst, technical analysis can seem a sort of cheat sheet, preventing development of proper understanding – and yet often giving infuriatingly good answers."

Most of my investing friends are long-term fundamental investors, whose reactions to drafts of this chapter tended to be grudging. One complained that buying upgrades and selling downgrades seemed a "slightly whiffy strategy"; another decried it as "a legal form of front-running." The fact that a day trader like Khalid trades successfully whilst never looking at accounting figures and knowing little about the underlying businesses of the 'names' he trades is irritating to those who spend long hours on fundamental research. To a fundamental analyst, technical analysis can seem a sort of cheat sheet, preventing development of proper understanding – and yet often giving infuriatingly good answers.

But there are no marks in trading for intellectual depth, and no penalties for plagiarism or vulgarity: all that matters is financial return. Leveraged compound growth above 40% per annum for the past six years is Khalid's answer to any principled critics.

KHALID: INSIGHTS AND ADVICE

10,000 hours of practice   Several years of indifferent results are not inconsistent with ultimate success as a trader.

CFDs for high-frequency trading   For a high-turnover trader with small expected profit margins on each trade, CFDs are a better instrument than direct shares or spread betting, because they offer the lowest commissions and no stamp duty.

Trading broker upgrades and downgrades   Acting on brokers' change in views can be a worthwhile short-term strategy – but only if you receive them early in their wider dissemination, through premium sources such as Bloomberg.

False but useful metaphors   To the fundamental investor, technical analysis may appear to be comprised largely of false metaphors, where prices are treated as having elastic, physical or graphical qualities. But to the technical analyst, these false metaphors can make money.

Monitor ratios of related prices   Indicators such as the relative strength indicator (RSI) can be used to monitor not just individual prices, but the ratio of prices of related stocks, e.g. HSBC and Barclays.

Give-and-take networking   Do not post on bulletin boards just to show how clever you are. In all interactions with other investors, aim for a lack of ego, and a degree of reciprocity: talk to people with whom you can both give something and learn something.

Low leverage   Use less than 50% of the maximum size of positions which your CFD provider would allow.

Trading is not a scalable business   As an activity which happens largely in one person's mind, trading is difficult to delegate and difficult to scale up.

VINCE
THE TAX EXILE

VINCE: FACTS AND FIGURES

Age at interview	64
Age at leaving last full-time job	33
Background	Schooling greatly disrupted by tuberculosis; left school at 17; miscellaneous entrepreneurial ventures; jobs in the motor industry and local government housing.
Style	Bottom-up scans of small caps for cheap value metrics; top-down thinking to switch from UK shares into German residential property from 2003 onwards.
Markets and sectors	UK small caps; UK large caps; UK commercial property; Real Estate Investment Trusts (REITs) in the US and Singapore; from 2003 onwards, German residential property.
Instruments	Shares, direct property.
Typical holding period	Months to years.
Performance indicators	ISA millionaire by 2003; many public announcements over the past 15 years of large shareholdings between 3% and 29% in UK-listed companies.
Quote	"When you find a good idea, buy enough of it to make a difference. Diversifying away risk also means diversifying away profit."
Phrases	Contrarianism; tax exile; absence of competition; profiling.

C ontrarianism in investment is like originality in art: all serious artists think they are original, and all serious investors think they are contrarian. But for most this is an affectation: conscious that being original or contrarian is often admired, they assure themselves and others that they are. To identify real contrarians, it helps to look at behaviour outside the investment arena: is the investor willing to hold unpopular beliefs in other fields?

"Contrarianism in investment is like originality in art: all serious artists think they are original, and all serious investors think they are contrarian. But for most this is an affectation."

Vince not only espouses some unpopular ideas himself, he actively promulgates unpopular ideas in general. The *raison d'être* of the small publishing firm he has run for two decades is to publish books which do not satisfy conventional commercial criteria, upset conventional wisdom, and which other publishers often will not touch. "I don't want to publish safe and inoffensive books. I want to publish books that change the world."

Although Vince has run his publishing firm for more than 20 years, and it is now a modestly profitable enterprise, publishing has never been his livelihood. In his late teens and twenties he pursued several small business ventures, spent a few years as a sales executive, and then had a short but rapidly progressive career in local government housing. He left his last job in 1979 at the age of 33. For many years he lived in London, where his elder son and daughter grew up. In early 2007 he relocated to Switzerland with his new partner and their infant son and daughter. His speech is staccato and restless, jumping back and forth between topics and decades, often alluding to many ideas in very few words; a listener needs to concentrate to keep up. His black-framed glasses sit on a quizzical, often expressively contorted face.

Tuberculosis

Vince was born in 1946, the son of a Durham miner who came to London in search of a better life working as a valet. Vince's childhood was dominated by ill health: between the ages of three and 12 he spent nearly five years in hospital with pulmonary and hip tuberculosis. Tuberculosis left him with two long-term effects: the physical effect of a slight limp, and the psychological effect of "an uncertain sense of entitlement", which he elaborated as follows. "When I left hospital aged 12 I left behind a close friend much cleverer and more accomplished than me. But he had muscular dystrophy whereas I only had tuberculosis, and at 16 he was dead. I am conscious that my success has been predicated on a lack of competition from absent others like him. I am not sure how much anyone really owns their own success."

Because of his disrupted early schooling, Vince never took the eleven-plus examination. He discovered the world of ideas not at his secondary modern school but through solitary reading in Hendon library. Despite his quick brain, university was never remotely on the agenda: "it was outside the range of possibility contemplated by family or my school".

> "The critical ingredient in financial independence was not so much running a business as having free capital."

On leaving school aged 17, after a couple of entrepreneurial false starts, he and a business partner took a lease on a tiny shop in Bishopsgate and opened a 17-seater sandwich bar. Turnover grew rapidly, but profit was more elusive. In 1968 they had the good fortune to sell the business to a buyer who paid more attention to the turnover than the profit. Vince's share of £2,750 from the proceeds – roughly equivalent to £30,000 in 2010 – provided his initial funds for stock market investment.

By this time he had realised that the critical ingredient in financial independence was not so much running a business as having free capital. His epiphany came when arranging to rent business premises from the Goodwins, a prominent family of Hampstead landlords. "I had an appointment to see the son in the family office at ten o'clock in the morning. I found him relaxing with the *Financial Times*, with breakfast on a tray, surrounded by high walls of paintings and books. I knew people who ran small businesses, but this was something different – the freedom of unencumbered capital. I realised at that moment that my object in life was to gain that freedom, and accumulating capital was the way to do it."

Vince spent 1969 doing various temporary jobs through the Manpower employment agency, and using the money from the sale of the sandwich bar for stock market investments. He was a typical tyro investor, naïvely following newspaper tips, neither making much money nor losing enough to put him out of the game. He then spent a year from October 1970 travelling to and around India – "chasing a girlfriend, but in the end we didn't work out" – and anxiously following his modest shareholdings in newspapers in the British Council reading rooms around the country.

A job is a means to a mortgage

On return to England, he took a sales executive job with Chrysler UK. He had no aspirations for a long-term career at Chrysler – "it was just a job, a way of making some money, and more importantly it enabled me to apply for mortgages". At the age of 25, he was already clear that his best chance of financial independence was through property and share investment, rather than a conventional career. As well as the epiphany in the Goodwin family office, his childhood experiences with tuberculosis were also a motivation: "I had been away in hospital for long periods. I had no confidence that I would always be able to work. I felt I had to do something which could support me even if I became incapacitated."

In late 1971 he bought his first house, funded by credit card loans and a mortgage, both of which were much more difficult to obtain than they are today. "Building societies would only lend if you were married, or said you were about to get married…you had to use the right mortgage brokers, keep increasing the limits on the credit card…and be a bit creative with receipts to demonstrate income." Over the next three years these tactics funded another three investment properties.

Because of his focus on property, he largely avoided the 1974 slump in shares. Price inflation combined with the lack of available credit – loan rationing, building societies only lending to owner-occupiers, no concept of buy-to-let lending – meant that in real terms, houses became very cheap in the mid-1970s, sometimes offering a 25% rental yield on the purchase price. Vince continued buying whenever he could scrape together sufficient finance, but rising interest rates over the course of 1974 made his position increasingly difficult. He rented out more and more of his own home, eventually retreating to live in only one room.

From 1975 he worked as a local government housing officer, being promoted several times but spending very little, saving all he could towards buying more properties. By the late 1970s rising property prices and falling interest rates meant that his ambition of becoming financially independent through investment started to look within reach again. In 1978 he realised that if he could buy a fifth investment property on a 25% yield, his rental income less mortgage payments would probably be enough to live off, so that he could give up his job. "It came to me in the middle of the night, and I remember getting up and writing out the figures." It took a long time and many abortive auction bids to buy the fifth property at a cheap enough price, but when he managed it in the summer of 1979, he resigned from his job. He was 33 years old.

Small-cap investor

After leaving his job Vince started a sociology degree at Bedford College in London. "I had an inferiority complex about not having gone to university… I thought the only way to deal with that was to do a degree." But a few months of the reality of first-year study in large classes neutralised the mystique he had attached to higher education. Having married in 1980 he felt he needed to focus on money-making, so he left the course at the end of the first year.

He prospered in the long bull market of the 1980s in both property investment and the stock market. He diversified from residential into commercial property, often buying ex-British Rail and similar properties where yields were around 15% but rent reviews were restricted by the lease, which tended to deter most investors. He cashed in most of his shares in the months leading up to the 1987 stock market crash – "it was easy to see the market was going crazy" – and reinvested in the immediate aftermath of the crash. He made larger profits in 1987-88 than in any year until the rebound from the credit crisis in spring and summer 2009.

Vince's share investments from the 1980s onwards until quite recently have usually been concentrated in obscure small companies. He offered two rationales for this strategy: the mispricing of insolvency risk, and excessive discounts for illiquidity.

On the mispricing of insolvency risk, he thinks that because of institutions' reluctance to be associated with the ignominy of corporate failure, the risks of failure of small companies are often over-discounted by their price.

"Institutions will often sell at any price if a company appears to have a substantial chance of going bust. Because of this, a company with say a 50-50 chance of either going bust or multiplying several times is often priced as if it will almost surely go bust."

On discounts for illiquidity, he thinks that for an institutional seller of small company shares, finding a buyer of a large block quickly at any price is often more important than achieving the best price. "On a Friday afternoon I have often been the only buyer in any size of a small company. If an institution needs to get out that day, you can often name your own price for a large block of shares, well below the mid-price, and sometimes even below the bid." These two factors together mean there is often little or no competition to buy a large block of shares in a troubled small-cap company. Vince stressed the advantages of this strategy: rather than trying harder to win, look for situations with an absence of competition. This point is similar to Warren Buffett's observation mentioned in Sushil's profile (Chapter 5), that "investment isn't Olympic diving", and Owen's advice (Chapter 9) to "look for easy decisions".

Because Vince dealt mainly in small companies, and with a concentrated portfolio, by the late 1980s he was occasionally accumulating notifiable holdings of more than 3% of a company's shares. By this time, having an interesting life was becoming more important than just making money. He was attracted to the idea of gaining control of a quoted company and using it as a vehicle for acquisitions – "not so much because of any clear financial advantage, but because it seemed like an interesting thing to do."

But rather than corporate finance, his venture into the world of books – as shareholder and eventually sole proprietor of a small non-fiction publishing house – provided a new interest in life. The firm specialises in psychoanalytical theory and related fields, with a focus on interdisciplinary titles or those which are contrarian within their own disciplines. Vince explained his motivation as follows: "I did not expect to make money from publishing, but I was attracted by the idea of publishing controversial books which nobody else would publish, and which might change the world."

Geographer and surveyor

It is difficult to label Vince as either the top-down (geographer) or bottom-up (surveyor) type of investor. He has made some big macro calls to exit the stock market, for example in the lead-up to the 1987 crash, and progressively from 2003 until early 2009. His scanning of the world investment universe is very wide, leading him into diverse asset classes such as German residential property, some currency trades, and Real Estate Investment Trusts (REITs) in the US and Singapore. But on other occasions an investment idea starts from detailed bottom-up research on an individual company. He also dabbles in option strategies detailed later in this chapter.

As an example of a top-down call, Vince cited his progressive switch out of UK shares and into German residential property from 2003 onwards. He had reinvested cash into UK equities in Spring 2003, and profited from the market turn around the time of the Iraq war. In the following months and years, almost all asset classes worldwide appreciated together. Searching for an unpopular asset class, he noted that German residential property had not risen in price in real terms for 15 years, and indeed had substantially depreciated relative to UK property: "In 1992 an average apartment in London was worth 0.7 of an equivalent one in Frankfurt, but by 2006 the same London apartment was worth two in Frankfurt."

He visited Germany, viewed properties, appointed agents and eventually accumulated a portfolio of around 200 apartments in a dozen blocks. Although German residential property was a good store of value over the period 2006-09, he emphasised that it is a very different market to the UK: "the property market in Germany has a completely different mentality – they prefer new properties, property is a depreciating asset, acquisition costs can be as much as 7-8%, rent increases are limited, tenants have high security of tenure, and there is no concept of a property ladder for owners."

As an example of detailed bottom-up research, Vince recalled a convertible loan stock issued by the retirement housebuilder McCarthy & Stone. In the early 1990s the company had large debts and its survival was in doubt, with the loan stock trading on a running yield over 30%. This would be very cheap if the company survived, which depended on a sufficient number of sales of retirement units. Vince described his research as follows. "I developed a systematic programme of ringing the site offices at their developments around the country to enquire about sales. The pretext was that my mother wanted to buy a retirement home but was nervous about being on her own, so could they please tell me how many units on their site had been sold? For a time I made several calls every week. As a result I had the confidence to buy large quantities of the loan stock at very cheap prices."

Vince screens for new investment ideas primarily by the simplest traditional value metrics. A combination of low price-earnings ratio and high dividend yield usually throws up enough candidates to investigate. For many years he subscribed to the *Company REFS* service for summarised financial metrics, but he now uses online tools at ADVFN. When he identifies promising candidates he will read recent RNS items, as well as the annual accounts including the notes. He sometimes scribbles his own comments on the accounts, but does not keep extensive paper files: because he holds only a handful of shares at any time, often fewer than a dozen, he can keep most of the facts in his head.

Discussing his process of selecting investments, Vince mentioned the concept of profiling. This means studying past investments to infer a list of characteristics of good or bad investments, which can then be used as a checklist.

Some examples of characteristics associated with successful investments might include:

- recent substantial director shares purchases
- the absence of a large number of naïvely enthusiastic posters on bulletin boards
- a recent substantial share purchase by a commercial rival (suggesting the possibility of plans for a takeover bid)
- a paucity of broker research coverage of the company.

Examples of characteristics associated with unsuccessful investments might include:

- the converse of most of those above
- a personality cult around the chief executive
- a gimmicky annual report
- "flagpoles and fountains" (glitzy company premises).

Portfolio management and debt

Vince is not a fan of broad diversification, and has often held the bulk of his portfolio in around six shares. "When you find a good idea, buy enough of it to make a difference. Diversifying away risk also means diversifying away profit." Over the years he has held notifiable stakes of over 3% of the shares in many small quoted companies. At the time of the interview he had recently built up a stake of over 20% in an AIM-listed property company focused on premises for medical practices and care homes.

He generally does not seek to influence management even at his larger holdings, and does not talk to company management before investing; usually his first contact with a company will be when he writes to notify a shareholding above 3%. This often leads to the company suggesting a meeting, and when based in the UK he used to oblige. "They usually give a presentation about the business, but the real agenda – usually unspoken, occasionally blurted out – is why am I buying their shares, what is this about, what is my ulterior motive? I have never had any motive other than passive investment for financial return, but they often have difficulty believing that."

Vince has always had some mortgage debt secured on his property holdings, but does not borrow directly for the purpose of increasing his investments in shares. He has never had a spread betting or CFD account. In the 1990s he dabbled in intraday short selling: at the market opening he would short the shares of companies which had announced poor results, looking to buy back later the same day. But he found this strategy became less effective in the 2000s, and he has now not shorted a share for several years.

Despite often taking large holdings in illiquid small companies, he has almost always managed to exit within a couple of years – by takeover, liquidation of cash-rich companies, or through selling in the market. He had one major setback some years ago when he lost around £400,000 on the highly indebted aerospace engineering company L Gardner Group. "I was impressed that the directors had given personal guarantees for some of the company's bank debt. But in early 2003 several of the directors resigned, then the company went into receivership, and the directors immediately bought the best part of the business from the receivers. In my opinion it was a bit of a scam, but I didn't want to spend years on litigation, so I chose to move on."

Options: covered straddles

At the time of the interview, Vince had "no good small-cap ideas". His main holdings were direct holdings of German residential property, real estate investment trusts in Singapore, and four very large FTSE100 companies: Shell, Glaxo, AstraZeneca and Vodafone. These household names were held as 'placeholders' in his portfolio – very liquid shares which could quickly be turned into cash, and so gave flexibility to change his stance quickly.

To generate more income from the placeholders, he writes options for income around these holdings. His main options strategy is covered straddles: that is, selling puts and calls on shares he already owns with the same expiry date and strike prices close to the current share price. A covered straddle produces a better result than just owning the share, provided the share price does not move too much (for a fuller explanation and an example see the next panel).

BACKGROUND: WRITING A COVERED STRADDLE

In the 'straddle' options strategy, the investor sells a put option and a call option which have a common expiry date, and exercise prices which 'straddle' the current share price. The straddle is 'covered' if the investor already owns the share (it is also possible to write a 'naked' straddle where one does not already own the share, but that will be ignored here).

Essentially, writing a covered straddle is a bet on low volatility: it produces a better result than just holding the share, provided the share price does not move too much. The graph shows an example: the payoff from the covered straddle (the heavy line) exceeds the payoff from just holding the share (the light line) provided the share price lies within the range (92, 113) at the expiry date of the options.

Payoff chart for covered straddle

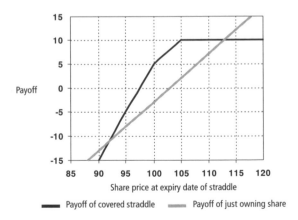

Source: drawn by author

The graph can be explained in detail as follows.

Suppose the current price of a share the investor already holds is 103. To write the covered straddle, the investor writes a put option for an expiry date say six months

---

forward with a strike price of say 100, and a call option with a strike price of say 105 and the same expiry date. The investor receives a premium for writing each option; on reasonable assumptions the total of the two premiums will amount to around eight.[1]

Let P be for share price at the expiry date of the options.

The light line in the graph shows the payoff (P - 103) from holding just the share: a gain (or loss) if the share is above (or below) its starting price of 103.

The heavy line in the graph shows the payoff from holding the share *and* writing the covered straddle. This comprises the option premiums received of 5 + 3 = 8, plus a contingent payoff depending on which of the options has value at the expiry date. There are three cases to consider (corresponding to the three directions along the length of the heavy line).

1. Share price P above 105 (the call option is 'in the money') at expiry:

- The call option is exercised against the investor; that is, the share he holds is bought from him for 105, giving a gain of 2 compared with its starting price of 103.

- The put option is 'out of the money' and so is not exercised.

- The total payoff is therefore 8 + 2 = 10 for *any* share price at expiry above 105.

2. Share price P below 100 (the put option is 'in the money') at expiry:

- The put option is exercised against the investor; that is, *another* share is sold to him for 100, causing an immediate loss (P - 100) compared with the market price.

- The call option is 'out of the money', so it will *not* be exercised; that is, the investor retains his original share, which also stands at a loss (P - 103) compared with its starting price of 103.

- The total payoff is 8 + (P - 100) + (P - 103). For P = 97.5, this is zero. For P < 92, this is less than the payoff (P - 103) from just owning the share.

3. Share price P between 100 and 105 (neither option is 'in the money') at expiry:

- Neither option is exercised; the investor is left holding the share, for a profit or loss of (P - 103).

- The total payoff is 8 + (P - 103).

A day in the life of a tax exile

Vince relocated to the canton of Zug in Switzerland in early 2007. To a large extent this was for tax reasons – "partly paying less tax, and partly the simplification of no longer having to think about tax in most investment decisions." He had always thought carefully about the interaction of investment and tax, for example concentrating his gains in tax-free vehicles wherever he could; over £1m had accumulated in each of his own and his wife's PEPs and ISAs by 2003.

He chose Switzerland over other low-tax jurisdictions partly because it is conveniently located between his apartment in Nice and his German property portfolio. He admires the Swiss culture of self-reliance and personal responsibility, which he feels will be a good milieu for his young children. Zug is astonishingly prosperous and yet egalitarian, combining discreet wealth with an absence of obvious poverty, the whole population floating on the obvious but unmentionable sea of black money. The canton levies a negotiable tax lump sum on foreign residents, based on guidelines related to the floor area of their Swiss residence, with no income or capital gains tax.

Vince has always been an exceptionally early riser: "I don't sleep much, and I tend to wake up at about 3.30am irrespective of when I go to bed. I do my best

> "Zug is astonishingly prosperous, the whole population floating on the obvious but unmentionable sea of black money."

work in the early morning." For a couple of hours he reads the newspapers, deals with overnight emails about his publishing interests from the Far East, and catches up on the ADVFN bulletin board. At 5.45am every weekday he leaves the underground car park at his house for the seven-minute drive to the swimming pool. After his swim he returns to breakfast with the children, and is back at his desk for 8am – equivalent to 7am in the UK, when the first batch of London company results and other news is released. He scans news on the Investegate website for any companies which he currently holds, or has followed in the past, or which present interesting headlines. Soon after the market opening he will usually speak to the UK stockbroker with whom he has dealt for 20 years.

In the morning he will work partly on investment and partly on his publishing business, answering emails from authors all over the world and queries from his property managers in Germany. He spends a good deal of time reading bulletin boards, particularly ADVFN, and also posts quite actively. His approach to bulletin boards has evolved over time. "In the early days I took it all very seriously. But I gradually realised that most posters don't want to take it seriously, so I adapted to that spirit. I still make some serious posts, but a lot of it is for amusement: at any time a few posters are baiting me, I bait them back, and it is all good fun."

He finds the boards useful for scuttlebutt – gossip from customers, suppliers, and employees – and he sometimes has the impression that particular posters are company officers or PR representatives. Overall he finds it difficult to think of an occasion when a bulletin board has been important to a decision, "but if it disappeared I would miss it."

School for the children finishes at 12 noon. In the afternoon the family often go out together, to the ski slopes in winter or the lake in summer. He takes a mobile phone on these excursions, leaving his broker instructions to call "if certain events happen, or anything else happens that he thinks I need to know." The UK number for the publishing firm also diverts to his mobile phone, and it is not uncommon for him to take a call from an author or publicist while out with the children, or on the beach in the south of France where the family spends the summer.

Reflecting on how his typical day has changed over the years, Vince highlighted the massive improvements in access to information and ease and cheapness of dealing. "When I started in the late 1960s, even finding a stockbroker to take you on as a client was not straightforward – you were expected to know somebody. And the mandatory minimum commissions set by the Stock Exchange for all brokers were crippling compared to today's rates." For share prices, he relied mainly on the *Evening Standard*, which printed a limited selection of intraday updated prices in each of its several editions through the day. Later, in the 1980s and 1990s, electronic services such as Prestel, Market Eye and Updata provided partial news services to private investors, but with four-figure price tags. Full real-time news provided by services such as Bloomberg and Reuters Topic carried five-figure price tags, far beyond what could be justified by even the most serious private investors. Nowadays, the full London Stock Exchange RNS is available in real time and free of charge on numerous websites. Even real-time prices are free to any registered user of sites such as ADVFN, with Level 2 prices available for a few pounds per month.

Vince was already a full-time investor before the two children of his first marriage were born. He thinks his children were probably confused by their father having no job, and found it difficult to explain to their peers what he did. Today they all circumvent the issue by describing him as a publisher. He had no qualms about his children enjoying a much higher material standard of living than he had had in his own penurious childhood. "I don't think children are spoilt by material things. But they may be spoilt if abundance prevents them from developing their own awareness of trade-offs and relative value." One way in which he encouraged his children's awareness of trade-offs was that as early as age ten, each child was given a generous allowance, but the allowance covered essential items such as school uniforms as well as frivolities.

Conclusion

Vince has spent a lifetime doing something different from his peers: focusing on investment rather than building a career in his twenties; studying sociology in his early thirties; selling before the crash in 1987; financing often radical social science texts (which would bemuse or irritate most of his fellow investors) ever since the early 1990s; and shifting progressively from UK small company shares into German property in the mid-2000s. His willingness to embrace the unpopular is reflected not just in his investment thinking, but in the unusual books he publishes and in his continuing admiration for unfashionable thinkers such as Marx. Contrarianism is not in itself a guarantee of success, and sometimes it is an affectation; one critic has described it as "a cheap way of allowing ideological hacks to think of themselves as fearless, independent thinkers". It is not enough to be contrarian, one also needs to be right; but if one can be both, the payoff is more direct and reliable in investment than in almost any other field.

VINCE: INSIGHTS AND ADVICE

Unpopular views   Contrarianism in investment is like originality in art: an affectation for many and a true characteristic of only a few. Real contrarians tend to espouse unpopular views in many areas, not just in investment.

A job as a means to a mortgage   Even if you have little interest in conventional career progression, it may be worth keeping a job as a means to a mortgage, or better terms on a mortgage.

Institutions shun embarrassment and illiquidity   Small company shares are sometimes under-priced because of the over-discounting of insolvency risk (institutions do not want to be associated with the embarrassment of a company which might go bust), and excessive discounts for illiquidity (if you are the only buyer in the market, you can name your price).

The absence of competition   A lot of success flows not from exceptional ability but from the transient absence of competition.

Profiling for profit   Investment 'profiling' can be rewarding: study past successes and failures to infer a checklist of characteristics which can be used to screen for good investments.

When you find a good idea, buy enough to make a difference
Diversifying away risk may also mean diversifying away profit.

Correct contrarianism pays well in investment   It is not enough to be contrarian, one also needs to be right; but if one can be both, the payoff is more reliable in investment than in most other fields.

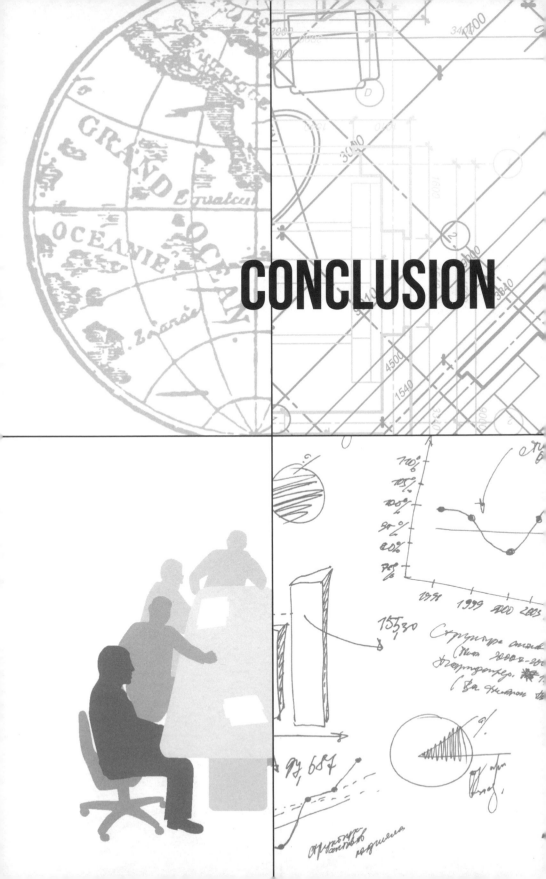

CONCLUSION

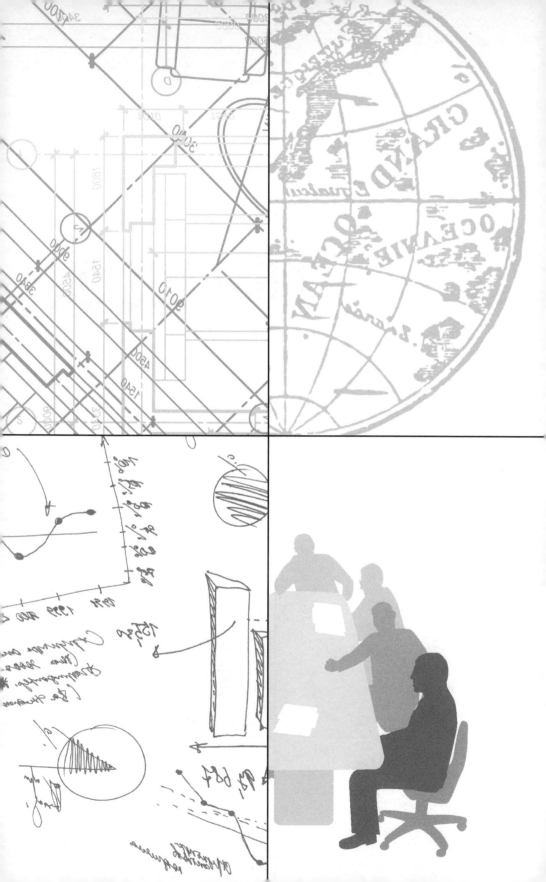

CHARACTERISTICS OF THE FREE CAPITALISTS

All of the people in the preceding chapters appear to have accumulated liquid wealth of around £1m or more (in many cases considerably more). Six of them have accumulated £1m or more in an ISA, which is arithmetically impossible without exceptional investment returns. As well as financial independence, investment has given them control of their own time to an extent unthinkable in any conventional career.

This chapter compares the investors' different paths to financial independence, identifying similarities and highlighting differences under the following headings:

- Life choices and chances – the sequence of decisions and events which led to their becoming independent investors

- Attitudes – the psychological traits and habits of thought characteristic of the investors

- Working methods – the techniques used by the investors.

No single blueprint

As a preliminary observation, it is worth noting the fact that there are substantial differences between the investors. Some have several academic degrees or strong City backgrounds; others left school with few qualifications and are entirely self-taught as investors. Some invest most of their money in a very few shares and hold them for years at a time; one makes several dozen trades every day, and holds them for at most a few hours. Some are social networkers, who spend their day talking to managers at companies in which they invest; for others a share is just a name, a number or symbol on a screen.

In summary, there is no single blueprint for stock market success. This is arguably one of the attractions of personal investing: there are no absolute entry requirements and many paths to success, so people with a variety of backgrounds and temperaments have a chance of finding a way which suits them.

LIFE CHOICES AND CHANCES

Future time perspective

Some interviewees were already interested in money-making schemes as teenagers: Eric was gaming for profit from 14, Owen stagged new issues from 16, and Peter and John made their first investments at 14 and 16. Those with less investment precocity were nevertheless level-headed youths, with a strong orientation towards and focus on the future. Apart from Taylor's trivial brushes with the law, there were no stories of teenage excess or delinquency. Nobody had turned over a new leaf after a previous financially undisciplined life of credit cards, interest and penalty charges.

In psychology there is a concept of time perspective, which describes how people parcel the flow of personal experience into a past, present and future, and the emphasis they place on each of these mental categories.[1] Some people have a primarily 'present' time perspective: they always live for the moment, with little thought or concern for the future. Others have a primarily 'past' time perspective: they dwell on memories, both good and bad, and see their current and future circumstances as determined largely by their past. A third group has a primarily 'future' time perspective: they focus on the future, and their actions in the present are shaped by long-term aspirations.

It is unsurprising that investors should adopt a primarily future time perspective in respect of their investment activities. But it is more interesting that all interviewees seem to have been strongly oriented towards this perspective from an early age, long before they ever thought about investing. A precocious interest in money-making is not essential, but a strong future time perspective may be. People with a stronger present time perspective may tend to spend rather than invest any increase in income which flows from career success, and so never get started as investors.

> "A precocious interest in money-making is not essential, but a strong future time perspective may be."

Few dependants

Several investors escaped from wage slavery to become full-time investors at early ages. Peter was the most extreme example: an enthusiastic investor from the age of 14, he dropped out of university at the age of 20 to concentrate full-time on investing. Others who became full-time investors after relatively short non-investment careers were Taylor (at age 31), Vince (33), Sushil (35), Owen (38), Vernon (38), and Bill (41). All these individuals were unmarried at the time they gave up employment. Becoming a full-time investor at an early age is a risky decision; a lack of family financial responsibilities makes the decision easier, and so does not having to justify one's eccentricity to a spouse.

Ambivalence about careers

Negative references to previous careers were couched as the mild disillusionment of a typical employee, rather than intense dislike. Vince regarded his earlier career as a motor company executive as "just a job, a way to apply for a mortgage". Nigel had grown weary of the politics of large organisations. Luke's career in investment banking had faltered in his mid-40s, with his new role as a treasury consultant never gaining traction. Sushil found his job miserable because of his disability, rather than because of the work.

Although they didn't hate their jobs, there is little evidence that interviewees gave up glittering careers to concentrate on investment. An unkind assessor might argue that several interviewees appear to have been career failures, albeit now financially successful failures. They drifted into independent investing via a period of dilettantish consultancy, and in some cases initially perceived themselves as between jobs: for example, Bill, Luke, Nigel, Sushil and Vernon. Eric spent a period working partly on investing and partly on his previous property management interests. Only Owen, Peter and Vince chose to leave well-paid jobs (or in Peter's case, to drop out of university) because they wanted to become full-time investors.

The lack of high-flying careers means that most interviewees had never spent much time thinking about organisational politics or how to progress in a hierarchy. They lack these skills for the happy reason that they have never needed them.

No overnight success

Most interviewees went through a long initial period in which they were largely unsuccessful investors. They either broke even or regularly lost small amounts of money, but not enough to deter them from trying again. Bill, Khalid, Nigel, Sushil and Vince all resorted to credit cards to finance investments and keep themselves afloat during this period. We cannot infer that persistence always pays off, because we cannot observe other amateur investors who may have been equally persistent but never became successful. But we can say that an initial period of indifferent results is common, it may last for several years, and it is not inconsistent with eventual success as a full-time investor.

Ill health as a career constraint

For some interviewees, ill health directed their focus towards investment rather than a conventional career. In the most extreme example, Taylor's ME left him incapable of doing any normal job; if he was not an investor, he would subsist entirely on disability benefits. Sushil's disability made him feel "acutely conscious that I probably couldn't carry on in a conventional career". Vince's history of tuberculosis led to similar worries: "I felt no confidence that I would always be able to work. I felt I had to do something which could support me even if I became incapacitated." The point is not quite that ill health motivates the individual to make money. Rather ill health closes down other career options, leaving investment as the individual's most realistic hope of a better life.

Technology as a facilitator

Many interviewees remarked on the dramatic improvement in the lot of the private investor which new technology has facilitated in recent years. Without this, they might never have become full-time investors. Khalid, Sushil and Vernon were amateur investors for several years in the early 1990s, but did not succeed in consistently making money. Sushil's "prices from rubbish bins" – scavenging bins at a suburban station for late-edition London evening newspapers discarded by home-coming commuters – vividly illustrates the difficulty in obtaining even basic information in the early 1990s.

Improvements since the mid-1990s have come in many areas. Brokerage costs have fallen substantially. Spread betting means that on many trades, stamp duty and capital gains tax can be completely avoided; it also makes it easy to short sell individual shares. Market-making spreads have been reduced by SETS and SETSmm trading systems, which enable the patient private investor to buy at the bid and sell at the offer. All these changes are examples of how the world of private investors has improved over the past 15 years.

> "Understanding how markets work is more important to an investor than understanding technology."

Technology was also a facilitator in another sense. For several of the investors, including Nigel, Owen, Sushil and Vernon, gains made in the technology shares boom of 1999-2000 were an important step towards giving up their jobs to become full-time investors. Vernon was the only one of these four who had much understanding of the technology. On the other hand Bill, an electronic engineer with a deep knowledge of technology, was very unsuccessful in this period, losing half his money on one share. Perhaps the lesson is that understanding how markets work is more important to an investor than understanding technology. In Bill's words: "I chose good growth companies, but you can lose money on a growth company if you pay too much for the growth. It took me a long time to understand that."

ATTITUDES

Money is about freedom, not consumption

A common trait for all interviewees is the attitude that investment represents first and foremost a source of quiet freedom, rather than a source of ostentatious spending power. Most interviewees appear to live modest lifestyles relative to their accumulated wealth. Nigel and Sushil explicitly identified reducing wants rather than increasing assets as a way of gaining freedom. Others are less ascetic, but still seem to lack the urge of many high earners to spend to the limits of their resources every year. This restraint in spending may be one of the mechanisms by which an investment fortune is accumulated.

Low appetite for leverage

Most of the investors use little leverage of any kind in their investments. Luke summarised the reason: "Leverage provides more juice, but in bad times that juice can quickly turn to hemlock."

For some this is a lesson learned through harsh experience: Peter had been substantially leveraged earlier in his career, but lost all his assets in market setbacks in 1976 and again in 1992.

Bill, Eric, Sushil and Owen have one or more spread bet accounts, but they are motivated mainly by a desire for short selling and tax-free capital gains, rather than a desire for leverage. Their actual leverage is always low compared to the levels potentially available from the spread bet firms.

Khalid, the day-trader, implicitly uses leverage on some of his intra-day CFD positions, but his leverage is typically only 50% of the maximum levels permitted by his CFD providers, and he closes most positions by the end of the day.

The general pattern of limited leverage amongst the successful investors contrasts with advertising by spread bet and CFD providers, which often emphasises the offer of lower margin requirements than competitors as a selling point.

Enjoying the process, not the proceeds

Most of the investors have now reached a level of wealth where they could afford to place their assets in passive investments and live on the income, spending their time doing something else. They carry on managing their own money because they enjoy investing, rather than from any financial necessity to generate an above-market rate of return.

> "They carry on managing their own money because they enjoy investing, rather than from any financial necessity."

This enjoyment was obvious from casual observation, and explicitly articulated in several interviews. John: "I am never happier than when I am writing, thinking or talking about [investment]." Or Peter: "I have never felt that investing is like working." Or Sushil: "To call it work is a travesty – I spend all day doing things I enjoy."

Not team players

The investors all work alone. They make their own decisions, and they appear to be little influenced by any form of group affiliation. Their mentality is captured by something Warren Buffett wrote about his investor friend Walter Schloss: "*I don't seem to have very much influence on Walter. That's one of his strengths: nobody seems to have much influence on him.*"[2]

WORKING METHODS

Foxes, not hedgehogs

The philosopher Isaiah Berlin divided writers and thinkers into two categories, foxes and hedgehogs. These terms originate from a remark attributed to the Greek poet Archilochus: "*the fox knows many things, but the hedgehog knows one big thing*". That is, foxes are eclectic, viewing the world through a variety of perspectives, with no allegiance to any single approach. Hedgehogs view the world through the lens of a single big idea – communism, capitalism, libertarianism or some other -ism.

The investors in this book are more foxes than hedgehogs. Their lack of allegiance to any single strategy makes their methods more robust (and incidentally, harder for an author to describe). This contrasts with professional fund managers, who often identify with a single investment strategy, which gives the business advantage of a succinct marketing message.

Applying sophistication in different dimensions

Some of the investors are wealthier than others, and some have more academic qualifications than others. Some are probably analytically smarter than others. Readers are free to make whatever inferences their own prejudices support about the PhD and Oxbridge graduates versus the early school leavers.

But greater wealth or analytical brainpower is not necessarily associated with greater sophistication in all relevant dimensions.

For example, the Cambridge engineer Bill has a high analytical intellect, but he chooses not to meet or speak much with companies because, by his own admission, he is "a poor judge of character". On the other hand, Eric has no higher education and relatively weak accounting knowledge, but exceptional social antennae: he attends AGMs almost every week, speaks frequently with company directors, and he is a very perceptive listener.

Khalid never speaks to a company director, never reads an annual report, and has only a superficial understanding of the businesses underlying the 'names' in which he invests. But his market information systems are the most sophisticated in the book: he is a heavy user of a Bloomberg terminal, for which he pays more than £20,000 per annum.

For Nigel and Vernon, sophistication was focused on psychological aspects of investing: the crowd psychology of cyclical markets for Nigel, and the cognitive psychology of individual decision making for Vernon.

In summary, investment sophistication is a multi-dimensional construct, not a linear one, and different interviewees are sophisticated in different dimensions.

Concentrated portfolios

Most of the investors hold concentrated portfolios, sometimes of fewer than ten shares (Luke, Owen and Taylor). Others such as Eric, John Lee, Peter Gyllenhammar and Sushil hold up to 60 shares, but this total may be misleading: for example Sushil mentioned that nearly half his portfolio is in his top six holdings. To the extent that portfolios are diversified, this tends to be driven by practical liquidity considerations coupled with the investor's large total funds, rather than a principled desire for more diversification.

Mainly smaller companies

Most of the investors have most of their portfolio invested in smaller companies, and they rarely hold shares in FTSE350 index companies. In other words, they largely ignore the top 90% of the stock market by market

> "The investors in this book largely ignore the top 90% of the stock market by market capitalisation."

capitalisation. When they do occasionally buy shares in a larger company it is usually just as a placeholder – a parking place for liquidity until a better idea comes along.

The investors mentioned various attractions of smaller companies: they are less well researched, yet easier to understand; the directors are more accessible to the private shareholder, and more likely to have meaningful shareholdings themselves; the companies are more susceptible to transformational external changes, and more likely to become takeover targets.

The exception to the focus on smaller companies is the day trader Khalid, who trades only FTSE350 stocks. Khalid doesn't disagree with the other investors on how easy the businesses of FTSE350 companies are to understand. But he deliberately does not try to understand the businesses, trading only on their headline news flow, and technical indicators and price charts.

Not taking advice

Provision of investment management or advice services to private investors is a large industry in the UK: wealth management companies, stockbrokers, tax advisors and so on. Although the investors were chosen for the book because they were self-directed, it might nevertheless be expected that some of them would delegate to third parties for part of their activities.

But in practice, the investors' reliance on third parties is minimal, and they take no advice whatsoever on which shares to buy. A consensus of expert opinion is often not useful in finance, because of its self-negating property: if something is widely anticipated, it is already in the price. But the investors' antipathy towards the concept of taking advice sometimes seemed to go beyond recognition of this point. John expressed the view that "authorised investment advice is a bit of a con"; Sushil said that he placed "almost no reliance on advisors"; Peter remarked that a small company where the management relied heavily on advisors displayed "a typical big-company mentality" (which was not a compliment). Comments like these suggest a psychological predilection for self-reliance and figuring things out for themselves.

Bulletin boards

There is wide variation in the investors' usage of internet bulletin boards. The geographers tend to post much more than the surveyors: both Luke and Nigel had made more than 30,000 posts, and Nigel had eventually grown sufficiently dissatisfied with mass-market sites such as ADVFN to start his own board. He saw little prospect of making any money from this: it was mainly a way of testing and refining his investment thinking. Amongst the surveyors and activists, Bill, Eric and Taylor are moderately prolific posters. Sushil and Vernon read a lot, but post little. John and Owen never look at bulletin boards.

These differences are not readily explained by differences in sophistication – Nigel, Luke and Owen, with very different bulletin board habits, are all former investment bankers, all with comparable levels of education (Harvard, the London Business School and Oxford). A more plausible explanation is that the geographers' top-down paradigm benefits more from broad debate drawing on a wide range of inputs, whilst the surveyors' bottom-up paradigm relies more on specific information obtained from company accounts and meetings rather than open-ended discussion.

A craft, not a science

None of the investors relies on modern portfolio theory as understood in the academic world ("like learning Physics to play snooker," said Vernon), or indeed on any sophisticated quantitative analysis. This is despite the fact that several – Bill, Luke, Owen, Sushil and Vernon – do have strong quantitative or business school backgrounds, as evidenced by their degree subjects and previous careers. When asked about this, each of these investors gave a similar answer: if a situation required sophisticated quantitative analysis, the decision was probably too close to call, and one was better off moving on and looking for a situation where the opportunity was more obvious.

In the first few interviews, investors were asked to name any investment books which they thought were particularly helpful. The answers seemed contrived and lacking conviction, so the question was abandoned for later interviews. Most of the investors have little focus on investment literature (the one exception is Taylor, the autodidact). Most have accumulated their investment knowledge gradually, from their own experience and from reading others' experience via bulletin boards, rather than from textbooks.

The paucity of definitive textbooks reflects the fact that successful investing is a practical craft, not an academic discipline, and certainly not a science. The craft of investing is comprised of heuristics: a toolkit of approximate, experience-based rules for making sense of the world. The rules are local rather than global, and slowly changing over time: sufficiently static to make experience valuable, but sufficiently fluid to keep the craft interesting. The investors derive satisfaction from the craft's process as well as its outcomes, but the outcomes have much to commend them. Autonomy, a low profile and sufficient free capital are probably some of the happier outcomes in life.

SUMMARY TABLE OF INVESTOR CHARACTERISTICS

Name	Age when first bought shares	Age at leaving last full-time job	Age at interview	Previous career (eclectic!)	Diversification (Typical number of holdings: low: <10 medium: 10-50 high: > 50)
Luke	23	47	55	Banking (debt origination)	Low
Nigel	22	47	56	Banking (shipping finance)	Medium
Bill	28	41	48	Electronic engineer	Medium
John Lee	16	50[*]	68	Member of parliament	High
Sushil	22	35	45	Economist	High
Taylor	23	31	46	Print estimator	Very low
Vernon	25	38	44	Management consultant (computer science)	Medium
Eric	25	39[†]	51	Property management	High
Owen	16	38	45	Banking (proprietary trader)	Low
Peter G	14	43[±]	56	Stockbroking analyst, corporate finance	Medium
Khalid	25	37	45	Family retail business (furniture)	Low
Vince	23	33	64	Local government (housing)	Low

[*] Lost seat as MP in 1992; part-time chairman of an NHS Trust, 1992-97.

[†] Last employment age 28; sold own property management business age 39.

[±] Completed Lindén Group workout age 43; continued working with Ulf Lindén on joint investments thereafter.

Typical holding period	Uses leverage? (As percentage of net worth: low: <25% medium 25-100% high: >100%)	Principal investment instruments	Uses bulletin boards?
Several years	Nil	Shares	Daily, >30k posts
Weeks / months	Low	Shares, index options, warrants	Daily, >30k posts (runs own board!)
Weeks / months	Medium	Shares, spread bets	Daily (mainly reads)
Years	Nil	Shares	Never
Months	Low	Shares, spread bets	Daily (reads), seldom (posts)
Months / years	Nil	Shares	Daily
Months	Low	Shares, index spread bets as hedge	Daily
Months / years	Low	Shares, spread bets	Daily
Months	Low	Shares, index spread bets as hedge	Never
Months / years	Nil for shares, some in property	Shares	Read occasionally
Minutes / hours	High	CFDs only	Never (Bloomberg chat instead)
Months / years	Nil for shares, some in property	Shares	Daily

A NOTE ON RESEARCH METHODS

The idea of this book first occurred to me in the early 2000s, but for several years two factors deterred me from writing it. Initially, there was my limited experience as a full-time investor: it seemed premature to write about a world in which I was new. Subsequently, in the bull market from early 2003 onwards, I was concerned that those whom the book presented as successful investors might later prove spectacularly unsuccessful in the next bear market. Although it was inevitable that this would be a book about lucky people, it seemed better for the integrity of the project to select interviewees *after* a period of large falls in markets. By mid-2009 a fall of nearly 50% from the highs of the FTSE100 meant that this condition was satisfied.

Subjects were recruited by several methods. I posted descriptions of the project on investment bulletin boards; I asked stockbrokers, CFD providers and spread bet firms for introductions to their most successful clients; I asked friends, and friends of friends.

Full taped interviews were conducted with 20 subjects, 19 male and one female (of whom 12 appear in the book). Particular effort was directed towards identifying more female interviewees, but without success. Perhaps I looked in the wrong places; or perhaps female investors are too rare, or too reticent, or both.

In the early stages of selecting the 20 subjects, there was simply a quality threshold: a potential subject qualified if he or she appeared to be a successful full-time private investor. As the book progressed, the quality threshold remained, but supplemented by a need for differentiation and balance. I wanted to include many different types of investor: geographers and surveyors, those who dealt many times every day and those who make only a few trades a year, and so on.

A standard list of questions was developed. This was tailored before each interview to reflect the subject's particular interests, to the extent that I could identify these before we met, and then emailed to the subject in advance of our meeting. Although the interview was the first time I had met most of the subjects, in some cases recruitment via a bulletin board meant that I was able to gain considerable insight by reading and making notes on the subject's history of posts over the past decade or so.

All interviews were conducted in person, except for Peter Gyllenhammar, based in Sweden, with whom there were a total of four telephone sessions each lasting between one and three hours. Other interview preparation included thorough internet searching; checking the Lexis database for press cuttings on the interviewee in the past 25 years; reading any other articles written by or about the interviewee (including some translated from Swedish about Peter Gyllenhammar); and speaking and corresponding with friends of the interviewees.

Taped interviews were usually conducted at the subject's home, and in every case lasted at least three hours, and usually rather longer. At the start of each interview, I gave a general outline of the project. The subjects were reassured that they would have the opportunity to see an early draft and suggest ways of obscuring any particularly sensitive or identifying details, but it was emphasised that they would not have copy approval: the final text and all judgments in the chapter would be my own.

The interviews were spread over a total of nine months, with writing-up being done as I went along. Interviewees were shown an early draft of their chapter. Only a minority of interviewees asked for further blurring of their identity; where required this was achieved by modifying biographical details, taking care to maintain the accuracy of the investment story. But most interviewees, rather than wanting to create distance between the portrait in the book and their real selves, actually suggested changes to make their story more accurate.

Eight full interviews were carried out but ultimately not included in the book. In some cases this was because these investors followed an approach too similar to someone already in the book. In other cases it was because I realised with hindsight that my line of questioning had been too technical – in one case, focused on the interviewee's self-developed computer systems – and therefore difficult to write up in a manner both anecdotal and informative.

ACKNOWLEDGEMENTS

My most important thanks are due to investors who gave interviews, commented on first drafts and responded to a welter of follow-up questions as I was writing the book. None of these people are selling advice or investment management services to third parties, so they had nothing tangible to gain from participation (and hence the need for anonymity to minimise their costs of participation). I was pleased that a few spontaneously mentioned that the self-reflection prompted by the interview process had been helpful.

Many people commented on drafts of this book. Colin Eastaugh reviewed some of my earliest drafts of individual chapters with his usual valuable frankness. Philip Cooper and Richard Sneller commented on early drafts of all 12 profiles. At a later stage David Holt, Andrew Howe, Calum Joglekar, Eddie Ramsden and Paul Stanley each read the full manuscript carefully and provided many detailed suggestions for improvement. Others who provided written feedback at various times included Dominic Connolly, Peter Hollis, Lee Samaha, Neil Thomas, Thalia Thompson, Martin White, and David Whitehouse. Not all of the advice given by these readers has been taken. All errors and inadequacies remain my own.

I thank Clem Chambers of the leading shares website ADVFN for allowing me to use data downloaded from the site to produce the charts in this book.

Finally, I thank Harriman House for taking on a first-time author, and in particular my editor Chris Parker for line-by-line improvements and the excision of much material better not inflicted on readers.

ENDNOTES

Introduction

[1] Bolton, Anthony & Davis, Jonathan, *Investing with Anthony Bolton*, 2nd edition (Petersfield: Harriman House, 2006), page 42.

[2] Huxley, Aldous, 'Wordsworth in the Tropics', in *Do What You Will* (1929).

1. Luke

[1] A sub-set of AIM stocks can be held in an ISA: those which have a dual listing on a foreign exchange recognised by HMRC.

[2] In an affidavit dated 6 March 2000, Daniel Loeb, the principal of hedge fund Third Point LLC stated as follows: "I used bulletin boards found on the internet...I find it is useful to exchange information with other interested persons...I find that such exchanges of information and opinions enable me to make more informed investment decisions...I posted these comments under my screen name Mr Pink." Mr Pink was an active poster on the Silicon Investor board between 1996 and 2006. In August 2010, several AIM-listed oil explorers – Empyrean Energy, Nighthawk Energy and Nostra Terra – all obtained *Norwich Pharmacal* court orders requiring ADVFN to disclose users' details, and threatened to sue authors of allegedly defamatory posts. Some CEOs post on bulletin boards: for example CEO of Whole Foods Inc, John Mackey, made 1,100 posts over seven years on Yahoo as the user Rahodeb ('Whole Foods Executive Used Alias,' *New York Times*, 12 July 2007).

[3] An independent ranking of sites by traffic is available at **www.alexa.com**.

[4] For a medical example see Haig, S., 'When the Patient is a Googler', *Time*, 8 November 2007. For a legal example see *Litigants in person: unrepresented litigants in first instance proceedings*, Department of Constitutional Affairs, 2006. For an

economics example, see the notorious paper by a staff member of the Kansas Fed: Arthreya, K., 'Economics is hard. Don't let bloggers tell you otherwise' (2010).

2. Nigel

[1] The poor risk-adjusted returns of shipping are noted in the definitive textbook by Martin Stopford (a former colleague of Nigel): "So it appears that the shipping industry is a high risk business...which offers little risk premium." (Stopford, M. *Maritime Economics*, 2nd Edition, (Routledge, 2003) page 71.)

[2] Delta is a measure of how the price of a put (or call) option changes in response to changes in the price of the underlying asset. Delta varies between 0 and -1 for a put option (0 and +1 for a call option). For example, a put option with a delta of -0.5 *rises* 0.5% for each 1% *fall* in the underlying asset. If the put option's delta is -0.5, the full value of the asset could be hedged by buying two put options.

Suppose an investor buys buy put options on the S&P500 as a hedge or insurance against a general stock market fall. To express the hedge of the portfolio on a delta-adjusted basis, the put options are re-expressed as an equivalent vanilla short position in the underlying asset. For example, suppose the portfolio is $100,000, the put options cover $40,000 of underlying index value, and the delta of the put options is -0.5. On a delta-adjusted basis, you are hedging 0.5 x $40,000 = $20,000 or 20% of the portfolio.

Delta is a local property; that is, the delta of -0.5 applies only for a particular date and value of the underlying index. As the index changes and the date of expiry of the option draws nearer, the delta changes. If the investor wants to maintain the hedge of exactly 20% of the value of the portfolio, the hedge will need to periodically rebalanced by buying or selling put options.

3. Bill

[1] Graham, B. *The Intelligent Investor*, 1st edition 1949, 4th edition (New York: Harper Collins, 2003).

[2] Some spread bet providers offer *guaranteed* stop-losses, where the provider guarantees (for a appropriate insurance premium) to close the spread bet at the stop-loss price (say 90p) even if the market price gaps lower.

[3] If these terms are unfamiliar, a good place to start is Leach, R., *Ratios Made Simple: A Beginner's Guide to the Key Financial Ratios* (Harriman House, 2010).

[4] The lessons of William James' philosophy of pragmatism as applied to investing are considered at length in Chapter 6 of Robert Hagstrom's *Latticework: The New Investing*.

[5] As above, these terms are explained in Leach, R., *Ratios Made Simple: A Beginner's Guide to the Key Financial Ratios*, (Harriman House, 2010).

[6] Chapter 13 in Morton, J., *Investing with the Grand Masters: Insights from Britain's Greatest Investment Minds*, (London: Financial Times Publishing, 1997). Nils Taube died at his desk in the City at the age of 79 in March 2008. Although his exceptional record, working with famous investors such as George Soros, was well known in the City, he was little known outside of it.

5. Sushil

[1] Chapter 12 of Keynes' *General Theory* describes the "beauty contest" metaphor for investment in this famous passage.

> "Or to change the metaphor slightly, professional investment may be likened to those newspaper competitions in which the competitors have to pick out the six prettiest faces from a hundred photographs, the prize being awarded to the competitor whose choice most nearly corresponds to the average preferences of the competitors as a whole; so that each competitor has to pick, not those faces which he himself finds prettiest, but those which he thinks likeliest to catch the fancy of the other competitors, all of whom are looking at the problem from the same point of view. It is not a case of choosing those which, to the best of one's judgement, are really the prettiest, nor even those which average opinion generally thinks to be the prettiest. We have reached the third degree where we devote our intelligences to anticipating what average opinion expects the average opinion to be. And there are some, I believe, who practise the fourth, fifth and higher degrees."

[2] For an entertaining non-technical account of 'Kelly' optimal betting see Poundstone, W., *Fortune's Formula*, (Hill and Wang, 2005).

[3] An investment which either rises 25% or falls 20% with equal probability has an expected return of $(1.25 + 0.8)/2 = 1.025$; that is, a positive return of 2.5% per period. But the expected logarithmic return is $(\log 1.25 + \log 0.8)/2 = 0$.

The median compound growth is found by exponentiating the log return: $\exp\{0\} = 1.0$; that is, a nil return.

An investment which either rises 50% or falls 40% with equal probability has an expected return of $(1.5 + 0.6)/2 = 1.05$; that is, a positive return of 5% per period. But the expected logarithmic return is $(\log 1.5 + \log 0.6)/2 = -0.0527$. The median compound growth is found by exponentiating the log return: $\exp\{-0.0527\} = 0.949$; that is, a negative return of 5.1% per period.

[4] The example graph is based on an investment which rises 30% or falls 15% with equal probability in each period. Before leverage, this has an expected return of $(1.3 + 0.85)/2 = 1.075$, that is 7.5% per period. But the expected logarithmic return is (log

1.3 + log 0.85)/2 = 0.0499. The median compound growth is found by exponentiating the log return: exp{0.0499}= 1.0511, that is 5.1% per period.

The theoretically optimal leverage L* in this example is 1.67, that is borrowing 67% of your net wealth. With this leverage, the investment produces either 1 + 1.67 x 0.3 = 1.501, or 1 – 1.67 x 0.15 = 0.745. The expected return is (1.501 + 0.745)/2 = 1.123, that is 12.3% per period. But the expected logarithmic return is (log 1.501 + log 0.745)/2 = 0.0589. The median compound growth is found by exponentiating the log return: exp{0.0589}= 1.0607, that is 6.1% per period.

The reader can verify by similar calculations that L* > 3.34 gives negative median compound growth, and L* = 2.34 gives the same median compound growth as no leverage.

In practical applications one would almost always use leverage lower than the optimal level from such calculations, because of the uncertainty about the true probability distribution of possible outcomes from the investment.

6. Taylor

[1] *Internal Control: Guidance for Directors on the Combined Code* was prepared in 1999 by a committee chaired by Nigel Turnbull, who subsequently became a director of Erinaceous.

[2] Chapter V in Lefèvre, Edwin, *Reminiscences of a Stock Operator*, (1923).

7. Vernon

[1] Fisher, K. *Super Stocks*, (Irwin Professional Publishing, 1984). See Chapter 1, 'Get rich with the glitch'. Ken Fisher is the son of Phil Fisher, the author of the legendary 1958 title *Common Stocks and Uncommon Profits*.

[2] The term 'hygiene factor' comes from the management writer Frederick Herzberg's dual structure theory of employee motivation. According to this theory, motivator factors such as achievement, recognition and responsibility energise employees' positive motivation; hygiene factors such as working conditions, benefits and relationships with co-workers have potential to create dissatisfaction if they are bad, but do not energise positive motivation even when they are good.

10. Peter Gyllenhammar

[1] Until recently 10% of the voting power was needed to requisition a general meeting, but as a result of the Shareholder Rights Directive, this was reduced to 5% with effect from 3 August 2009.

[2] 'Ensamvarg bland rovdjur', *Veckans Affarer*, 10 June 2003.

[3] Slater, J.D. *Return to Go*, (London: Weidenfeld & Nicholson, 1977).

[4] The Swedish Corporate Governance Board gives more details of Swedish nomination committees: see **www.corporategovernanceboard.se**. Documents on the site refer to the "stronger role of the shareholder in the Swedish – and indeed entire Nordic – corporate governance system than in some other parts of the world."

11. Khalid

[1] Gladwell, M. *Outliers: The Science of Success*. (Little, Brown, 2008).

[2] Lo, A.W., Mamaysky, H. and Wang, J., 'Foundations of technical analysis: computational algorithms, statistical inference and empirical implementation', *Journal of Finance*, 55: 1705-1765 (2000).

[3] Irwin, S.H. and Park, C-H., 'What do we know about the profitability of technical analysis?', *Journal of Economic Surveys*, 21:786-826 (2007).

[4] Green, T.C. 'The value of client access to analyst recommendations', *Journal of Finance and Quantitative Analysis*, 41: 1-24 (2006).

[5] Busse, J. and Green, T.C., 'Market efficiency in real time', *Journal of Financial Economics*, 65:415-437 (2002).

[6] Kim, S., Lin, J. and Slovin, M., 'Market structure, informed trading, and analysts' recommendations', *Journal of Finance and Quantitative Analysis*, 32: 507-524 (1997).

[7] Welles Wilder, J. *New Concepts in Technical Trading Systems*, Trend Research, (1978).

12. Vince

[1] With an interest rate of 2% per annum, no dividends and assumed volatility of 18% per annum, the Black-Scholes model gives the put and call option premiums as 4.79 and 3.37 respectively.

Conclusion

[1] Zimbardo, P.G. & Boyd, J.N., 'Putting time in perspective: a valid, reliable individual-differences metric', *Journal of Personality and Social Psychology*, 77: 1271-1288 (1999).

[2] Buffett, W. *The super-investors of Graham & Doddsville* (1984). Walter Schloss worked alongside Buffett at the Graham-Newman Partnership in the period 1954-56.

INDEX

A

academic research 103–104
account trading 215
acquisitions 113–114
ADVFN. *see* bulletin boards
advice, investment 82, 95, 105, 197, 204
All-Share index 79–80
alternative energy sector 43
Alternative Investment Market (AIM) 21, 76
Amex Gold Bugs Index 40–41
analyst research 22, 27, 225
 profit forecasts 128
 research notes 219
annual general meetings (AGMs)
 asking questions 161, 163
 attendance 22, 76, 151
 non-attendance 63
 time vs. effectiveness 101
arbitrage 37, 170, 171–172
asset valuation
 banking 61
 oil exploration 22
 ratios. *see* valuation ratios
 under-valuation 196
Authoriszor 37
autonomy 249–250

B

banking sector 21, 32
 asset valuation 61
 crises 78–79

Baruch, Bernard, *My Own Story* 112, 117
Battle for Investment Survival, The. see Loeb, Gerald M., *The Battle for Investment Survival*
Ben Bailey 156–157
bid failure 129
bid-offer spread 15
blogs. *see* bulletin boards
Bloomberg 221, 244
board representation 199–200
bombed-out shares 192
 discount to net asset value 196, 197–198, 204
bookmaker's spread 57, 58
bottom-up investment 3, 17, 81, 237–238
BP 75
Bre-X Minerals 37
Britannia Group 193–194
Buffett, Warren 61, 76, 101, 104, 119
bull markets 31, 45
 gold mining shares 40–41
bulletin boards 22–25, 43–44, 62, 243–244
 information sharing 24–25
 insight to market sentiment 44, 45
 research 100, 202
 'tail-coating' 65–66, 67
business angel investing 155

C

Canada 39, 40
capital gains taper relief 76
capital gains tax 78
capital return 79–80, 175
capital structure arbitrage 172
Cawkwell, Simon 58–59
charity 104
closed-end funds 167, 176
 arbitrage 172
closing auction 226
commodity derivatives 35–36
commodity markets 17, 36
Common Stocks and Uncommon Profits. see Fisher, Philip, *Common Stocks and Uncommon Profits*
company announcements 99, 123
 bad news 123, 127–132
company directors 82, 103, 205
 shareholder representation 199–200

company reports 63
company reserves valuation 36
company structure 192, 200
    restructuring 193–194
compliance 173
Computer Investments Group 33
concentrated portfolio strategy 25, 112–113, 177
    vs. diversification 118–119, 239–240
contracts for difference (CFDs) 21, 40, 213, 216–217, 228, 229
    trading platforms 218, 220
    vs. spread bets 218
contra-cyclicality 34
contrarian investing 123, 127–143, 233, 245–246
    case studies 133–139
    stock selection 131–133
    timing decisions 139
copper 42
corporate governance 36, 103, 199–200, 203
Countrywide, estate agent 59
covered straddles 241–242
credit cards 32–33
credit limits 59
cross-market intelligence 42–43, 45
crowd psychology 249–250
currency options 33
cyclicality 31, 34–35
    cross-market intelligence 42–43
    Kondratieff cycles 34
    long and short cycles 45
    and mal-investment 44
    and market sentiment 35
    shipping finance 34–35

D

day trading 213, 225–228
Deal4free 218, 219
debt origination 16
debt securities 16–17
defensive pessimism 67
defensive value 71, 74–75, 85
delta-adjusted position 42
Diamond Fields 37
discount to net asset value 176, 192

discounted cash flow (DCF) 61
diversification 20, 105, 131–132
    and risk 94
    vs. portfolio concentration 113, 193, 239–240
dividends 71, 74–75, 77, 85
double and sell 45
downgrades 219–221, 222, 225, 229
downside risk 20
dumb money 20

E

earnings forecasts 61, 127
economic cycles. *see* cyclicality
Education of a Speculator, The. see
  Niederhoffer, Victor, *The Education of a Speculator*
environmental issues 44
equity markets 17, 170
Erinaceous 113–115
EV/sales ratio 61
    the value spider 63–64
exchange traded funds (ETFs) 42, 117
Execution Management System (EMS) 221
expected returns 97–98

F

final salary pension schemes 200–201
Fisher, Ken 123
Fisher, Philip, *Common Stocks and Uncommon Profits* 114, 118
forums, online. *see* bulletin boards
fraud
    Bre-X Minerals 36
    Erinaceous 113–114
FT30 index 79
FTSE100 index 79–80
    futures 96–97
full bids 196
    Takeover Panel rules 199
fully listed stocks 21
fund managers 82, 93
fundamental investment 223, 228
fundraising, equity 36, 38–39

G

gambling 97
game theory 53, 89, 105
gearing 40
Geist, Richard, *Investor Therapy* 118
'glitches', company 123, 127–132
    case study 130–131
    investment research 131–132
global markets 17, 25
GNI Touch 220
gold mining shares 40–41
Graham, Ben, *The Intelligent Investor* 56
Green Energy Investors 23, 43
Growth at a Reasonable Price (GARP) 111
growth companies 56, 77

H

Halifax House Price Index 59
Hansard International 135–138
Haynes Publishing 133–135
hedge funds 82
    redemptions 176–177
hedging 42, 96–97, 159, 177
Hemscott Company Guide 81, 111–112
heuristics 139, 143
Horace Small 173–174, 177
house building shares 42, 193–194

I

idiosyncratic risk 94
income shares 175
index demotion 128
Individual Savings Accounts (ISAs) 21, 77–78, 177
    ISA millionaires 5
inheritance tax 76
insider information 114–115
insolvency risk 236–237, 246
institutional investors 155, 170
insurance sector 194
Intelligent Investor, The. see Graham, Ben *The Intelligent Investor*
Interactive Investor. *see* bulletin boards
interest rates
    and cyclicality 34

the dollar 43
Internet, the 57, 62
Internet forums. *see* bulletin boards
Intuitive Trader, The. see Koppel, Robert, *The Intuitive Trader*
investment cycles 34
investment funds 93
investment research 81, 100–101, 202, 239
    analyst research 22
    broker research notes 219
    company directors 103, 160
    contrarian investing 131–133
    corporate governance 103
    cross-market intelligence 42–43
    microeconomics 95
    oil exploration 22
    property sector 156–157
    small cap companies 155, 163
    vs. academic research 103–104
Investor Therapy. see Geist, Richard, *Investor Therapy*

J

James, William (philosopher) 61
junior mining 39, 40

K

Kelly, John 97
Kelly betting 97–98
Keynesian demand stimulus 44
Kondratieff cycles 34
Koppel, Robert, *The Intuitive Trader* 118

L

Laramide Resources 40
Lefèvre, Edwin, *Reminiscences of a Stock Operator* 115–116, 118
leverage 59, 139–140, 177, 249–250
    mining sector 40
    oil sector 21, 27
    and risk 113, 193
    and spread betting 97–99
    and stop-loss orders 60

liquidity 76, 93, 94, 105
listening skills 160, 163
Loeb, Gerald M., *The Battle for Investment Survival* 112, 117
long positions 59
    and contracts for difference (CFDs) 216–217
long-term investment 25, 77, 82
luck 6–7, 140, 143

M

macro trading 117
macroeconomics 15, 95, 105
    Kondratieff cycles 34
mal-investment 44
management. *see also* annual general meetings (AGMs)
    accounting decisions 129
    proprietorial companies 74
    and shareholder activism 173
margin call 59, 227
    and contracts for difference (CFDs) 217
marked to market 57
market capitalisation 74, 75
    company demotion 128
    micro cap companies 191–192
    and reserves valuation 36
market cycles. *see* cyclicality
market data services 219, 220, 221, 244
market expectations 127
market exposure 42
Market Eye 244
market makers 201
market risk 42, 94
market sentiment 31, 35, 128–129
    insight from bulletin boards 44, 45
market spread 57, 58
market swings 43, 45
market timing 31, 79
mean reversion 167
medium-term note market 16–17
merger arbitrage 171
metrics, financial 67, 99–100
    the value spider 63–64
MF Global 220
micro cap companies 190, 191–192, 204

microeconomics 95, 105
Microsoft Network (MSN) 159
mining sector 31, 36–37, 61
    Canada 39
    copper 42
    discoveries and acquisitions 36–37
    equity fundraising 36, 38–39
    gold mining shares 40–41
    junior mining 39, 40
Money Masters, The. see Train, John, *The Money Masters*
mortgages 233, 240, 246
Motley Fool. *see* bulletin boards
multiple share classes 175–176
My Own Story. see Baruch, Bernard, *My Own Story*
'My Portfolio', *FT* column 79

N

NASDAQ 174
natural resources 20
negative working capital requirements 194, 204
nested cycles 34–35
net asset value 22, 61, 176
    discount to net asset value 192
networking 151, 161, 163
New Issue Share Guide 169
new issues 17, 168, 169–170, 181
New Money Masters, The. see Train, John, *The Money Masters*
Niederhoffer, Victor, *The Education of a Speculator* 117

O

oil sector 19–21
    asset valuation 22
    exploration 19–20
    leverage 21, 27
    overlap with technology sector 20
    overnight transformations 27
    swaps 35
opening auction 225
optimal betting 97–98
optimal compound growth 97–98

option arbitrage 171
optionality 17
options 42, 175–176
over-confidence 59
over-trading 59
ownership structure 204

P

pensions 198, 200–201, 205
Pensions Act 1995 200
percentage price falls 99–100
performance record 4–5, 79–80
Personal Equity Plans 21, 77–78
philanthropy 104
placeholder investment 75, 85, 240–241
politics 73
Polly Peck 111
portfolio concentration 112–113
    in a bear market 116–117
    vs. diversification 113, 193
portfolio management 76–78
    and debt 239–240
    leverage 139–140
    mining sector 40–42
    spread betting 158
positive working capital requirements 194
possible reserves 20
Prestel 244
price doubling 40, 45
price exhaustion 222
price monitoring, indicators 229
price-earnings ratio 56, 60–61, 74
    the value spider 63–64
price-sales ratio 61
privatisation 54–55
probability 96, 125
profiling, investment 239, 246
profit warnings 127–128, 129
property market 233
    market slump 1990s 18, 190
property sector 31, 35, 74, 234, 238
    house building shares 42
    rental market 154–155
    residential market, Gemany 238, 240
proprietary trading 171–172, 173
proprietorial companies 74, 85, 157
Proquote 99, 220

proven and probable (2P) reserves 20
proven reserves 20
psychology 31, 249–250
    market sentiment 35
public relations 114–115, 120
put options 176

Q

quantitative analysis 63, 96
QXL Ricardo 130–131

R

Ratner, Gerald 214–215
record-keeping
    bulletin board posts 24
    contrarian investing 139–140
    electronic files 177
    note taking 67
    spreadsheets 62
relative strength indicators (RSI) 222, 223–224
Reminiscences of a Stock Operator. see
    Lefèvre, Edwin, *Reminiscences of a Stock Operator*
research notes 221, 225
retail sector 194, 214–215
rights issues 188
risk
    arbitrage 171
    aversion 177, 179
    and diversification 94
    downside 20
    income vs. capital investment 175
    insolvency 236–237, 246
    market 42, 94
    and return 175
    upside 20

S

S&P500 index 42
'scuttlebutt' concept 114–115, 158, 244
secondary fundraising 39
securities markets 18

self-invested personal pensions (SIPPs) 92, 109, 112
selling 139
    top-slicing 158–159, 163
semiconductor shares 42
settlement system, stock exchange 215, 216
share issue privatisation 54–55
shareholder activism 3–4, 22, 102–103, 161, 167, 178
    board representation 199–200
    corporate engineering 185
    investment research 177
    management response 173
shareholder influence 193, 200, 203, 240
shipping industry 31, 33–35, 72
    cycles 34–35
    freight rates 42
short positions 59
    and contracts for difference (CFDs) 217–218
short-selling 21, 159
    and spread betting 58–59, 96, 126
short-term investment 82
small cap companies 74, 75, 85, 237
    corporate governance 36
    insolvency risk 240
    investment research 155, 163
    liquidity 76
    reserves valuation 36
SmallCap index 79–80
split capital trusts 129, 175–177, 181
spread betting 21, 40, 57–58, 139
    leverage 97–99
    and short selling 58–59, 126
    and tax 57, 96, 97
    vs. contracts for difference (CFDs) 218
    vs. share purchase 158
spreadsheets 62
stagging 54, 55, 168, 169–170, 181
steel industry, Sweden 187–188
stock brokers 39, 82, 99, 100
    commission-free services 220
    contrarian investing 139
stock selection 131–137
    hygiene factors 132
Stockopedia. *see* bulletin boards
stop-loss orders 40, 59, 60, 67, 227
substance over form 54, 67
sum-of-the-parts valuation 22

T

takeover bids 61
    bid failure 129
    Takeover Panel rules 199
tax
    capital gains taper relief 76
    capital gains tax 78
    exile 243
    Individual Savings Accounts (ISAs) 77–78
    inheritance tax 76
    and investment decisions 96
    Personal Equity Plans 77–78
    spread betting 57
TD ('Tom DeMark') indicators 222
technical analysis 221–224
technical indicators 219, 222–224
technology sector 55, 101–102, 126
    bear market 2003 92
    overlap with oil sector 20
    the technology 'bubble' 91–92, 126, 155, 173–174
telecoms sector 58
telephone broking 63, 81, 100, 158
Thorp, Ed 97
time allocation 141–142, 143
    and efficiency 179–180
    full bids 196
    vs. rationality 15
timing decisions 31, 79
    contrarian investing 139
top-down investment 3, 15, 17, 25, 238
    cyclicality 44
    oil sector analysis 19–21
Toppel, Edward Allen, *Zen in the Markets* 118
top-slicing 163
Toucan Gold 37
trade journalism 114–115
trading calendar 215
trading volume 40
Train, John, *The Money Masters* 118

U

UK Corporate Governance Code 199
unsustainability 44
Updata 220, 244

upgrades 219–221, 222, 225, 229
upside risk 20

V

valuation ratios 61
    EV/sales ratio 61
    price-earnings ratio 61, 74
    the value spider 63–64
value investing 56, 60, 75
value spider 63–64
Vodafone 75
voice broking 63
voting rights 193, 204

W

warrants 39, 40
working capital requirements 193–194

Y

yield 75, 79
    the value spider 63–64
YJ Lovell 195–196

Z

Zen in the Markets. see Toppel, Edward
  Allen, *Zen in the Markets*
zero dividend preference shares 175
zero-sum game 53, 89